DON GIOVANNI LA BOHEME I P

CARMEN AÏDA CAVALLERIA RUSTICANA
DON CARLO NORMA FAUST TURANDOT
RIGOLETTO IL TROVATORE SIEGFRIED
LA TRAVIATA KHOVANSHCHINA TOSCA
IL TABARRO DIE GÖTTERDÄMMERUNG
SALOME DIE ZAUBERFLÖTE WERTHER
TRISTAN UND ISOLDE COSI FAN TUTTE
ANGEL OF FIRE DIE WALKÜRE OTELLO
MADAMA BUTTERFLY DON QUICHOTTE
PARADISE LOST FIDELIO LA FAVORITA
DON PASQUALE SEMIRAMIDE ELEKTRA
MACBETH I DUE FOSCARI BILLY BUDD
EL AMOR BRUJO DER ROSENKAVALIER
I PAGLIACCI MARIA STUARDA WOZZECK
FALSTAFF LE NOZZE DI FIGARO THAÏS
THE HARVEST NABUCCO LA GIOCONDA
PETER GRIMES LUCIA DI LAMMERMOOR
FEDORA SIMON BOCCANEGRA JENUFA
LA FANCIULLA DEL WEST TANNHÄUSER
OEDIPUS REX PRINCE IGOR IDOMENEO
SAMSON ET DALILA BORIS GODUNOV

CAGO OPERA

TEXT BY CLAUDIA CASSIDY
FOREWORD BY SAUL BELLOW
RECOLLECTIONS BY CAROL FOX
GRAPHIC DESIGN BY R.D. SCUDELLARI

THIS IS A LYRIC OPERA OF CHICAGO BOOK, PUBLISHED BY LYRIC OPERA OF CHICAGO.
TEXT AND PHOTOGRAPHS COPYRIGHT 1979 BY LYRIC OPERA OF CHICAGO
TEXT COPYRIGHT © BY CLAUDIA CASSIDY
FOREWORD COPYRIGHT © BY SAUL BELLOW
ALL RIGHTS RESERVED UNDER INTERNATIONAL
AND PAN-AMERICAN COPYRIGHT CONVENTIONS.

LIBRARY OF CONGRESS CATALOGING IN PUBLICATION DATA:
LYRIC OPERA OF CHICAGO:
CASSIDY, CLAUDIA   BELLOW, SAUL
79-90902
ISBN 0-9603538-0-1
MANUFACTURED IN THE UNITED STATES OF AMERICA

EDITOR:
ROBERT E. WEISS

EDITORIAL ASSISTANCE:
ANN CAIN
ALFRED GLASSER
JAMES J. PETZKE
RICHARD TURNER

PHOTO CREDITS:
LYRIC OPERA OF CHICAGO
ROBERT CAHEN
DAVID FISHMAN
GERALD RITHOLZ
PHOTOGRAPHY SKREBNESKI
NANCY SORENSON
CHICAGO AMERICAN
CHICAGO DAILY NEWS
CHICAGO SUN-TIMES
CHICAGO TRIBUNE

PRINTED AND BOUND BY: **R.R. DONNELLEY & SONS, COMPANY**

FOREWORD BY SAUL BELLOW

Readers of this book on Chicago's Lyric Opera will be intrigued, amused, charmed and touched. These pleasures need give them no anxiety. To be charmed by Miss Cassidy is perfectly safe—she knows what she is talking about. It is clear, moreover, that she is not one of your coldblooded pundits. She adores her subject, she has immersed herself in it for decades. Composers, conductors, orchestras, tenors and divas have filled her thoughts and perhaps even her dreams. And, as most Chicagoans know, she is not invariably sweet; she can be exacting, sharp and tough. She prefers, however, to write enthusiastically and generously. In writing about opera one cannot be stingy with metaphors. Miss Cassidy seldom offers a flat statement on any subject. Of a performance of *The Magic Flute* conducted by Furtwängler, she writes, "It was above all human Mozart, filled with joy and sorrow, innocence and evil, generosity and greed, ennobled by the eternal striving to reach from darkness into light." Journalists seldom speak of "ennoblement" in the papers but Miss Cassidy has established her right to the high tone. She speaks of Bartoletti's orchestra, "darkly beautiful and menacing", the Lyric's "most powerful asset." She speaks of "feathery" coloraturas, of the "triumphs of heartbreak" of great tenors, of di Stefano's "molten glow" and "blandishing" talents, of Bjoerling's piercing sweetness, of a voice that flashes "like a drawn sword" (we do not often see swords drawn in Chicago except on the stage, but there a drawn sword really flashes as it should). She has not forgotten Mary Garden and she eulogizes Maria Callas as often as she mentions her. She reminisces richly, and she seldom indulges in gossip. There is not a touch of malice anywhere in this chronicle. Miss Cassidy's devotion to opera is far too pure and wholehearted for that.

"Without the Lyric," she tells us, "Chicago would be underprivileged. A city," she continues, "is more than tall buildings, crowded streets and, in our case, a magnificent lakefront." The plug for the lakefront we could not reasonably expect, in self adulating Chicago, to be spared. But she is dead right about the Lyric.

About fifteen years ago, a wellknown local coffee company promised in a breathless radio-commercial, "We will bring a mountain to Chicago." This mountain was of course a coffee mountain. Now without coffee a civilized city is inconceivable; but coffee, when all is said and done, is only a commodity. The real mountains of Chicago are its cultural institutions. What would this city be without them?

The Italian novelist, Moravia, when he came to the United States in 1955, wanted to see all the famous sights and asked me to take him out to Coney Island. We went there on a gloomy March day, and after he had looked at the cheerless skeletons of summery entertainment and smelled the vapors of Nathan's hot-dogs and heard the rattling of the shooting gallery and stood on the empty boardwalk staring at the gray Atlantic, he said to me, "How long would it take to get to the Metropolitan Museum? Let's see some paintings. I need an antidote." I was better able than Moravia to bear Coney Island in winter, for I am after all an American, and a Chicagoan at that. I can go without art for a longer time, as camels can without water. But without art and intellect no community has the right to describe itself as a city. My sole objection to Miss Cassidy's statement about the importance of Lyric to Chicago is that it is too narrow. Without its universities, libraries, museums Chicago would indeed be what one of its bitter detractors called it, a place to which people came for the sole purpose of making money. In a society in which men *think* they know what they live by (machines, commodities, politics, journalism, popular entertainment) these institutions of high culture offer us what is really essential. For whether we know it or not these art collections, libraries, centers of research and teaching, these musical organizations save us from utter dehumanization. They are admittedly imperfect. Most of them are to a large extent staffed and dominated by philistines. Indeed, the standards of what Matthew Arnold called Sweetness and Light have so far deteriorated that it becomes harder and harder for us to make out the Philistine, to discern his true outline, or even to identify the philistine elements in ourselves. There was a time when business tycoons, machine politicians, journalists and taxpayers in a solid phalanx put down the "fads and frills" of poetry, art and music. (We should in pure objectivity remind ourselves that even the great Sir Isaac Newton referred to poetry as "preposterous fiddle-faddle"). But no society that denies human beings their indispensable nourishment is safe from disorder and madness. Mountains of coffee beans, oceans of gasoline, cannot preserve us. And slave-labor camps in totalitarian states have not succeeded in eliminating the art-impulse from human beings. "The Imagination," said William Blake nearly two hundred years ago, "is Not a State: it is the Human Existence itself." By Human, Blake meant Divine.

Chicago's cultural institutions have done much—even literally, physically—to hold the city together. During Lyric performances I have sometimes thought of the desolation of the West Side, just beyond the river. If the walls of the Opera House were suddenly to become transparent, the audience might be able to make out West Madison Street and the County Hospital just behind *Tosca* or *Figaro*. As your car turns off the Expressway eastwards towards the Loop you may occasionally see one of the derelicts who take shelter under the highway structure. A moment later you pass the arcades of the Lyric.

Robert Morss Lovett, who came to the University of Chicago from Harvard in 1893, records in his autobiography that the city then was very melancholy. He tells us how bleak and grim the University campus looked—a mere sandlot with a swamp in which frogs croaked. "For a month we enjoyed the Fair," he wrote, "but the contrast between its artificial glory and the squalor of the real city is appalling." He notes, however, the achievements of Chicago's ambitious millionaires, some of whom, like Martin A. Ryerson, were cultivated men. It was Ryerson in the 1890s who bought a famous collection of Dutch paintings and gave it to the Art Institute. As for the Columbian Exposition, Lovett called it "the triumph of the feudal barons under whom the city has grown great." These barons meant to change Chicago's reputation for "materialism, cruelty and clownishness." Soon after this moment of pride came the economic collapse of 1893. Lovett, a lifelong liberal, a friend of Jane Addams and an editor of the *New Republic*, was impressed by the way in which Chicago's magnates "stood up to their responsibilities in the face of danger and depression."

A very different sort of visitor, Henry Adams, was also struck by the grandeur of the Exposition and tried to guess what it augured for the culture of the city and the country. Could the achievements of the Beaux Arts, artistically induced to spend a summer on the shore of Lake Michigan, be expected to remain? Would art ever be at home here? Adams observed that the American at first had the air of enjoying his imported art, of being on top of it all. "If he had not done it himself, he had known how to get it done to suit him . . . Perhaps he could not do it again; the next time he would want to do it himself and would show his own faults; but for the moment he seemed to have leaped directly from Corinth and Syracuse and Venice over the heads of London and New York, to impose classical standards on plastic Chicago."

What Adams notes here is a powerful American cosmopolitanism, capable of taking from the world precisely what it wanted, whether in the form of machinery or ideas or arts, and offering in return its own innovations, its will to originality. Some Europeans judged Americans to be a rootless hybrid population with whom culture had no future, undoubtedly projected on America the anxious fears that the masses of their own countries caused them. But these "rootless hybrids" have surprised everyone.

Opera audiences are large in Chicago. The Company as a rule performs to full houses. Our Chicago subscribers are perhaps less sophisticated than the opera lovers of London, Munich or Milan, but there are thousands of Chicagoans who are musically educated and knowledgeable, good judges of singing. The Lyric can meet the most exacting standards in the world. Chicago is at the very heart of populist America. Yet in spite of its lowbrow reputation, so tragically well-deserved, it is not isolated from international art and culture. Patrons and philanthropists have on the whole spent their money wisely and even City Hall has recognized the contributions made by cultural institutions to the stability of Chicago. I suppose that a certain number of people attend concerts or get themselves up to listen to *Aida* in order to distinguish themselves from the bleacher bums at Wrigley Field and other rowdies and yahoos. But for the most part the Lyric audiences come in from every quarter of the city to satisfy a genuine need for music and spectacle—for art. Cosmopolitan culture sustains itself with difficulty (but not without energy) amid heavy industry, desolate slums, and crime. This is as true for Milan with its great factories and its terrorists as it is for Chicago.

I am inclined to think that the descendants of European immigrants are among the most important supporters of Chicago's concerts and operatic performances. I am told by Miss Carol Fox that most of the singers in the Lyric chorus—the same chorus that went abroad with Penderecki's *Paradise Lost* and was stormily applauded at La Scala and again in the Vatican—are of Polish origin.

People shut up in their apartments by the difficulties and dangers of getting about after dark, more or less captive, victimized by the mind-disintegrating forces of television, come out in large numbers to attend performances of *Tosca* and *La Traviata*. They would not venture out in vile winter weather to watch and hear wigged and costumed figures if their desire for full expression were not great, if they did not require storms of harmony, blasts of emotion.

Such needs, it must be said, would remain unsatisfied without the work of Carol Fox, Bruno Bartoletti, and their principal assistants Ardis Krainik and Daniel Newman. Miss Fox will be remembered, together with Jane Addams of Hull House and Harriet Monroe of *Poetry* magazine, as one of Chicago's greatest women.

—SAUL BELLOW

DON GIOVANNI LA BOHEME I PURITANI
CARMEN AÏDA CAVALLERIA RUSTICANA
DON CARLO NORMA FAUST TURANDOT
RIGOLETTO IL TROVATORE SIEGFRIED
LA TRAVIATA KHOVANSHCHINA TOSCA
IL TABARRO DIE GÖTTERDÄMMERUNG
SALOME DIE ZAUBERFLÖTE WERTHER
TRISTAN UND ISOLDE COSI FAN TUTTE
ANGEL OF FIRE DIE WALKÜRE OTELLO
MADAMA BUTTERFLY DON QUICHOTTE
PARADISE LOST FIDELIO LA FAVORITA
DON PASQUALE SEMIRAMIDE ELEKTRA
MACBETH I DUE FOSCARI BILLY BUDD
EL AMOR BRUJO DER ROSENKAVALIER
I PAGLIACCI MARIA STUARDA WOZZECK
FALSTAFF LE NOZZE DI FIGARO THAÏS
THE HARVEST NABUCCO LA GIOCONDA
PETER GRIMES LUCIA DI LAMMERMOOR
FEDORA SIMON BOCCANEGRA JENUFA
LA FANCIULLA DEL WEST TANNHÄUSER
OEDIPUS REX PRINCE IGOR IDOMENEO
SAMSON ET DALILA BORIS GODUNOV

"The three finest things in creation," said Gustave Flaubert, "are the sea, *Hamlet* and Mozart's *Don Giovanni.*" "If we are to have a flourishing world of the arts," said Bruno Walter, paraphrasing Hugo von Hofmannstahl, "the roots must be more splendid than the foliage." "I've been poor and I've been rich," said Sophie Tucker, "and believe me, rich is better." Sitting for that historic first time on the Lyric aisle, I said, paraphrasing Sophie, "I've known Chicago without and with a major opera company, and believe me, with is better."

Why did we know, against all odds, that gleaming *Don Giovanni* night of February 5, 1954, that Lyric of Chicago was a major opera company? Perhaps it was in the air, even before it was on stage. The stars were right. After all, less than four months earlier, on October 15, 1953, Fritz Reiner walked on the stage of Orchestra Hall and Chicago got its orchestra back. There is nothing like the best to remind you that fair to middling is no substitute.

Yet between orchestra and opera there was a major difference. The Chicago Symphony Orchestra, which began at the top with Theodore Thomas, had never been lost, just shunted to the sidelines of splendor by incompatible leadership. It was right there, waiting. But the sumptuous resident opera in Chicago and at intimate Ravinia had been dealt a lingering death blow by the depression. Ravinia, which had always had the Chicago Symphony Orchestra in the pit, became its festival summer home. But for seven years before Lyric's *Don Giovanni* Chicago had had no resident opera at all.

This was an echoing, incalculable loss. Visitors were welcome, but not a substitute. The Metropolitan Opera came at season's end, often tired and depleted. The New York City Opera was often adventurous, but never a replacement for the real thing. Then, suddenly, out of the blue, there was the Lyric, the real thing, right in front of us, in our own Opera House. By a kind of miracle, for nothing else really explains the survival of the major arts in a difficult time, Lyric is still there—or, in the sense of our proud possession, here—on the threshold of its 25th season.

I don't attempt to explain miracles, just to enjoy them. Out of the blue, and the operatic blue at that, which is more dizzying than your average empyrean, three young newcomers—Carol Fox, Lawrence Kelly and Nicola Rescigno—had conjured one of those "three finest things in creation," Mozart's *Don Giovanni.*

There was Bruno Walter's foliage, glistening and luxuriant, and more of that in a moment. How about the roots? Lyric's timing was apt, for in that opening night audience were Giorgio Polacco, Rosa Raisa and Edith Mason, who in the great nights of Chicago opera had been conductor, Donna Anna and Zerlina of radiant *Dons*, with Vanni-Marcoux and later Ezio Pinza of the single earring. Their matchless Leporello—and Toscanini's at Salzburg—was to have been Lyric's, but Virgilio Lazzari did not live to make that longed for return.

A great one who did make it was Giovanni Martinelli, heroic tenor of the Metropolitan and of Ravinia, where Louis Eckstein always began the twin bill with *Pagliacci*—he said that Martinelli's Canio would explode backstage if *Pagliacci* had to wait. Martinelli, a superb Otello, was often Chicago's guest. It was here he sang his only Tristan with Kirsten Flagstad in 1939. The roots were truly splendid. They spoke for a glorious past.

So what was I doing, paraphrasing the ineffable Sophie, who on our first meeting gave me a piece of motherly advice? She said "You'll never get anywhere in that dress. Too plain. Now look at mine"—blue brocade embroidered, beaded, tasseled and sequined—"what more

could you get for $65?" Sophie knew that rich was better. So, on my own shopping list, did I.

It was a dazzling list into which I tumbled with what you might call a blank check. When I started to work on the vanished *Chicago Journal of Commerce* I was the keeper of a full set of opera tickets airily designated for our non-existent society editor. I got the leftovers, if that is the right term, for such exotica as Mary Garden's Melisande, Jongleur and Honegger's Judith. Addiction followed as the night the day. When the editor suddenly put me on the aisle seat the floodgates opened. Each opera season, downtown and at Ravinia, staged 30 or more operas. My first Auditorium visitor on the aisle was Sol Hurok, inviting me to supper with Pavlova. There were no male chauvinists on the Ravinia aisles. On the contrary, they welcomed me for truly personal reasons.

In those days, if the opera kept giving *Tosca*, the lady might be Rosa Raisa, Claudia Muzio or, at Ravinia, the blandishing Yvonne Gall. The men in the press room said they were relieved that I too was smitten by the French charmer—"we were afraid she just batted those eyelashes at us and over we went, spouting superlatives."

Well, this is not an autobiography on the opera aisle. I just want to explain how pampered I had been in the lustrous world of opera, and how bitterly I missed its outpouring of music, theater, ballet, stage direction and scenic design. This was intensified when in the aftermath of World War II Europe had that ravishing renaissance of the only opera worth doing, the real thing. Naturally, dozens of people wanted to try it here. The three who did it made their felicitous decision at a Metropolitan Opera performance of *The Marriage of Figaro*. Felicitous because they wanted only the best.

That is a dazzling and a dangerous goal. In opera as in all stagecraft, some things look better on paper than on stage. Sometimes—in fact, much of the time—great voices and great conductors are in short supply. The cost, never negligible, keeps soaring. Ticket prices must be held down to a fraction of those charged at European festivals. Most of all, to aim high is to risk missing.

George Bernard Shaw said "Only the second rate are safe." Ashton Stevens said "Mediocrity is always at its best." Lyric is neither second rate nor mediocre—it is neither safe nor always at its best. It has had its problems, its disappointments, its failures as well as its spectacular triumphs. It was almost blown off the map after two seasons by the managerial dispute that turned Lyric Theater of Chicago into Lyric Opera, and left Carol Fox in sole charge. It

LEFT: NICOLA RESCIGNO, CAROL FOX AND LAWRENCE KELLY. CENTER: ADVERTISEMENT FOR THE OPENING OF LYRIC THEATRE. RIGHT: NICOLA RESCIGNO, BIDU SAYAO AND GIORGIO POLACCO.

took a fearful risk in cancelling the 1967 season because of an impasse with musicians and unions. But it survived.

Why? Because Chicago without the Lyric is unthinkable. Somehow, we all knew that from the start. The artists, a resonant gallery, gave the young company their heart's blood—there was no other way to explain those dazzling early seasons skyrocketed to instant fame by Maria Callas. Ardent audiences swept through the ticket racks like devouring locusts, and no one denies the lures of that drum beating Pied Piper, Danny Newman. But if you asked me what has kept the Lyric so radiantly alive, I would say, primarily Carol Fox.

It was sad to lose the brilliant imagination of Larry Kelly and the flowering of Nicola Rescigno's lyric talent. The triumvirate was unique. But we did not lose Carol Fox, and that turned out to be paramount. She has tenacity. She does not give in, or give up. Because we still have Lyric, much has been done, and anything is possible. Just once before, in the season of 1921–22, a woman was running Chicago opera. Mary Garden herself, the dazzling *directa* (her word) of our first million dollar opera deficit. It has been noted, here in Chicago, that Mary and Carol have the sound of Christmas. But then nothing is more festive than a great night at the opera.

What we rejoice in is the foliage, the coming together in splendor of taste and talent, which can amount to genius. But how deep are the roots? As deep, and as old, as opera. Chicago's first opera came overland, or by lake boat, and its luxurious Crosby Opera House had little satin sofas in the boxes. Adelina Patti opened the Auditorium in 1889 and from then on the sky was the limit. Tamagno in the brand new "Otello," Nordica, Lilli Lehmann, Sembrich, Maurel, the de Reszkes, Tetrazzini, Fremstad, Gadski, Journet, Plançon; a little later, Caruso, Toscanini, Farrar.

Our resident opera brought Mary Garden and a golden rain of French opera to the Auditorium in 1910–11—the company which as Oscar Hammerstein's Manhattan had fought New York's Metropolitan to a draw in an operatic duel rarely rivaled. It was a glorious era of spectacular opera—Cleofonte Campanini's reign which ended with his funeral service on the Auditorium stage in the temple scene of *Parsifal* with Rosa Raisa, his special protégée, singing the *Inflammatus* from Rossini's *Stabat Mater*. As time moved on, Chaliapin was there, Tito

NICOLA ROSSI-LEMENI AS **DON GIOVANNI,** 1954. AT LEFT AND RIGHT, CENTER, FROM LEFT: GEORGE LAWNER, MRS. NATHANIEL LEVERONE, ELEANOR STEBER, LAWRENCE WHITE, LAWRENCE KELLY, CAROL FOX, NATHANIEL LEVERONE, NORMAN ROSS, AT A DINNER PARTY, 1954.

TOP LEFT: OPENING NIGHT, NOVEMBER 1954. MARIA CALLAS AS **NORMA,** BACKSTAGE. TOP RIGHT: MARIA CALLAS AND NICOLA ROSSI-LEMENI BACKSTAGE. BOTTOM LEFT: ROSSI-LEMENI AND CALLAS IN PERFORMANCE. BOTTOM RIGHT: CALLAS AND MIRTO PICCHI.

Schipa an adored favorite, the repertory enormous, the relatively untaxed wealthy generous.

When the depression struck, opera had moved into the new Civic Opera House, where Egon Pollak headed a matchless German wing—Lotte Lehmann, Olszewska, Leider, Maison, Bockelmann, Nissen, Habich, Kipnis. It was there in 1940 that Fritz Reiner gave us *Der Rosenkavalier* and Artur Rodzinski his *Salome*—there that Rodzinski gave us his unique *Tristan and Isolde*, a Chicago Symphony Orchestra pension fund concert to welcome Kirsten Flagstad back after ugly exile.

Then for seven long years we had no opera of our own. None. One season we lost held a special Lyric root. It was in 1947 that the Scotto troupe came to town and never opened, because it ran out of money and was snagged in union trouble. It held major Italian, German and French artists little known here in that aftermath of World War II. To give you an idea, a newcomer named Maria Callas was to sing *Turandot*. A newcomer named Nicola Rossi-Lemeni had been engaged by San Francisco and the Metropolitan. And there they all were except Callas, who was still to arrive, stranded.

Telephones are remarkable instruments. Mine at the Chicago Tribune rang and a beautiful voice full of Chaliapin shadows sang to me. That settled it. We would at least have a benefit concert, and we did. Not enough, but a taste, a tantalizing taste to tell the opera fan what he had missed. A few of them did something about it. Nicola Rossi-Lemeni was Lyric's first Don Giovanni. After that, he told Callas to come to Chicago. So much for roots and history.

Even so, as Sarah Bernhardt used to say, enclosing the world of art—*Don Giovanni?* No more glorious, or more demanding, opera ever was written. It was a wonderful idea. But the Lyric in 1954 did not exist except in the minds of its founders. Any opera worth the name takes money, imagination, taste and the courage of a pride of lions. *Don Giovanni* takes miracles. The major miracle was that it got them.

I sat there that first night, remembering Flaubert's "The three finest things in creation are the sea, *Hamlet* and Mozart's *Don Giovanni.*" For we can look at the lake through a salt spray, if necessary. We can read *Hamlet*, though not many of us will get from it what a great actor can. But if we want *Don Giovanni*, make believe won't do the trick. *Don Giovanni* takes talent, carloads of flesh and blood talent, and a touch of genius helps. And there it was, a wonderful *Don Giovanni*, when the Lyric made its astoundingly successful debut.

It was Mozart to do credit to an established troupe of long standing. That it was conjured out of the air by a company which did not really exist until the curtain rose was a kind of authentic miracle, born of love.

It was, primarily, such a joyous performance, keyed to the exuberant vitality of Nicola Rossi-Lemini's Don. It was a big, bold performance with the full quota of stage bands, a performance so Mozartean in its play of light and shadow that it spun all of a piece the splendor of Eleanor Steber's Donna Anna, the silky textured tenor Léopold Simoneau bestowed on Don Ottavio, the mischievous glint of Bidu Sayão's Zerlina, and the other sides of the comic face, from the rue of Irene Jordan's Elvira, the peasant-not-quite-bumpkin that was Lorenzo Alvary's Masètto, and the knowing Leporello of John Brownlee, who used to sing the Don.

Nicola Rescigno's conducting was fortunate in its orchestra—lots of Chicago Symphony men—and more fortunate in knowing Mozart. William Wymetal's staging was simple and alive. Lyric had arrived, fortunately, to stay.

———

There was a second *Don Giovanni* set off by demand for the first, then the three who were Lyric set off for Europe to arrange the 1954 season of three weeks opening in November, and to plan for the 1955 season extended to five weeks. This would be impossible today when all major opera houses plan years in advance to snare their share of splendor. But in 1954 the operatic renaissance sweeping Europe in the wake of World War II had not yet reached us in full flood, though lustrous operatic recordings had created a band of aficionados unrivaled since Victor's spotted terrier cocked a listening head at Caruso and Galli-Curci. Lyric skimmed the cream.

Looking back, no doubt it is possible to overestimate those extraordinary seasons. Lyric had to build an orchestra, as the Chicago Symphony in full season was not available. It had to create a chorus, which is precisely what Michael Lepore did. It had to improvise settings from the splendid but aging wealth of the old Chicago opera warehouse, and that is what Gerald Ritholz did. It had to create a company in the true sense of that battered term, in depth.

This could not be done overnight, though precisely that seemed to have been done in that luminous *Don Giovanni*, yet while it was happening that stage gleamed with such a wealth of song, such a revelation of singing actors, such a radiant reminder of just what opera is all about, that inquisitive newcomers were captured, and the richest memories reinforced. I always remember what a man wrote me after a Callas performance. He said, "I see now what you mean. I just never heard opera before."

So we come back to Maria, then Meneghini, Callas. It isn't entirely fair, for those two seasons gleamed with song. But she did put the Lyric instantly on the international map. Her debut as Norma and the six roles she sang here found her—with the possible exception of the Luchino Visconti nights at the Scala—at her matchless crest. It was a brief, dazzling trajectory, as she soared, glittered and splintered in the astonished sky. I for one could never pay my debt to Lyric for the chance to hear her at that time.

She was at that time slender, blonde, with great, myopic eyes in that Greek mask of a face, that marvelous, haunting voice piercing the very heart of equilibrium, the very center of the phrase, as a great dancer does in flight. She had a very human woodwind sound—some said the clarinet. I heard the oboe and the mourning dove. Her descending scales were chromatic marvels, yet I never thought of that at the time—just of falling leaves spinning patterns.

When she came here she was shifting from the great dramatic roles—no more Isoldes, for one—and there was sometimes a slight unsteadiness when she pierced the stratosphere. But in those six roles—Norma, Violetta, Lucia, Elvira in *Puritani*, Leonora in *Il Trovatore* and her first Butterfly—we were all enriched beyond counting.

As Norma she had Giulietta Simionato as a glorious Adalgisa, and the supreme Rossi-Lemeni as the high priest resembling Michelangelo's Moses. For a new opera company to begin its first season with such riches was to have all the good fairies at the cradle, and no Carabosse.

Her Lucia with the ardent Giuseppe di Stefano had people remembering Garbo and John Gilbert. Ettore Bastianini was a notable newcomer in the stellar *Puritani*. No less than Jussi Bjoerling and the renowned Ebe Stignani joined her in *Trovatore*, the night Rudolf Bing threw in the sponge and came out to lure her to the Metropolitan. She had always had to hurry away from Lyric to open the Scala.

OPPOSITE PAGE: THE CALLAS **NORMA.**

That last time was the extra *Butterfly* sung to appease the disappointed, the night the luckless process server confronted a Callas fresh from hara-kiri, who suddenly turned into Medea with all the stops out.

But that last Cio-Cio-San for Lyric had been altogether extraordinary. From the start she had been fascinating, a kind of Kabuki figure with a touch of the Chinese marvel Mei-Lan-Fang. That last night her death scene was pure Callas distilled into heartbreak. As she struck the fatal blow her coiled hair flew out like a wild thing to shield her face. When the faithless Pinkerton called her name from outside, joy touched her, meeting death on the journey.

Have I forgotten her Violetta? No. Even in that company and in the coloratura realms of Lucia of the feathery scales, of Leonora spinning embroideries in the shadow of death, her Violetta was unique. Her beauty, of course. Her exquisite costumes by Biki, granddaughter of Puccini's Elvira. Her sensitive musical intelligence capturing in one unbroken line the theater of Dumas, the poignant lyric drama of Verdi. The glittering brilliance of feverish excitements, the quality of presence. She rivaled Garbo's Camille.

At its crest this was singing in an all but vanished style. Mesmerizing beauty was a part of it, a part of operatic revelation. Without Lyric we would not have heard that Callas. Callas in operatic concert, perhaps—she drew benefit houses. But Callas in the opera house, her home, probably not. The loss would have been irreparable.

The 1955 season had opera fans noting with some awe, "You have them both." Meaning that Renata Tebaldi had made her Lyric debut in *Aida* with Tullio Serafin, Italian opera in person, majestically in charge in the pit.

A few nights later, all but true dyed-in-the-wool Lyric fans thought it had gone mad. It is well known, say the cynics, that you just bill *La Boheme,* open the doors and, no matter who sings it, get out of the way of the mob. Lyric had Serafin in the pit, with Tebaldi, di Stefano, Rossi-Lemeni and Tito Gobbi for Puccini. A hard act to follow, but a lovely one to remember.

Tito Gobbi. What took me so long? This extraordinary singing actor is practically the Lyric's godfather. His obsidian Scarpia has been to our time what Antonio Scotti's was to Caruso's days at the Metropolitan. His Lyric roles have ranged the baritone galaxy, from Rigoletto to Rossini's Figaro, Iago to Gérard in *Andrea Chénier,* Renato in *Ballo* to Gianni Schicchi, Amonasro to the *Simon Boccanegra* he considers the *Boris* of baritones. His silky baritone could curl with delight or cut like a lash. Always an enormous favorite, he has turned to a new love, stage direction, where all he really needs is a mirror of his own performance.

There you have most of the singers and much of the repertory of those extraordinary first and second seasons. Not quite all. The 1955 *Ballo,* with Bjoerling and Gobbi, introduced what should have become the next great dramatic soprano. Anita Cerquetti. She was a big girl with an avalanche of a voice pouring like lava. But something happened, one of those inexplicable things that halts and destroys great promise. Just the same, to have heard that promise was to have known what can be.

It was 1955 when Rossi-Lemeni—both times with Serafin—sang his marvelous quack Dulcamara in *L'Elisir d'Amore* and his powerful blind king in *L'Amore dei Tre Re,* which brought Carlo Bergonzi as Avito and Dorothy Kirsten as Fiora, the role Mary Garden sang downtown and Lucrezia Bori at Ravinia—both with Virgilio Lazzari's Archibaldo. Another Rossi-Lemeni collaboration with Serafin was *Faust,* with Bjoerling soaring in the cavatina.

There were two triple bills that vivid 1955 season—that was before Lyric realized that while a triple bill may be three times as much fun, it is also three times as much work. Still, from out front you just see the fun.

The first bill held Gobbi in *Il Tabarro*, the murderous third of the Puccini triptych; a rare Monteverdi masque from ducal Mantua, *Il Ballo delle Ingrate*—to warn ungrateful wives—with Ebe Stignani and Teresa Stich-Randall to sing, and Zorina herself as Venus; and Ruth Page's *The Merry Widow*, with the feathery Alicia Markova.

At the second, Stignani and di Stefano sang *Cavalleria Rusticana*; Markova danced Page's *Revanche*, a ballet *Trovatore* designed by Antoni Clavé; and Lyric introduced *Lord Byron's Love Letter* (later recorded), a poignant short opera based by Raffaello de Banfield on Tennessee Williams' play. The score matches the story in the high, ecstatic tessitura of the supreme experience remembered. Astrid Varnay, Gertrude Ribla, a glimpse of Carol Lawrence, Rescigno's sensitive handling of the music, the crumbling house of memories—I have always wanted to hear it again.

So it was with Lyric Theater in its two radiant seasons, a time so extraordinary that when *Carmen* fell on its face a subscriber wrote, "Here's an extra five dollars. I was beginning to think you couldn't do anything wrong."

To the outsider, all was more than serene, it was glowing like a sunrise. But temperamental differences blew up a storm and when it was over Carol Fox was in charge of Lyric Opera, and her ex-collaborators Kelly and Rescigno had gone to Dallas, taking Maria Callas along.

It was like starting all over, only more so. Rescigno had conducted almost every performance, with Serafin the second season's honored guest. Major conductors are scarce and booked far in advance. They can also be generous in time of need. When Lyric opened its 1956 season with a roistering *The Girl of the Golden West*, adding the powerhouse Mario Del Monaco to Steber and Gobbi, Dimitri Mitropoulos rode to the rescue in the pit.

Georg Solti was lured from Europe—*Salome* with Inge Borkh, *Die Walküre* with Birgit Nilsson, a Rossi-Lemeni *Don Giovanni*, and what is generally conceded to be one of the matchless Lyric performances, *La Forza del Destino* with, count them, Tebaldi, Simionato, Richard Tucker, Bastianini, Rossi-Lemeni and the buffo Melitone, Carlo Badioli.

This *Forza* was Chicago's first performance since 1945, though it had been a great favorite here in the days of Raisa and Muzio, who loved to sing it. Lyric's cast speaks—or sang—for itself, magnificently. The staging by Aldo Mirabella Vassallo made it an opera, not a series of episodes. Solti's brilliant direction was both ardent and exact. He got what he wanted in that pit and on the stage, and what he wanted was the voice of Verdi. If it were possible to collect a Golden Dozen of Lyric's finest, *Forza* would leave you a choice of eleven.

Another welcome newcomer that season, the one who came and stayed, was Bruno Bartoletti. He declared himself with a fiery *Tosca*—Tebaldi, Bjoerling, Gobbi. Quite a declaration.

You can't have forgotten, unless you are very young, the rivalry not so much between Callas and Tebaldi as between their vociferous fans. I find this at the top of my *Tosca* review that October morning in 1956:

"In the unscheduled but not unpublicized bout between La Divina and La Superba, both of whom I admire enormously (you don't get me in the middle of this one) La Superba recently was characterized by an incautious umpire as 'intimidated.' Now I am quite aware that La

Divina, meaning Maria Meneghini Callas, can stalk her prey like a lithe lioness, emitting roars. But last night in the Civic Opera House La Superba, meaning Renata Tebaldi, came out of her *Tosca* corner like a hungry tigress defending her young."

She was pounds thinner, radiantly beautiful, and in voice so opulent it was both sumptuous and dangerous. She set the wonderful old thriller blazing. Gobbi's Scarpia was evil, carnal, ruthless, an aristocrat of style. Bjoerling's Cavaradossi had his own blazing fire, plus his own special gentleness for *E lucevan le stelle*, which Puccini set like a veiled star in the fading night.

It was a night of stars brightly shining, and Bartoletti the young Florentine was one of them, in command in the pit. Nor was all the glitter on stage. In the audience were Rosa Raisa, our great Tosca of older days, and Fritz Reiner, remembering *Toscas* of his days with Dresden opera. It was opera to send long memories back to the Auditorium when it still had the horseshoe curve of boxes. If Mary Garden was not singing, she was waving a handkerchief from the artists' box at the proscenium right. It just could be Queen Marie of Rumania in that box directly opposite the one where Mrs. Rockefeller McCormick was wearing her emeralds. If I ever build an opera house it will have encircling boxes, tiers of them. Remember the Scala as the lights slowly dim on jewels and red roses. Remember the time when Chicago opera, trying to be democratic, decreed that Wednesday was "don't dress" night, thereby enraging every woman who was planning a grand entrance. Remember when Callas came to the Lyric after her debut, and the audience stood up and applauded. She said, "That never happened to me before." Opera is something more than a performance and an audience, it is a state of mind.

On the big nights there can be one dazzling, overwhelming performance transcending all else. There can be a night many good things come together in strong rather than stellar focus. On rare nights all the stars are out—the singers, the conductor, the stage director, the designer, sometimes the ballet, often the sharing audience. That is when you discover, or rediscover, the opera itself.

I said earlier that the Lyric triumvirate which launched that crucial *Don Giovanni*, made its irrevocable decision in a Metropolitan Opera box at a performance of *The Marriage of Figaro.* To be born of Mozart is a challenge of sizable dimensions. The first Lyric *Figaro* was disappointing. But luxury came to the Opera House with the Viennese production of 1960. This is how it was:

"Opera theater has few rivals in the world of entertainment when *The Marriage of Figaro* captures the winged Mozart style. The Lyric's production last night was not only swift and gay and superbly sung, it was Viennese Mozart and that means a special enchantment.

"It means a lightness of touch never unintentionally shallow, a warm amusement that floods over the footlights, and in high places it means magnificent Mozart song. If you say what high places you can't possibly have looked at the cast.

"For it was right out of Vienna's top drawer, most of it, with the stellar quality *Figaro* demands and the expert ensemble it implores. So it ran all of a piece, with the arias swung on ribbons of by-play and the set pieces glinting in the interplay of accustomed performance. Christopher West had staged it simply and deftly, and Josef Krips' conducting did justice to the singers, the audience and the score. That is, we all heard and enjoyed each other, so that the audience was a part of the performance. The torrents of applause at all sorts of places would have scandalized a Viennese, but it worked out fine. *Figaro* blooms on applause, for as comedy a good performance is in everyone's vernacular.

"Where do you begin with such a cast? With Elisabeth Schwarzkopf, Christa Ludwig, Walter Berry and Fernando Corena, so warmly welcomed back? Or with the brilliant newcomers, Eberhard Waechter and Rita Streich? The truth is that in *Figaro* they are inextricable in glowing, knowing Mozart song.

"Schwarzkopf, never more beautiful than in the Countess' radiance and rue, began a little dryly with the merciless *Porgi amor*, warmed quickly to exquisite song, and was in her full splendor, which is matchless, for *Dove sono.* Ludwig, a chubby, adorable but never 'cute' Cherubino, sang like so much warm velvet. Streich, a superb Susanna with the swift hands of a born comedienne, has a pure crystal voice that embroiders Mozart ensembles with *diamante.* When she and Schwarzkopf sang the letter song I remembered with pride that I have a copy from the Salzburg Mozarteum, autographed by two of their predecessors, Claire Dux and Edith Mason.

"Berry, rather under wraps when he sang Figaro here three years ago, was as much at home this time as on the stage of the Staatsoper, gay, wry, debonair, and in beautiful voice. Corena etched Bartolo in drypoint on a carrying scale.

"Which brings me to Eberhard Waechter, whose Almaviva was a memorable debut. Without using makeup, or visible makeup, he can look like any role he plays, and in some curious way he can also sound like it. Here was an overprivileged grandee up to his ears in intrigue. A young grandee, and this, with Schwarzkopf's touch of mischief, made the Almavivas a part of things rather than onlookers. A grandee who took his position for granted and who could take in stride the big aria of revenge, *Vedrò, mentr'io sospiro*. Such an Almaviva rounds out the whole opera, for the man is often made pompous and stupid, two things Mozart's count is not.

"This was a true *Figaro* in all its cosmopolitan delight—Viennese, from the French, in Italian, with that crucial understanding of the Spanish sense of caste."

Memory exaggerates? Of course it does. Looking back can intensify. When the Ballets Russes considered reviving dazzling Russian ballets that had stunned Paris in debut engagement,

Serge Diaghilev said "We must intensify the colors—they will have been exaggerated in memory." Which is why, saluting Lyric on the eve of its 25th season, I trust not what I remember, but what I wrote, instantly for next morning's Chicago Tribune, or, subsequently, next Sunday's WFMT. From where I sit, and have sat since the Opera House opened in 1929, this is how it was.

Undeniably, though, there are times when a great performance takes on a special poignancy because of what comes after. It was 1958 when Lyric captured Artur Rodzinski for its first *Tristan*, ten years after his glorious and tragic season with the Chicago Symphony Orchestra. This is how it was:

"To know and cherish the singing splendor of Artur Rodzinski's Wagner is never to be quite prepared for what happens the next time he puts all his skill and his whole heart into incandescent performance. It happened at Ravinia and in Orchestra Hall time and time again. It happened 11 years ago in the Opera House when he conducted the Chicago Symphony Orchestra's *Tristan and Isolde* with Kirsten Flagstad at her zenith. It happened again Saturday night when with that same opera he returned to set the Lyric a new standard of music drama and to introduce in her richest role Birgit Nilsson, the next great Nordic Isolde.

"For this was a miraculous performance, ending on the dot of midnight, but in no danger of turning into a pumpkin coach in the matter of losing its audience, had it gone on a full hour more. Its secret was the secret of all great music drama, the glory of what happened in the orchestra pit. Skeptics doubted that it could be done with the Lyric orchestra, which is comparatively new, and recruited for a short season. It certainly is not like having the Chicago Symphony Orchestra.

"But an orchestra will give its heart and soul and perhaps its union card to a great leader. What that orchestra did for Rodzinski, for Wagner, and for the audience was to pour out the molten gold of the score as if mesmerized. Perhaps it was mesmerized. In that packed theater, why should the orchestra be an exception?

"For the stage was held in the music's thrall, and the audience is the stage's reflection. What we saw was an extraordinary performance, though not all that went into it was so. Some of the singers were below the higher Wagner quality, and some of the smaller roles

LEFT: TITO GOBBI, **LE NOZZE DI FIGARO**, 1957. RIGHT: MARIANO CARUSO, ANNA MOFFO, TITO GOBBI AND GIULIETTA SIMIONATO, **LE NOZZE DI FIGARO**, 1957.

TOP LEFT: ELISABETH SCHWARZKOPF, RITA STREICH, AND CHRISTA LUDWIG, **LE NOZZE DI FIGARO,**
1960. TOP RIGHT: LISA DELLA CASA, RITA STREICH, AND TERESA BERGANZA, **LE NOZZE DI FIGARO,** 1962.
BOTTOM: SCHWARZKOPF, **LE NOZZE DI FIGARO,** 1960.

probably ranked as first time performances. But the autumnal beauty of the old Chicago Opera settings looked down on a *Tristan* of youth and poetry that held its own dignity and repose. It knew that music alone brings the legend to life.

"When that music is matched by the kind of voice for which it was created something close to divine fire burns in the opera house.

"It burned most fiercely for Nilsson, who has all it takes to be a magnificent Isolde. The soaring, all but tireless soprano, the personal beauty, the serenity, the style. Not all of it is fully developed, and there are times when she is not quite cradled in the center of pitch—that wonderfully comfortable place to sing which focuses her voice like a golden trumpet. But her first act already is magnificent, and once she is fully in command of the role she will have audiences hanging from the rafters. They are shouting the house down for her now.

"Karl Liebl is a Tristan of quality—no clarion heldentenor, but a good tenor of knightly quality and baritone shadows. Grace Hoffman, the new Brangaene, has a big, voluminous mezzo soprano of gorgeous colorings, and she sings the warning in the dusk with great beauty. Walter Cassel is a Kurwenal who understands the knight's squire, puts him squarely in the picture, and has the baritone to keep him there. William Wildermann is Marke part way—the man is bigger than that, in voice and poetry.

"But in this case the sum of the whole was larger than the parts because the music magnified it. As for the audience, as Schumann said of one at the Beethoven Ninth, 'I do not recall that ever before has it (the music) been received so enthusiastically. Saying this we do not mean to praise the work, which is beyond praise, but the audience.' "

So there is no counting the worth of a major opera company—there never was, and there never will be. Lyric's first *Tristan* brought us that preview of the next great Nordic Isolde and, though we did not know it at the time, Artur Rodzinski's glowing farewell.

Though no one will believe this except other occupants of professional aisle seats, it is sometimes such a pleasure to be wrong. When in 1964 Lyric announced that it would do *Ariadne auf Naxos*, my reaction was one of Gilbertian modified rapture. Let me explain myself, as of the next morning:

"It was something close to a miracle, Lyric's first *Ariadne auf Naxos*, affectionately spun of brilliance, tenderness, buffoonery and high skill. It really was not in the cards to happen, not a success like this. For no Richard Strauss opera is simple, and this one is fantastically complex, having a way of blowing bubbles that when you least expect it turn into something more like tears. Besides, it belongs in a jewel box theater like Munich's Cuvilliés—not in our huge hall.

"But there it was, a triumph. It was borrowed from all over the hospitable globe, with Oliver Messel's beguilingly baroque stage coming alive in Josef Witt's gleaming stagecraft, with a cast summoned as if by magic, and with the Lyric's own orchestra sounding bewitched by Eugen Jochum, whose strong, vital conducting went straight to the ecstatic heartbeat of Strauss.

"When *Ariadne* goes with such a flair—it doesn't very often, even in the most richly equipped houses—I mourn the loss of Strauss' original version with the music of *Le Bourgeois Gentilhomme*.

"Still, the way it is—with a serious opera and a harlequinade performed simultaneously at the whim of a *nouveau riche*—it is quite complicated enough to tax a theater's ingenuity.

"When it works, it is one of the more diverting Strauss-Hofmannstahl collaborations, for like *Der Rosenkavalier* it has three wonderfully contrasting roles for sopranos, and the Lyric had the sopranos. Irmgard Seefried for the Composer who would be Octavian's equivalent. Régine Crespin for Ariadne, not exactly a Marschallin, and Reri Grist for Zerbinetta, who is enchantingly, bewitchingly herself. Wonderful how Strauss, and his audience, falls in love with each in turn.

"It is possible to say that Seefried does not now have the full splendor of the voice that once poured from her as Strauss' passionate young composer constantly fighting for his music, and constantly falling in love. Possible, but not really important.

"For she has such ardor, such warmth of heart, such depth of musicianship, and she so unaccountably makes you think of the young Beethoven. I had never before seen the Composer's scene with Zerbinetta when it brought tears to your eyes, as the scene of the rose can with Octavian and Sophie.

"Crespin is a sumptuous woman, wittily amusing in the prologue where her jealous prima donna is a rainbow of curl papers, stunning in the opera where Ariadne is forsaken by a mortal and loved by a god. Her voice has the French rather than the Viennese timbre, and at times the sound is wrong. But in the apotheosis she soars, and never was a beautiful woman happier to be rescued.

"Little Grist—now there was a debut. She is tiny and dainty and amusing in a thistledown sort of way, and she sings the birds right off the trees. She handles Strauss' *Grossmächtige Prinzessin*—a kind of fabulous coloratura jest—with the airy elegance of the effortless. It is a marvelous piece of singing, pure and true, but what you remember is that she sings with complete and utter delight.

"Too much space has run by and too many people are waiting in the wings. Consider this a salute to cast, orchestra and crew. To Jean Cox for his handsome ease as Bacchus, a rather churlish Straussian gesture to tenors. To the special skills of Erich Kunz's Harlequin, Morley Meredith's Major Domo, Gerhard Unger's Dancing Master and Brighella, and to Bernard Izzo for his droll lackey, neither too little nor too much.

"The size of the house? I should have remembered Wilhelm Furtwaengler. When I asked him which was the best house in Europe, he said, 'The one with the best performance.' "

Turandot is in a sense a Chicago opera possession. Rosa Raisa, the regal beauty whose voice was royal purple streaked with gold, created the title role with Toscanini at the Scala, and he was not at all pleased that the crystalline Edith Mason, the chosen Liu, was having a baby. Raisa gave her costumes, including that fabled 40 foot train, to the Lyric.

Here is the Lyric's *Turandot* of '59:

"It was a stunning *Turandot*, even finer than last year's, which was a Lyric triumph. The old fire was back, the old brilliance took command, and the big house glowed and glittered with Puccini song.

"It came from quite a cast, quite a conductor, and increasingly, quite an opera. For years *Turandot* was patronized as a Puccini afterthought, a dim echo of richer song. But as the years go by its barbaric beauty takes a deeper place in admiration and affection, and the sorrow is that Puccini died before it was finished. As things are, the opera really dies with Liu, for her suicide is the place where the faithful but uninspired Alfano took over. When I don't leave at

MARIO DEL MONACO, *PAGLIACCI*, AND GIULIETTA SIMIONATO, *CAVALLERIA RUSTICANA*

LEONTYNE PRICE AS **THAÏS,** 1959.

RENATA TEBALDI AND GIUSEPPE DI STEFANO IN **FEDORA,** 1960.

RENATA TEBALDI AS **TOSCA,** 1960 (TOP PHOTO) AND AS **FEDORA,** 1960 (BOTTOM PHOTO).

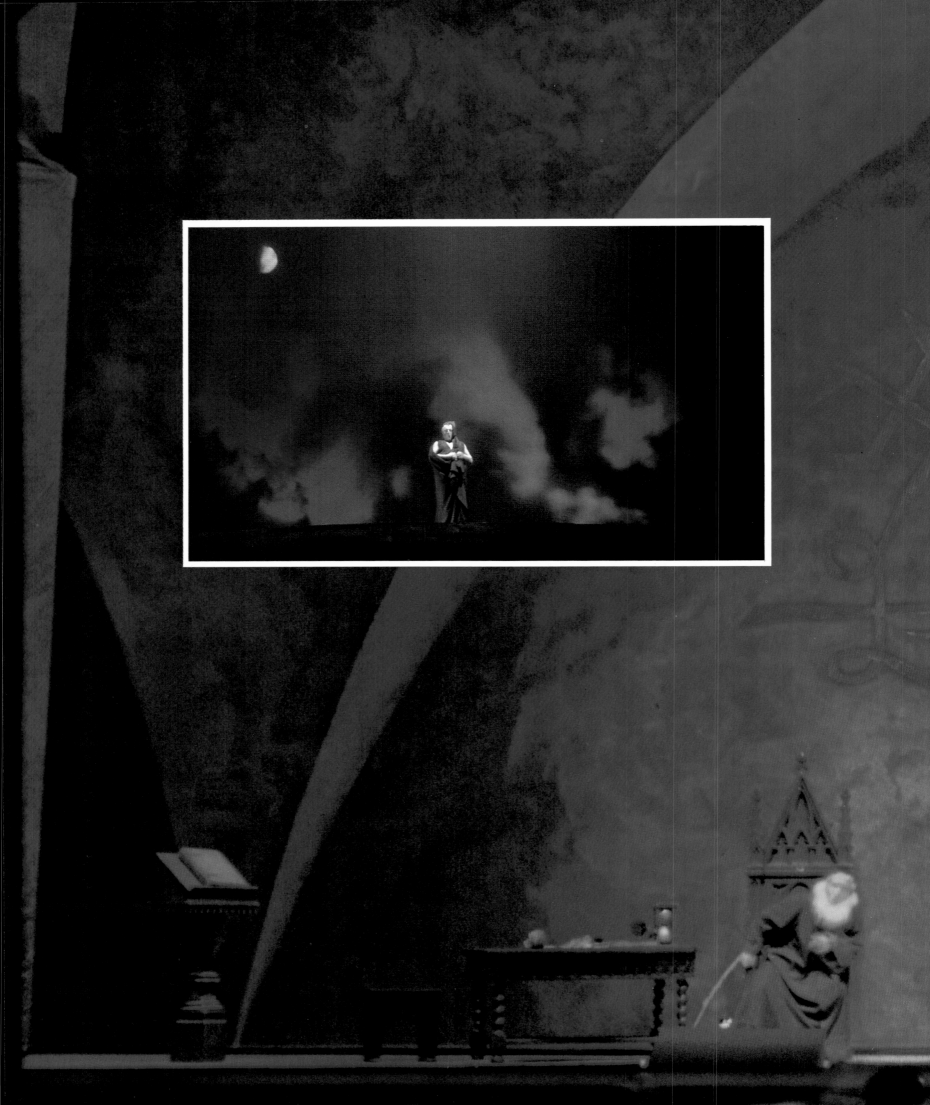

BORIS CHRISTOFF AND CARLO BERGONZI IN **MEFISTOFELE,** 1961. INSERTS: CHRISTOFF AS **MEFISTOFELE.**

BIRGIT NILSSON AND GIUSEPPE DI STEFANO, **TURANDOT,** 1959.

TOP: RIGHT TO LEFT: LEONIE RYSANEK, TITO GOBBI, JUSSI BJOERLING, KENNETH SMITH,
GIULIETTA SIMIONATO, AND WILLIAM WILDERMANN, **AIDA,** 1958.
BOTTOM: ASTRID VARNAY IN **LORD BYRON'S LOVE LETTER,** 1955.

TOP LEFT: REGINE CRESPIN, **UN BALLO IN MASCHERA,** 1963. TOP
RIGHT: SENA JURINAC, **OTELLO,** 1963. BOTTOM: ELISABETH
SCHWARZKOPF AND CHRISTA LUDWIG, **COSI FAN TUTTE,** 1959.

TOP LEFT: ALFREDO KRAUS, **LA FAVORITA,** 1974. TOP RIGHT: NICOLAI
GHIAUROV, **DON CARLO,** 1964. BOTTOM LEFT: TITO GOBBI, **OTELLO**
1963. BOTTOM RIGHT: FRANCO CORELLI AND GRACE BUMBRY,
IL TROVATORE, 1964.

that point, I always wish I had. For there is a burnished beauty about the best of *Turandot* and that I want fresh to remember.

"On almost every front this was a memorable performance.

"Gianandrea Gavazzeni had the orchestra playing better than it can play, which is no contradiction but an occasional phenomenon heard on a big night when the whole is greater than its parts. True, he could have used more and richer strings, and far finer winds and brass. But there he was, working on the top level and getting some wonderfully effective Puccini sound. As Puccini gives his own stage directions with every note, a good Puccini conductor is worth every cent you have to pay.

"The four leading roles held two singers from last season—Birgit Nilsson and Giuseppe di Stefano—and two welcome newcomers, Leontyne Price and Ferruccio Mazzoli.

"Nilsson's Turandot is not (was not then) Puccini's woman of ice melted by the fire of love, but when that cold steel voice soars it is as thrilling as a drawn sword forged in Toledo. Price's Liu poured one of the loveliest lyric voices of our time into the poignant pattern Puccini loved so well he was planning to extend the role (for Edith Mason) when he died.

"Caught between two such voices, a heart-slasher and a heart-breaker, di Stefano, who can grow moodily morose when bored, sang Calaf with all the poetic ardor at his command, which is about as much as our generation has to offer Puccini. *Nessun dorma* had the melting textures of the night, yet knew its dangers. When he guessed the riddles he challenged Nilsson, which takes doing.

"Ferruccio Mazzoli, the sad old king of Tartary, underscored the promise heard in *Simon Boccanegra*. He is a picturesque young bass with a big, dark and beautiful voice. The company is richer for having him. The chorus did some of its finest work. The flaws were minor, the performance major. When you go to the opera, that is what counts."

OPPOSITE PAGE: OPENING NIGHT, 1978.

ABOVE: ANTONIO GADES, **EL AMOR BRUJO,** 1969.

Great singers, great conductors, great composers are not available for cloning. They come in their own time and not to use them while you can is to flout Shakespeare's time and tide. The Lyric was not really ready for *Otello* in 1957—its fourth season, the second after the schism. Yet how penny wise and pound foolish it would have been not to risk the gamble. When it paid off, the odds were spectacular.

Stellar performances by Renata Tebaldi, Mario Del Monaco and Tito Gobbi, a powerful orchestra under the command of Tullio Serafin, a good chorus, a series of spectacular stage pictures, some vivid staging, an *Otello* of smouldering fires and some fierce spurts of flame—not quite the molten glow that is the revelation of incandescence. And yet, who could forget it in the gallery of ultimate Verdi? This is how it was:

"With honors to spare for all, Del Monaco's is the crucial casting. He has the voice for Otello, and such a tenor can skip whole generations. It is a big beautiful voice with the ring of steel, the hurt of anguish, the spectacular range, and the noble style of declamation. If he were a great actor he would be a magnificent Otello. Instead, he is a striking one, handsome in barbaric splendor, superbly costumed, and with a voice that rejoices in rather than strangles on the score. Without him we could put *Otello* back where it has been far too long, on the operatic shelf.

"His catlike foil is Gobbi's Iago, who has the face of an impish, evil child, the supple voice of a man who knows how to make it say what he isn't thinking. His *Credo* pours out no torrent of tone, but it stirs depths dangerously stagnant.

"Between them stands Tebaldi's Desdemona, no doormat, but a beautiful woman unable to accept rejection and so doomed to press it to destruction. The beauty of Tebaldi's voice is a wonder of our time, but I think it was never more beautiful than this opening night when it poured out in all its splendor, or touched the *Willow Song* with the poignancy of despair."

It was a special Lyric benison in that early time to have the honored Venetian, Serafin, veteran of all the great opera houses. Serafin was conducting that Metropolitan *Falstaff* in 1925 when Lawrence Tibbett's Ford launched a career by stealing the show. If you heard him in Italy, no matter how celebrated the cast and how frenzied the applause, it reached its ultimate decibel when the Maestro appeared. There was a splendor about him, once known, always cherished.

Of course, cherishing is what your opera aficionado is all about. He can be found in any gathering, waiting to pounce on any expression of admiration with "Ah—but you should have heard . . ." Everyone knows about this in the worlds of the soprano, the tenor, the sumptuous mezzo-soprano and the resonant baritone. The stellar bass is more rare, even in the annals of La Scala, which opened August 3, 1778 with a Salieri opera demanding an orchestra of 70 and 36 horses, but whose playbill neglected to name the composer, though the Archduke and his Princess were present in person and in the larger type. The stars had to be right in the Chaliapin heavens for Lyric, one eighth the Scala's age, to have snared for such wealth of sharing first its inaugural Nicola Rossi-Lemeni, then Boris Christoff, and now Nicolai Ghiaurov. All these have worn and magnetized the *Boris* crown.

Rossi-Lemeni's value, especially in those crucial early years of Lyric flowering, is beyond computing. His mesmeric voice and presence, his generosity enriched every stage. I once said to Callas, "There is just one person on that stage who matches you." She said, "Oh, yes—Rossi."

OPPOSITE PAGE: RERI GRIST AND IRMGARD SEEFRIED, **ARIADNE AUF NAXOS**, 1964.

50

Oddly, or perhaps not at all oddly because he always sees them coming, I had first heard both Christoff and Ghiaurov at Salzburg in Herbert von Karajan's *Verdi Requiem*. Without Lyric, we probably would have lured them to Chicago, perhaps in recital, perhaps with the orchestra. With Lyric they have enriched not just our opera stage, but its repertory.

When Christoff made his Lyric debut in 1957 with the Solti *Don Carlo* he was a man of presence and authority whose voice poured out in a voluminous dark flood with the sumptuous shadows of *mezza voce*. His foil was his brother-in-law, Tito Gobbi, a Rodrigo both lyrical and Spanish as the marquis with the misfortune to be shot in the back by an arquebus.

Christoff's *Mefistofele* gave Chicago its first performance since 1936 of Boito's version of *Faust*. All the anthracite in that voice came out for this magnetic Lucifer of a flaming Brocken scene whose projected scenery and writhing dancers suggested Dali's Inferno holding open house in *Goyescas*. A minor Mephisto would have been dwarfed in so flaming a production.

Not so Christoff. He was as tautly mesmeric as the gray friar as when he strode in scarlet—perhaps more so, because the friar holds the lure of mystery. He even had the shrill Chaliapin whistle. He also had the strong conducting of Antonino Votto (call him Antonio at your peril), Carlo Bergonzi as Faust, Ilva Ligabue as a Margherita all promise, and a creamily moonstruck Helen of Troy, Christa Ludwig. This was a revival of imagination and style, staged by Riccardo Moresco, its soaring flames and triptychs the projections of Enzo Deho.

So what of the falcon? It sounds like the name of a television series, but it was 1962's *Prince Igor*, the opera and the famed Polovetsian dances. Where Christoff was the Tartar chief with a monkey fur wig and a live falcon clawing at his wrist, the real Tartar was Rudolf Nureyev, a feral, catlike warrior leaping like a fully bent bow, and pouring dynamite into the *grande pirouette*. Igor Gorin came for the title role, brilliant young David Poleri was the ardent tenor of the song of night and love.

Borodin's *Igor* was twice raided, by Diaghilev for the dances and by "Strangers in Paradise" for the popular song. As opera it is not fully a triumph, though Rimsky-Korsakov

LEFT: TITO GOBBI, RENATA TEBALDI AND MARIO DEL MONACO, BACKSTAGE DURING **OTELLO**, 1957. RIGHT: DEL MONACO AND TEBALDI ONSTAGE, **OTELLO**, 1957.

52

TOP LEFT: GEORG SOLTI ARRIVES FOR HIS AMERICAN OPERATIC CONDUCTING DEBUT WITH LYRIC OPERA, 1956. TOP RIGHT: ARTUR RODZINSKI. BOTTOM LEFT: TULLIO SERAFIN. BOTTOM RIGHT: GIANANDREA GAVAZZENI.

FOLLOWING PAGES, LEFT TO RIGHT: NELL RANKIN, ANITA CERQUETTI, TITO GOBBI, BRIAN SULLIVAN AND BORIS CHRISTOFF IN THE AUTO-DA-FE SCENE, **DON CARLO,** 1957.

and Glazounov worked on it, but it does have rich choruses, grateful arias, outbursts of the oriental, a kind of refreshing exotica. The Lyric's Oskar Danon made the most of it. Ruth Page staged the dances she had danced years before with the original warrior, Adolf Bolm. It was welcome on Wacker Drive with the powerful Christoff and the magnetizing Nureyev on the threshold of world fame.

Timing is all, sometimes a gift, sometimes a disappointment. Because Rossi-Lemeni, a wonderful, haunting Boris, was here before Lyric was ready to tackle Moussorgsky's overwhelming opera, that honor went to Christoff's blackly brooding portrait of the mad Tsar. That performance was a time of burgeoning splendor veiled in sorrow. What turned out to be Rodzinski's fatal illness forced him to cancel the *Boris Godunov* planned to follow his *Tristan*. Georges Sebastian was the able rescuer.

It is rare for three singers of *Boris* caliber to converge in Lyric's brief span, yet there came its three "Russian" basses, whatever their slavic roots. Rossi-Lemeni hailed from Italy and La Scala and, magnifying the unlikely odds, the two Bulgarians were here in the 1963 season.

Christoff returned as the powerful Pizarro in *Fidelio*, as the cavernous Basilio in a rollicking *Barber*, and in the historic *Nabucco*, that operatic turning point for the young Verdi, whose requiem by Toscanini and the Scala chorus was its nostalgic lament, *Va, pensiero*. Ghiaurov made his American debut as Lyric's Mephistopheles in *Faust*.

I mentioned earlier that I had heard both Bulgarian basses in the *Verdi Requiem* with Karajan. That *Requiem* summer of 1949 Christoff was mesmerizing Verona's Roman Arena in an Italian *Lohengrin*, whose willowy Elsa was Renata Tebaldi. Ghiaurov's *Requiem* in 1962 was the same summer he sang Padre Guardiano in London's *Forza* with Solti. Without Lyric as showcase they might have remained lustrous names in a distant gallery.

OPPOSITE PAGE: SONIA AROVA AND RUDOLF NUREYEV, IN A GALA PERFORMANCE FOR LYRIC OPERA, 1962. NUREYEV MADE HIS AMERICAN OPERA DEBUT WITH LYRIC OPERA EARLIER THAT SEASON.

ABOVE LEFT: SONIA AROVA AND RUTH PAGE, **REVANCHE**, 1955. RIGHT: OLEG BRIANSKY AND ALICIA MARKOVA IN REHEARSAL FOR **THE MERRY WIDOW**, 1955.

No portrait gallery of opera is richer than that of the great Mephisto. Here is what happened the night of Ghiaurov's American debut:

"This is a tremendous voice, used rather more in the tradition of Journet and possibly Plançon than in the more familiar guise of Chaliapin. It is a huge black column of a voice in the grand manner, of full range and wonderful color, a voice peremptory by its very sound. I doubt the ear exists that is not impelled to listen. That voice commands the stage, fills the theater, and fulfills the composer. It is like a black mirror of satanic moods, capturing evil, mockery, contempt, even fear.

"With the voice goes a tall, supple Mephisto with the dark face to command the peaked and feathered cap, the elegance to carry the courtier's garb flicked with flame, glinted with jewels, mocking with gloves like a cardinal's with the ring. He has everything the role demands, including the flair for all the sulphuric tricks. He chalked up one of Lyric's great triumphs."

So Ghiaurov came back the next season as the most extraordinary *Don Giovanni* since Ezio Pinza. A striking young Don of high spirits, volcanic energy, vivid stage presence and a huge singing bass to dazzle the champagne aria and to wrap *Là ci darem* in velvet.

Except for Nicoletta Panni's silkily mischievous Zerlina the men outshone the women, from Josef Krips' knowing Mozart in the pit to Erich Kunz's Leporello, a marvel of gaiety, wit and servile stance. Few who saw it can have forgotten his masquerade when Don Ottavio looked with dismay on what he believed to be a grovelling grandee. Don Ottavio was a grandee himself, with an aristocrat's tenor, and Spanish at that, despite his name, Alfredo Kraus.

Yet it was not as Don Giovanni that Ghiaurov made his bow that 1964 season. Boris Christoff was in a Rome hospital recovering from surgery—he has long since resumed his career, but not with Lyric. He had twice sung Philip of Spain in the Lyric's *Don Carlo*—this third time it was Nicolai Ghiaurov.

It was astonishing how much they looked alike, those two stellar Bulgarians—no doubt in part the stamp of La Scala. Dour, grim, in the end, tragic. The figure in black with the walking stick Ghiaurov ignored in his own apartments, as if it were merely a prop of state. The Philip voice to match, big, black and brusque except in grief. Ghiaurov's was a lava flood in the powerhouse of his youth, his great aria one of pride shipwrecked on grief.

A tantalizing might have been is that Martti Talvela, another lava outpouring, had been engaged as the Grand Inquisitor, but had withdrawn until a later season. Imagine that confrontation. Along with Fiorenza Cossotto's soaring Eboli, the stellar Richard Tucker and Tito Gobbi, and Bartoletti's singing Verdi in the pit.

Of course, opera fans are insatiable. It goes with the territory. When I think of that stellar triptych I regret every performance lost to Lyric. Rossi-Lemeni's Boris that mesmerized Verona's huge arena. His Philip II, which I heard at La Scala in 1952, two years before Lyric was born with his Don Giovanni.

It had been a Verdi pilgrimage, from Roncole and Busseto to Milan with Giorgio Polacco, a Verdi venerator, into the Scala museum and Verdi's Home for the Repose of Musicians, where he lies in the courtyard beneath D'Annunzio's inscription, "He wept and loved for all." From

there to the Scala to be captured forever by Rossi-Lemeni, the magnetic man closer to Chaliapin than any I have heard, a superb singer with that touch of the shadowed baritone heard in the basso cantante, a voice all imagination and mystical shadows. His somber soliloquy will haunt me all my *Don Carlo* days. The more great performances, the richer the opera house.

Each artist of this mighty triptych has enriched Lyric uniquely. Nicolai Ghiaurov restored Mussorgsky's *Khovanshchina* to the repertory in 1969 (and 1976), and added Massenet's *Don Quichotte* in 1974. By the grace of operatic forces which sometimes meet in full tide, both were superb performances. Both were originally Chaliapin operas, though Vanni-Marcoux, Chicago's Don from the time of Mary Garden's Dulcinée, sang the Paris première soon after Chaliapin's at Monte Carlo in 1910.

But they were considered one man shows, and sometimes not even the mightiest man was enough. When Chaliapin introduced *Don Quichotte* at the Metropolitan in 1926, Lawrence Gilman, critic of the Herald-Tribune, saluted him as a true Don Quixote—but Mr. Gilman had this to say about Massenet, "This intrepid composer, gifted with the spiritual distinction of a butler, the compassionate understanding of a telephone girl, and the expressive capacity of an amorous tomcat . . . did his worst."

This would be mildly discouraging to all revivals. Just the same, Vanni-Marcoux restored *Don Quichotte* to the Chicago season of 1929-30 with the Russian conductor Emil Cooper. It was a *tour de force* in which a knightly dreamer leaned against a tree and sagged, almost imperceptibly, in defeat.

Even to long memories, this indelible glimpse had just one rival, the sight of Chaliapin in the frayed film with George Robey as Sancho, and with music by Ibert because disagreement

with the producer turned Ravel's music into his song cycle, *Don Quichotte à Dulcinée.*

This was Chaliapin at 62, with the fading but still resplendent voice, that quality of brooding over the world, of striding beside you into the whirlwind. Chaliapin the ex-stevedore who invisibly but unmistakably wore a crown, his voice mysterious and terrible, seductive and sardonic. Even in the frayed film you see the great clown he made of Basilio the music master peering through the mad Tsar of the Russias. Could any new production, however gifted the protagonist find its own way through such clinging cobwebs of memories?

It could and it did. In performance, staging and design, with a magnetic Don whose magnificent voice is full of slavic shadows, this is how it was:

"With Andrew Foldi's powerful, faithful but not foolhardy Sancho, Viorica Cortez' inimically alluring Dulcinée, Jean Fournet's understanding elegance in the French style, shared to a reassuring degree by Italo Tajo's staging, this *Don Quichotte* is picturesquely and lavishly designed by Pier Luigi Samaritani, with lighting to set it off by Gil Wechsler.

"Of course, it would not be opera without its whimsies. This *Don Quichotte* has been moved from the Middle Ages to the 19th century, I've no idea why, and all that handsome scenery gives you too many long intermissions. Considering how brilliantly Mr. Samaritani handled the cyclorama projection of the Don's vision—a kind of sepia Chagall swirl of his beloved, his imagined adversaries, and even a tumble of what might be Faust's forbidden books—he could have given us a dream *Don Quichotte* with no intermissions at all.

"But lots of people love intermissions, they dote on applauding scenery while interrupting the music, and this *Quichotte* solution works admirably on its own terms. The idealist is an anachronism in any century, and only the Dulcinée scenes—first in the Spanish town of dusky perspective, and then in a kind of gardens of the Alhambra—carry a hint of the calendar.

VIORICA CORTEZ AND NICOLAI GHIAUROV, **DON QUICHOTTE,** 1974.

"The forests of great, gnarled trees and moonstruck nights are as timeless as bandits wrapped in huge capes, carrying serrated knives, and struck to their knees by the guileless knight they meant to hang, after cutting his throat.

"After all, Massenet wrote a romantic opera in Cervantes adaptation and sometimes eloquent, sometimes perfumed music to match, with more than a dash of Bizet in the hanging gardens. Do it with style, the precise, understated French style, and it works.

"Tajo held his staging within the freedom of that frame. The one exception was the intrusion of the two clowning valets, which he probably made a note of from the third row. In general, this was top-drawer staging: Dulcinée's almost imperceptible rejection of her suitors, always indicating that it might be different the next time—surely the courtesan's major lure; the handling of the crowd, the delightful ballet with its bedecked and tipsy bull, its novice matadors, even the scurry of the children, who seemed to live there. My heart went up at once, and stayed there. The Lyric's luck was in, even to the risk of a real Rosinante and two donkeys, all trying to trip their descending riders.

"Nicolai Ghiaurov's Don is quite his own, and yet at times he made me think of Marcel Marceau's Bip entangled in dreams of chivalry. A kind of sweetness in the face of the impossible—the wholly vulnerable point of unjustified view. When he gets his lady's guerdon, her handkerchief, he is in bliss; when she brushes his cheek with a kiss, it all but fells him. Nothing in his gaunt, tottering courage had armed him against such joy. He makes the faintest of deprecating gestures, but life at that moment is almost more than even Don Quichotte had ever imagined.

"This could be wholly French. But not the death of the Ghiaurov Don. He does not wear the rusty armor, he does not lean against the tree. He lies exhausted on the great mossy bank, with Sancho mourning. He dies like Boris, the mad tsar of all the Russias, in a great surge of splendor as suddenly vanished as summoned.

"Many people call opera an anachronism. Assuming that they could be right, which I seriously doubt, is that bad—considering a great night with Massenet's *Don Quichotte* in honor of the Don Quixote of Miguel de Cervantes Saavedra?"

If *Don Quichotte* is a rare operatic item, *Khovanshchina* is even rarer. Chaliapin sang it at St. Petersburg, Marcel Journet was its protagonist in Paris with Serge Koussevitzky conducting. Both Christoff and Rossi-Lemeni sang it at La Scala. Even in such company, call the Lyric blessed. That November night in 1976, this is how it was:

"Count *Khovanshchina* high among the reasons why Lyric is a Chicago treasure, restoring the only kind of opera worth the name, much less the cost. The real thing in all its manifold splendors of music drama.

"This is a powerful opera in the stunning Benois production, staged by Sonja Frisell and conducted by Bruno Bartoletti, with the great singing actor Nicolai Ghiaurov heading the strong cast.

"In *Khovanshchina* the protagonist is the Russian people, and the Lyric chorus rose to the challenge both as actors and in song. The catalyst is Peter the Great, here given a token appearance at the end of the pardon scene, which isn't entirely fair as Peter never pardoned anyone. Still, it makes a striking curtain.

"*Khovanshchina* has no single role as overwhelming as Mussorgsky's Boris, but it does have a kingpin conspirator, Prince Ivan Khovansky. Ghiaurov makes him all but overwhelming. First of all, there is that voice. Magnificent in size and quality, in overtones and undertones, with a latent ferocity as deeply Russian as its shadows. If he just stood there and sang you would be satisfied. But not Ghiaurov. He is a powerful figure—barbaric, ferocious, yet with a courtly air quite betrayed when he has too much to drink. He has an eye on the throne, and on his dancing girls—he even catches the one who leaps into his arms. Ghiaurov is not the only strong figure on that stage, but he is the riveting one. What a death fall he takes as climax.

"There is too much on that stage for one short report. Old Russia in all its splendor, the Moscow of great log houses and Byzantine Christs, of Saint Basil's domes and princely palaces. The times when pure Mussorgsky comes through in stark signature, the times when Rimsky-Korsakov stamps it indelibly.

"The wealth of men's voices, always a Russian delight. Here Norman Mittelmann a strong Boyar, Peter Lagger the poetic priest, Jack Trussel and Frank Little the good tenors with a sense of character, Florindo Andreolli as the letter writer so necessary to operatic plotting—these and more, with Viorica Cortez soaring as Martha, who almost gets drowned for divining bad luck. A beautiful, powerful, authentic *Khovanshchina*, a rarity in any opera house."

To balance the triptych of three magnificent basses—Rossi-Lemeni, Christoff and Ghiaurov—striding our resonant galleries of opera in roles as adventurous as magnificent- what to choose from the Lyric's luster of sopranos? Any choice would be just that—a choice— and so, arbitrary. But I cherish opulent, generous gestures by which artists are pampered in risking new repertory. It doesn't always work, but it stretches the horizon and when it does work, the audience is pampered, too.

The very young Lyric encouraged three sumptuous sopranos in what seems to be every soprano's ardent desire at birth, the chance to sing Puccini's *Butterfly*. I spoke earlier of Maria Callas' first and last Cio-Cio-Sans sung here in 1955. Renata Tebaldi in 1958 sang the first American performance of a role she had just tested in Europe. In 1960 it was Leontyne Price's American debut in a role just tried out in Vienna. For the collector, these were priceless opportunities impossible without a major resident opera company.

From the start, Chicago had deep roots in *Butterfly* lore. Its conductor that strange and terrible opening night at La Scala, which Puccini called "a Dantean Inferno," was Cleofonte Campanini, who in 1920-11 came to head Chicago's first resident opera company, in sumptuous residence at the Auditorium.

It was February 17, 1904 with Puccini's rising star, you would have thought, ascendant. The production was under the direction of Giulio Gatti-Casazza, in later years general manager of New York's Metropolitan, the renowned "Mr. Gatti." Tito Ricordi of the great publishing house was the producer, the celebrated Parisian Jusseaume was the designer. The focal cast held Rosina Storchio, introduced to the Scala by Toscanini, the tenor Giovanni Zenatello, and the renowned Giuseppe De Luca.

The audience hissed the house down. Referring to Puccini's illness complicated by a car crash, a headline said "Diabetic Opera—Caused by an Accident." Puccini withdrew the opera, refunded the production fee, and made a few minor changes. Three months later, at Brescia's Teatro Grande, *Butterfly* was a triumph.

Arturo Toscanini was by then the conductor, with Salomea Krusceniski in the title role, as Storchio had gone to Buenos Aires, where she and Toscanini had another triumph in the first foreign production. Campanini, meanwhile, introduced *Butterfly* to London's Covent Garden, with Emmy Destinn and two destined to mark the opera, presumably as long as recordings last, Enrico Caruso and Antonio Scotti.

It was February, 1970, when Caruso and Scotti introduced *Butterfly* to the Metropolitan, with that beauty whose hordes of idolators included the Gerry Flappers, Geraldine Farrar. The three of them sang it here at the Auditorium that April—the troupe also held Fremstad, Eames, Schumann-Heink, Plançon and Stracciari.

How did Puccini feel about all that? You never know about composers. He went to New York for the Metropolitan premiere and wrote to a friend:

"I have had all I wanted of America—at the opera all is well, and *Madame Butterfly* was excellent, but lacked the poetry I put into it. The rehearsals were too hurried and the woman was not what she should have been. Also as regards your god *(entre nous)* I make you a present of him—he won't learn anything, he's lazy, and he's too pleased with himself—all the same his voice is magnificent."

So Giacomo Puccini on Farrar and Caruso. Heinrich Conried, then in charge of the Metropolitan, agreed on at least one count. He said any opera was fine if Caruso was in it.

The picturesque Campanini of Parma and points international, brother-in-law of the dazzling Tetrazzini, was a fiercely devoted man and a practical joker. Edward Moore's *Forty Years of Opera in Chicago* tells what happened when Campanini and Gatti-Casazza had in wartime to cross a suspicious border. Campanini delayed his friend by whispering about invisible ink written on the skin. On the other hand, Chicagoans at the opera, knowing Campanini's superstitious nature, strewed pins in the vanished tunnel between the Auditorium and the Congress, knowing that he would stoop to pick up every one.

Campanini came to Chicago when the desperate Metropolitan Opera finally bought out Oscar Hammerstein's spectacular Manhattan troupe which had among many other things the impresario's running publicity battle with Mary Garden. Example: Miss Garden: "Mr. Hammerstein treats me like a chorus girl." Mr. Hammerstein: "Miss Garden owes me $5,000; no chorus girl ever did that."

So Chicago's first resident opera sprang full blown into Auditorium splendor with, among other things, matchless French repertory. Mary Garden's immediate impact as Mélisande, Louise and Salome (sung in French) was not rivaled until 44 years later when Maria Callas came to set the Lyric skyrocketing as Norma, Violetta and Lucia.

It was November 29, 1910 when Campanini first walked into the Chicago orchestra pit for *Butterfly*, with Farrar and Scotti, the tenor Amadeo Bassi. Later, Maggie Teyte was Cio-Cio-San, and so was Florence Easton, so was Tamaki Miura. The season of 1920-21 planned a glorious reunion, but when Rosina Storchio, the first Butterfly, came to sing it, Campanini, its first conductor, was dead.

Mary Garden, his dazzlingly improvident successor, opened her 1921-22 season with Muratore, d'Alvarez and Polacco in *Samson et Dalila*. Then *Tosca* with Raisa, Pattiera and Baklanoff. The third night opened a new era in *Butterfly* lore with the debut of Edith Mason, whose Pinkerton was Edward Johnson. Over the years the tenors changed, and over the years

wonderful sopranos sang Cio-Cio-San. Amelita Galli-Curci for one, Rosa Raisa, for another (no one who was there has ever forgotten the night Raisa and Martinelli sang the love duet at Ravinia in the nights of the little pavilion).

But Cio-Cio-San was Mason's role. She studied it deeply, costumed it superbly, and was so radiantly a Puccini singer that Butterfly stirred a tragic opulence you might not have suspected in that lovely voice had you heard, say, only her crystalline Sophie in *Der Rosenkavalier*. The combination made her a close friend of the Puccini family, a special favorite of Toscanini, and, of course, twice the wife of the great conductor, Giorgio Polacco.

There was toward the end of this period, another Cio-Cio-San utterly exquisite, Hizi Koyke, who later coached Callas in the role. Some of us called her a Japanese Garden because in her flower-like blown-with-the-breeze magnetism she understood two major Garden attributes: the value of stillness and silence.

Many others have sung *Butterfly*, of course. But these set the Chicago background for Lyric to embroider. Because of Tamaki Miura's success as Butterfly, Chicago opera gave her Messager's *Madame Chrysanthème*. Because of Edith Mason's success, and also because Mrs. Rockefeller McCormick loved the opera, Chicago gave her, or both of them, Mascagni's *Iris*. They were a part of the resonance set off that long ago night at La Scala where it is more courteous to call the uproar a cabal than to put it down to bad taste.

Secretly, or, more often, otherwise, sopranos of the world have yearned to sing Butterfly, one of the most exacting roles ever written because it never lets down from the floating entrance song to the doomstruck hara kiri. If you collect performances, you are forever in Lyric's debt for the luxury of its indulgence, first of Callas in 1955, then Tebaldi in 1958, then Leontyne Price in 1960.

That Callas was a supreme artist is to some of us a basic premise of music drama. We had the unique experience of seeing her create her own Cio-Cio-San and to move into almost total triumph by her third performance. This was not the soaring ardor of full-throated Puccini—rather, it was brushed almost from the start by the shadow of tragedy to come. It set the mounting urgency of the man against the muted ecstasy of the woman. It told which one kissed and which one turned the cheek. It had its own magic.

Even the first night, Callas had worked out the complicated role to its geisha fingertips. As a decoration she was exquisite. As a tragic actress, she had the unerring simplicity, the poignant power that thrust to the heart of the score. There was curving beauty in her song and a deep tenderness in *Un bel dì*. It was an incomplete performance, in terms of Callas, who demanded more of herself than anyone else could, but by that third night—the last time we saw her in Chicago opera—she was magnificent.

Nicola Rescigno was the ardent conductor, the Pinkerton was the one and only Giuseppe di Stefano. Young, handsome, romantic to a degree, with that beautiful, blandishing tenor, he had precisely Pinkerton's ardor for what he wants, the indifference, even the contempt, for what he does not value.

Di Stefano was authenticity incarnate as Pinkerton, and so, in quite another fashion, was Robert Weede as Sharpless. Remember that this was 1955. Watching Mr. Weede I kept thinking of John Foster Dulles, who had troubles enough of his own without being Pinkerton's apologist.

When Renata Tebaldi in full bloom of that glorious soprano came for the 1958 *Butterfly*, di Stefano was again the best of Pinkertons, in ravishing voice, negligently at home in Navy whites, in the lord of creation attitude, and in the charm to remind you that even on his side *Butterfly* is in its way a love story.

The conductor was the eloquent Russian Kyril Kondrashin, who worked with Van Cliburn that Russian night of Tschaikowsky triumph. That sweeping, almost languishing approach had its Puccini splendors, sometimes losing the direct line of climax. What should have flamed sometimes flickered.

But it was quite a night for Renata Tebaldi, provocative, fascinating, an adventure, a great conversation piece. Her voice at that time was one of the wonders of opera, big, lustrous, soaring and with the lasting power of the big roles. Her beauty, sweetness and dignity held true, and sometimes a proud inner fire smouldering into flame. The potential, had she gone below that lovely surface, was enormous. Even so, to hear her sing Puccini was a special Lyric gift.

The third of Lyric's highly provocative Cio-Cio-Sans was Leontyne Price—in 1960, with the enormous plus of Gianandrea Gavazzeni's brilliant, powerful, authoritative direction. Just to show you how wrong I can be without trying, I felt that November night that of the three special Lyric gifts to *Butterfly* Leontyne Price was the most likely to make the role a focal point of her career. Nothing of the sort happened.

Yet she had what it takes—temperament, voice, staying power, appearance and style. She had so much temperament she would have had to control it, for Puccini wrote *Butterfly* as almost no other role has been written for the soprano who can sing it. It does not need and will not tolerate embroideries. A little trill of laughter diminishes rather than heightens its gaiety, and sobs destroy the stark desolation of Puccini's *Triste madre*. These were things she probably would not have done twice.

For she had the role in her blood. Her voice was darker than the limpid lyric so beautiful for the music, but it was a lyrical darkness that carried the entrance song to ecstatic climax. She sang *Un bel dì* with moving simplicity, she understood the difference between coquetry and coyness, her scenes with the child were unaffected, her death scene was strongly traditional. There were miscalculations in a role almost endlessly demanding. Far more important were the strength, depth and beauty of her performance. Why she turned away from what it might have been I've no idea.

Because you always wonder. One of the great gifts to an audience is the opportunity to see, to hear, to compare, to be enriched by various interpretations rather as if a jewel turned new facets to the changing light. It is why, once lured to the arts, you never tire of the search for discovery, but are constantly refreshed. That is why we pour into opera, concert, theater, and ballet. Here, too, as in art galleries, light changes with the point of view. We learn. We grow. No one watching and listening is quite the same after the revelation of rich performance.

But where the Art Institute can hang the masterworks of the centuries in its great halls, where the Chicago Symphony Orchestra can, to a degree, keep the masterworks of music within performance realization, and where classic theaters strike root and flourish from the great plays of the past, opera peering into its past must rely on scholarship, imagination and inspiration. Scholarship is imperative, but it needs discretion. Just scholarship in the opera house is exhumation, and not much fun.

Perhaps Lyric's richest adventure in this reverberation of the past was its 1975 *Orfeo ed Euridice*, which gave an historic opera its beauty, even its nobility, and yet had for it a freshness, an almost debonair ease, and at the same time a witty approach. This means a highly civilized world of opera. It underscored Lyric's value not just as a necessity, but as a luxury for all to cherish.

We have all seen Gluck's masterwork when it sits on a pedestal with no Pygmalion to bring it to life. But this was a fascinating *Orfeo*, beautifully sung, vividly staged and quite marvelously designed by Pier Luigi Samaritani, subtly conducted by Jean Fournet, and with George Balanchine himself turning the ballet into Balanchine dancers.

The stage was like the core of a tunnel swathed in black veiling—the center opened and closed, swirled and altered, but always in that frame of mourning. It might house Greek temples, a whimsical golden baroque fantasy of Venus' chariot—rather like the work of that E.T.A. Hoffmann goldsmith who so disliked selling his work that he murdered the buyers to get it back.

For the entrance into Hades that tunnel was a dark swirl of Balanchine Furies. For the journey back to earth it shifted mysteriously until Orfeo and Euridice were helplessly caught in its gauzy beauty. Richard Stilwell and Ileana Cotrubas made you believe. Balanchine swirled it all in the furious dusk. The lighting was magical.

This was no token obeisance to Gluck. It was a fresh light on ancient splendor.

Mozart's *Idomeneo*, which came in 1977, was musically beyond price. He was about 25 when he composed this third of his opere serie, as if age meant anything in the Mozart world except to define his short span. Its haunting ambiance, at once unique, individual and universal, would have rejoiced in a poetic production of purest imaginative simplicity. It survived Jean-Pierre Ponnelle's pseudo-baroque production borrowed from Cologne—a production dominated by a huge, drowsy head of Neptune, whose heavy-lidded eyes opened at the instant of godlike intervention.

You could forget the setting. You could forget the complicated story sometimes a problem to disentangle. What was important was Mozart, magnificent Mozart, with a memory of Gluck and radiant intimation of the Mozart to come. Most of all, it was Mozart walking fully robed and crowned into his kingdom. If you could hear that purely Mozartean continuo of cello and harpsichord without holding your breath, you weren't listening.

You sometimes wonder where to begin, in describing so valiant a venture whose florid demands are often believed to be beyond contemporary resources. A brilliant find was Eric Tappy the Swiss tenor as Idomeneo, strikingly handsome, with a hint of King Lear in extremity, with a beautiful voice of heroic timbre, brilliance and skill in ornamentation.

A priceless presence was that of John Pritchard, that inheritor of Glyndebourne tradition, in the pit. This was not just competent Mozart, it was the shadowed, dappled Mozart of the great nights, all splendor, heartbreak and that burnished depth not just of tone but of feeling. It was music for singers, which is surely what opera is all about.

In lesser hands, or routine performance, *Idomeneo* could seem just one spiraling aria after another, with now and then the commenting chorus. Yet in this three act version running more than three hours, with some often omitted music restored, *Idomeneo* was lyric theater of heroic overtones. It is deeply Italian—as Romain Rolland said, "how much grace and *morbidezza*."

TOP: ERIC TAPPY AS **IDOMENEO,** 1977. BOTTOM: GEORGE SHIRLEY,
IDOMENEO, 1977.

Anyone can agree that *Idomeneo* is voluptuous, but to agree with Rolland that Mozart is less passionate than Gluck or Beethoven, there I for one am not so sure.

Idomeneo's classic tale of Greeks and Trojans, gods and men, oaths and human sacrifice is not a cool, collected situation—it is elemental. The action is in the music. The voices are the protagonists.

At Lyric's brilliant revival the Martinique soprano Christiane Eda-Pierre had the haunting, womanly sound of the Countess in *Figaro*—a gentle, yet a glorious performance. Carol Neblett was a brilliant, sulphuric Electra, unaccountably dressed in old Spain with a red Infanta wig. Maria Ewing, more a little girl than the king's son, spun that extraordinary voice of sometimes burnished bravura. George Shirley as Neptune's high priest was an ebony custodian singing superior Mozart.

Encountering *Orfeo* and *Idomeneo* all these years after their original triumphs, we can only wonder what the castrati really sounded like, those idolized men who embellished the vocal stratosphere. In quality of sound and endurance of compass I can only offer my favorite solution.

When the young Ethel Merman was flabbergasting her first Broadway shows by capturing a note and walking several times around the block with it, Arturo Toscanini was taken to hear her. He said "Castrato!", causing Miss Merman a trip to the dictionary. It is at least an authoritative clue to roles we now hear transposed for tenor or mezzo-soprano or baritone.

Sometimes transposition is caused by nothing more than the desire to hear a beautiful voice in a role not born for it. Rosina began life as a mezzo soprano in Seville and returned to that voice with the emergence of some bravura singers—meanwhile she had become a coloratura soprano interpolating a song recital into the lesson scene.

Lyric recently startled its public by announcing that 1980 will bring a new *Don Giovanni* with Richard Stilwell. Richard Stilwell is a baritone. So is Don Giovanni, or was. Many purists found it unthinkable that another bass should share that stage with Leporello. For years the role was baritone property—Stabile, Maurel, Renaud, Jean de Reszke before he became a tenor, Scotti in his Metropolitan debut, Luigi Lablache before he became the great Leporello, the brilliant Frenchman Vanni-Marcoux so much a part of Chicago memories. Even Manuel

LEFT: JEAN PIERRE PONNELLE AND LYRIC OPERA'S CHORUS MASTER
GIULIO FAVARIO IN REHEARSAL. RIGHT: JOHN PRITCHARD IN A
REHEARSAL OF **IDOMENEO**.

García sang the Don and he was a florid tenor. He was also a remarkable man, father of Malibran, of Viardot and of the junior García, the teacher of Jenny Lind and the tenor Nourrit—to skim some cream.

It was Ezio Pinza of the velvet voice and the single earring who convinced the world that Don Giovanni is a basso cantante, a tradition Rossi-Lemeni and Ghiaurov have done nothing to diminish. It will be interesting to discover how the Lyric world readjusts its ears.

At least, *Don Giovanni* has flourished in the repertory since that magical October in Prague when Mozart took rooms at the Lion's Inn with Da Ponte across the narrow street, so that romantics like to think that they leaned out their windows and exchanged ideas, as housewives shared recipes and gossip. It is known that at rehearsal Mozart sneaked up and pinched Zerlina severely, to make her scream as if she meant it, but that was before the trade union put the composer in his place.

There is just one *Don Giovanni*. But there are some dazzling operas languishing in the archives because the day of the dazzling technician is over—or almost.

Lyric has more than once reached back to the days of Pasta, Grisi, Malibran and Viardot to display Callas, Simionato, Sutherland and Caballé, to name four. Its *Puritani* quartet of Callas, di Stefano, Bastianini and Rossi-Lemeni stirred historians to look back to Grisi, Rubini, Tamburini and Lablache. Bravura opera is in its own way another Sleeping Beauty, held prisoner in a thicket of technicalities only the superlative singer can penetrate.

It is easy enough to say, and almost believe, that when any theater, operatic or otherwise, turns into a museum, it becomes a caretaker, perhaps admirable, but also dull. But a true museum is not just a place of preservation of works of art, but of restoration, of display in the most revealing light—of wide open doors inviting the world to come and look.

Before Lyric's sumptuously staged *Semiramide* of 1971—with Joan Sutherland and Marilyn Horne engaged in a four hour *bel canto* duel—many had known Rossini's opera only for its overture, a preview of the score, and for *Bel raggio* transferred to the concert hall from its original locale in the hanging gardens of Babylon.

Even in the never-never land of opera you don't come across a *Semiramide* every day in the week, or season. In four acts and ten scenes it is rather like one continuous cadenza, sometimes in duplicate, triplicate or quadruplicate, with occasional comments by the chorus. It adores the bravura, the agile, the *scala trillata,* the elaborations they used to call divisions, the cabaletta, the cavatina; it embellishes the embellished, and bursts into the full flower of fioriture.

It is, among other things, a field day for the exuberant opera fan, who doesn't really have any fun unless he can salute both singers and scenery in a range of *brava, bravo, bravi, braviss'*—a man sitting near me ended in a piteous caw.

Old timers used to say that *Semiramide* might work if you had a Patti and a Scalchi to sing *Giorno d'orrore.* Everyone knows about the legendary Patti, who opened our Auditorium in 1889 tactfully remarking—"Chicago seems to be getting everything now. Really, I wonder what is to become of New York." Sofia Scalchi was a contralto from Turin with a range, they said, of two and a half octaves, adored from Milan to London, New York to St. Petersburg.

So at Lyric out came Joan Sutherland and Marilyn Horne to tackle what as *Day of Horror* sounds rather fierce, but is actually a kind of double coloratura cadenza. They coaxed the bel canto birds right off their elusive trees—it was a subtle dazzler in spun silk.

It is true that once a *Semiramide* singer starts to sing, he displays no inclination to stop, but then, that is how it is written. Cynics believe that Rossini was annoyed at improvisations in his operas—he said to one such singer "That was pretty—who wrote it?" So in *Semiramide* he left no time to invent—it is all the singer can do to survive.

So you don't do it without the singers, at least the two women. The men are less important—what do you expect of an opera where the "tenor" is a contralto commander of the Assyrian army—and sometimes bearded to boot?

What counted was that Miss Sutherland had the range, the agility, the capacity and often the magnificence for *Semiramide* and Miss Horne sang like a bird turned loose in a honeycomb—it was dazzling, cajoling and caressing.

So *Semiramide* was precisely what it is, a display piece—conducted by Richard Bonynge, who had taken the trouble to study the music, to persuade the orchestra to play it beautifully, and whenever possible to restore an all but lost opera to life. If you really listened to Rossini, you heard intimations of famous things to come—for one, Rigoletto's *Cortigiani*.

In a time when many stage designers have become as inexplicably self-indulgent as their stage director counterparts, Pier Luigi Samaritani's production from Florence was a loving tribute to Rossini, buried there in the pantheon, Santa Croce.

Its ten scenes of temples, tombs, hanging gardens, palaces and royal tents looked monumental, but seemed to move in scene changing like a breeze, the colors bronze, dull gold and the soft pink ranges of rose and apricot.

It was a welcome adventure in the operatic night.

It is always risky to say that any venerable opera is having its first Chicago performance, unless you can prove world premiere. Some astonishing operas were coming overland and by lake boat long before the Auditorium was even a gleam in the eye of civic pride.

What was believed to be the first Chicago performance of Donizetti's *Maria Stuarda* opened the Lyric's 1973 season with Montserrat Caballé as Mary of Scotland and Viorica Cortez as a carrot top Elizabeth who signed Mary's death warrant in a forest, sitting on what seemed to be the stump of a giant sequoia. This was not untypical of a strange, often rearranged libretto, which flies not just in the face of fact, but of less than unrestrained fantasy.

This one, too, sings and sings and sings. It is a spill of cadenzas, an outburst of cabalettas, and its overtone is that of gentle melancholy with a dying cadence. Pier Luigi Pizzi's Florentine production held the somber note even to the soaring curve to the headsman's block—where Mary of Scotland changed from black to more becoming scarlet.

Caballé, with that first name taken from Catalonia's sacred mountain said to be the setting of Wagner's *Parsifal*—Monsalvat for Montserrat—Caballé who bewitches so many was a joy in the limpid phrase, the fragile embroidery, the spinning legato. She was not at her best in dramatic moments, and soon canceled engagements. One curious result was that Cortez, given a Caballé replacement, promptly stole the show.

Franco Tagliavini was the tenor and Bruno Bartoletti, his heart in the music, let it sing. That was the opening night after the opulent pink velvet curtain was destroyed by fire, and briefly replaced by the smaller one from the little Civic next door.

Lyric then was beginning its 19th season, yet it even then had opera fans indulging in that famous game of looking back over the shoulders. This time they said, wistfully, what if *Maria Stuarda* had been sung with Callas, Cossotto, di Stefano, Bastianini and Rossi-Lemeni? Ah, *brava*, *bravo*, *braviss* . . .

Cossotto? Fiorenza, that is. Another example of why bravura revivals are born. Donizetti's *La Favorita*—or *Favorite* in its Parisian birthplace, was written for Rosine Stoltz, a fiery mezzo famed in lyric tragedy whose life outdid her librettos—she married in turn the manager of an opera house, a baron, a count and a prince. Viardot was another renowned Leonora in an opera often rearranged under political pressure. Such voices are not common in any century, so the Metropolitan revival of 1905–06 was arranged to display Caruso, along with Scotti and Plançon. The lady was Edyth Walker.

But by 1962 La Scala had its Leonora. Gavazzeni restored *La Favorita* in Benois production with Cossotto, Bastianini and Ghiaurov. Lyric imported it in 1964, with Cossotto in American debut, along with Alfredo Kraus, Sesto Bruscantini and the conductor, Carlo Felice Cillario. It was a glowing night of song and when Cossotto was asked next day what she thought of the glowing reviews she said "I don't know. I can't read English."

There was a sumptuous revival in 1974, again with Cossotto, Kraus, the brilliant lyric baritone Piero Cappuccilli (reminding many a listener of Bastianini), a handsome new production by Ming Cho Lee, on loan from San Francisco, what had been the Ruth Page ballet newly in charge of Maria Tallchief, and the return of Nicola Rescigno, a Lyric founder, to the orchestra pit.

LEFT: FIORENZA COSSOTTO AND SESTO BRUSCANTINI, **LA FAVORITA,** 1964. RIGHT: COSSOTTO AND ALFREDO KRAUS, **LA FAVORITA,** 1964.

COSSOTTO AND KRAUS IN **LA FAVORITA**, 1974.

La Favorita makes absolutely no sense except as a showcase for singers, which in the opera house is more rewarding than an intelligent opera that can't sing. Cossotto's glorious voice was even warmer than before, a glowing mezzo held in a luminous sheath. *Favorita* was sung to the rafters in a setting whose Mr. Lee of Shanghai had fallen in love with Spain and the Moors and the Moors filtered through the Portuguese. A brazen cyclorama with a sun disk, a ramped stage of porticoes and pavilions and terraces, Spanish baroque façades hung in the dark sky—an invitation to imagination as Donizetti is to song.

When an opera company becomes part of a community, it inherits obligations as custodian of the repertory. Many operas can happily be staged with stellar singers and a competent conductor, orchestra and chorus. Some, and *Der Rosenkavalier* is one of them, are enormously complicated musically, physically and above all emotionally. Lyric waited 16 seasons, until 1970, to tackle Richard Strauss' enchanting Viennese comedy with shadows about the Marschallin and the Knight of the Rose she sends to woo Sophie by proxy.

Many an opera fan will tell you that *Rosenkavalier*, which had its Dresden premiere in 1911, is the last internationally and apparently permanently popular opera. Even the best opera houses sometimes vulgarize it beyond recognition. As the Marschallin says, "But in the *how* lies all the difference." A great *Rosenkavalier* is one of the treasures of music; even a good one is invaluable.

The challenge is formidable. Everyone cherishes the recording with Lotte Lehmann, Elisabeth Schumann and Richard Mayr. Fabled casts are collector's items. Chicago opera opened its 1925–26 season with a superb production conducted by Polacco with Raisa as the Marschallin, Kipnis as Ochs and Mason as Sophie, the role of her Metropolitan debut with Frieda Hempel. Cortis was the Italian tenor, sung in 1978's Salzburg production by Pavarotti.

The settings, ideal but vanished, were from the designs of Alfred Roller, Mahler's collaborator in their Vienna era of "painting with light and music." The stage director was the European George Moor, of infinite understanding and tact.

Into this wittily elegant ambiance came the early 1930s invasion of Chicago's great German wing under Egon Pollak's direction, which had first Frida Leider and then Lotte Lehmann as the Marschallin, with Maria Olszewska a magnificent Octavian and again Kipnis as Ochs. The Fritz Reiner revival of 1940 had another enchanting Octavian, Risë Stevens.

So some of us went with hopeful fingers crossed to the Opera House that September night in 1970. Could the Lyric in its short season and relatively short life hope to conjure the brilliant, teeming, bustling *Rosenkavalier* stage so imperative as background for the splintering, soaring ecstasies of its radiance, relinquishment and rue?

The odd thing was the Lyric had that kaleidoscopic marvel of a *Rosenkavalier* stage the very first night—it just did not have, the whole way, the stars. The stunning one from start to finish was Yvonne Minton as Octavian—tall, knightly, elegant, vulnerable, charming, and a singer to boot. When she left the Marschallin at the end of the first act she gave a single rap at the double doors with her riding crop, knowing that they would be opened. She knew instinctively what the young Count Rofrano would have done.

Christa Ludwig's Marschallin had the creamy opulence of voice, but not the teasing indulgence of the love scenes, the heartbreak of the monologue, the anguished ecstasy of the trio. Walter Berry's Ochs got a dry start, the Sophie was disappointing.

But—and in the but lies all the difference—the miracle happened at a most unlikely point, when the curtain rose on the vivid stageful of the Marschallin's Hogarthian levee. Suddenly, there was *Rosenkavalier*. Dozens of smaller roles, some of them mute, bustling without confusion, rich in character vignettes. Ottavio Garaventa as the gently parodied Italian singer. Florindo Andreolli and wasp-waisted Elena Zilio up to their pricked ears in intrigue. A hairdresser who dressed hair. A devoted major domo. A marvelous lout with the mischievous resemblance to Baron Ochs, his doting, illegitimate son, played by Casimir Zielinski.

From then on it was a good performance with Guenther Schneider-Siemssen's decors simultaneously taking your breath away and making you smile and Christoph von Dohnanyi's orchestra promising any minute to spill the music's prodigal wealth of allusion, implication, recollection and faint parody—that crystalline beauty splintering the Straussian universe. Basically, at long last, the Lyric had a *Rosenkavalier*.

In a truly resident opera company, such as we once had at the Auditorium and at Ravinia, where artists came to live for the season, it is simpler to keep a work lustrous in the repertory. As things are in the jet age residence means a few performances between other engagements, and far more cancellations. You really start all over again every time.

Lyric's second *Rosenkavalier* in 1973 lost Yvonne Minton by cancellation, but gained a true Marschallin when Helga Dernesch took command of the stage after the first Ludwig performances. Judith Blegen's Sophie was a pretty, spunky parvenu. Hans Sotin was a find as Ochs, the right age—about 35—the flair for comedy and a magnificent voice of full range and beauty of velvet tone. Ferdinand Leitner, later to return for the *Ring*, was the competent conductor. The stage direction was appallingly coarse. In such cases I always remember Maestro Polacco's quivering reaction to an unfortunate conductor's *Otello*—"Assassino!"

Probably some of you are fuming in the wings in that matter of *Rosenkavalier* as the last universally popular opera, demanding, how about Benjamin Britten? Certainly there is an argument to be put up about *Peter Grimes* and Lyric put up quite an argument in 1977.

Jon Vickers, who had always been a superior protagonist, walked over that mysterious line to magnificence. Either the role now possesses him or he possesses it—with a major artist it is not always possible to be certain.

Up to that night I had considered a Vickers Parsifal at Bayreuth the crest of our many meetings over the footlights, but this *Peter Grimes* moved into that same rarefied realm of precisely what you would choose if you had limitless choice.

In an otherwise good, even superior, performance, Vickers was more than the dominant figure. In that brooding seascape he was the undertow, the sea spray, the hallucinated and the hallucinating. It was a powerful, brutal performance of the shunned outsider. It was a poetic, superbly sung performance climaxed by the vocalise on his own hated name.

At the end he was like Wozzeck, as thick-witted as thin-skinned, totally uncomprehending of all but the necessity of death. You wait a long time for such a performance; when it comes, it is worth the wait.

From the start, the Lyric was fortunate with *Peter Grimes*, which is to say sympathetic. The bleak North Sea settings by Carl Toms have a kind of sunless poetry of grey skies and misted moon and the spell the sea casts over bleached villages and fishermen worn out by the struggle. The most commanding scenic solution is extraordinary. Caught high between steep

cliffs is Peter Grimes' cockle shell of a hut, an upturned boat made halfway habitable. It is all isolation and danger, a frightful place for a child, whose fall is both terrible and inevitable. It is a haunting stage for a drama all fugal choruses, vocalises, chanties and those *entr'actes* the knowing audience lets you hear.

Along with Vickers, Bruno Bartoletti's orchestra and the all-important chorus held the audience spellbound. Staging was by Geraint Evans, an old Britten hand who shared Balstrode with Morley Meredith. The mesmerizing boy who fell from the cliff was H. L. Silets, much younger than he sounds.

Part of an opera company's obligation to the art and the audience is to explore and extend the repertory. When Lyric offered the first American stage production of the 1961 revision, it came as no surprise that Britten's *Billy Budd* was no *Peter Grimes.* It never was.

Yet it might have been. Melville's powerful, mystical story, here told with the aid of E. M. Forster and Eric Crozier, has a sunny boy with a stammer press-ganged by a British frigate and destroyed by the malignant Claggart. In that 1797 terror of mutiny on the high seas, floggings and drumhead court martial are more than ever a way of death. Claggart might have said of Billy Budd as Iago of Othello, "He hath a daily beauty in his life that makes me ugly." Captain Vere, the "Starry Vere" of Billy's adoration, knows the malignity. But he goes by the book and Billy hangs from the yardarm.

Lyric gave us every chance to see the opera at its best. John Piper's Covent Garden production with Geraint Evans the original Claggart, Theodor Uppman the justly admired protagonist, and Richard Lewis the Captain originally Peter Pears.

TOP LEFT: GERAINT EVANS AND THEODORE UPPMAN, **BILLY BUDD,** 1970. TOP RIGHT: JON VICKERS AS **PETER GRIMES,** 1974.

TITO GOBBI AND JON VICKERS DURING THE DRESS REHEARSAL OF
OTELLO, 1966.

MARIA TALLCHIEF, DIRECTOR OF THE LYRIC OPERA BALLET SCHOOL OF
CHICAGO.

But a powerful story challenges opera to meet it, or if possible transcend it, on its own high ground. *Billy Budd* is a letdown. There are many reminders in the ambience. Claggart as Iago, Claggart as Mephisto summoning his powers. Billy Budd as the sublime innocent, the guileless fool, the predestined victim, the beauty that evil cannot tolerate. The Captain in Faustian old age and scarlet dressing gown, looking back in self-justification hard to share. In the mists you may even wonder if this is a kind of *Flying Dutchman* journey in search of salvation.

Yet Britten's music, largely incidental, weakens the story of what often turn out to be womanish men. In times of stress, they make you wait while they vocalize. Melville's story is shorn of its power, its mysticism, its redemptive beauty.

As *Billy Budd* recedes into the mists, what some of us remember most vividly is Geraint Evans' Claggart of evil pride and total corruption. The Mephistophelean summoning of evil forces before the false accusation. After his death, his hat and stick held in the spotlight, demanding retribution.

In the Lyric world of Benjamin Britten, the fascinating rival to *Peter Grimes* was his haunting chamber opera *The Turn of the Screw*, in the Piccola Scala production staged by Virginio Puecher for the Opera School (which some of us call the Little Lyric) at the 1975 spring season in the Civic theater, that miniature of the rose and gold opera house next door, designed for just such intimate performance.

Henry James' haunting ghost story of the two possessed children has had three lives. Its own, fragile and clinging as cobwebs. William Archibald's subtly provocative play in Jo Mielziner's haunted country house with wraithlike music by Alex North. Britten's music, some of his finest, is obsessed with theme and variations on a pervasive sense of evil and the turning of childhood games into a mocking litany.

Puecher's production was a bold and powerful dislocation moved to a kind of reverberant, distorted mirror image gleaming in the dusk, its own obsessive variation on a theme. The magical performance was that of the boy Miles, the same H. L. Silets who plunged in terror from the cliff in *Peter Grimes*.

It was in the second act that he came into his own as a natural actor. He suddenly took on the boy's charm, his terror, his sinister sense of the possessed. In the role's strange aura of the dutiful and the diabolical, he felt and shared the spell.

There have been other valuable Opera School productions, notably Italo Tajo's silky spinning of Cimarosa's *Il Matrimonio Segreto*, and fresh young ballet augmented by George Balanchine in compliment to Maria Tallchief.

The little theater could be to Chicago what the jewel box Cuvilliés is to Munich, the Piccola Scala to Milan, an intimate showcase. It needs M. and Mme Maecenas to subsidize it as airily as Harold McCormick when he paid off Mary Garden's spectacular deficit, saying, "It's a pleasure."

Years later, that brilliant, costly Mary Garden season carried its echoes into Lyric repertory in Prokofiev's *The Love for Three Oranges* and *Angel of Fire*.

The Love for Three Oranges was not a Garden commission. When Prokofiev came to Chicago as pianist-composer-conductor with Frederick Stock and the Chicago Symphony Orchestra, directors of the Chicago Opera asked him to write an opera for the company, in those days an unusual if not unique procedure. When Carlo Gozzi's satirical fairy tale came up in discussion Cleofonte Campanini, the opera's general director, cried, "Ah, my dear Gozzi," and that is how *The Love for Three Oranges* was born.

But Campanini died and it was Garden who presented the Russian opera on an Italian fairy tale—in French. Prokofiev conducted the world première at the Auditorium December 30, 1921 and thought it went well. When the company took it to New York on one of its then renowned coast to coast tours, he said of the critics, "It was as though a pack of dogs had broken loose and were tearing my trousers to shreds."

Chicago having been more appreciative—though noting that at $130,000 *The Love for Three Oranges* cost $43,000 per orange, a high price for operatic fruit bearing two Auditorium performances—an exuberant Prokofiev planned that Mary Garden should create Renata in his *Angel of Fire*. But in the volatile way of opera, Miss Garden resigned as *directa* (her word), *Angel of Fire* drew official Soviet reproof as "decadent," and only the adventurous Serge Koussevitzky played some of the music at one of his 1928 Paris concerts.

More than 40 years after Prokofiev's hopes were dashed, Chicago saw *Angel of Fire*. Lyric imported Rome's Teatro dell'Opera production in 1966, its own adventurous season which also held *Boris*, *L'Incoronazione di Poppea*, *Les Pêcheurs de Perles* and the Oscar Kokoschka production of *Zauberflöte*. The Renata was Felicia Weathers.

One of the more disturbing mysteries of music is what Prokofiev might have done with total freedom of artistic choice. It was such an extraordinary gift of power, sardonic wit, suddenly murmurous romanticism and, as pianist in his own music, massive, mordant brilliance. You heard this authentic voice most powerfully in *Angel of Fire* in Bartoletti's clangorous entr'acte devil music, and in the hag-ridden chorus of possessed nuns.

But in general in this Rome production the music said one thing, the Italian version of Luciano Damiani and Virginio Puecher, another. A Gothic tale emerging from the Middle Ages was placed in a realm of surrealist metaphysics, the action unaccountably on the housetops. Prokofiev's ending of execration and anathema by devil-ridden women as the Inquisitor sends Renata to the stake became a brilliantly lighted cathedral triptych signifying redemption and transfiguration.

It was fascinating, though often baffling, to encounter *Angel of Fire* in any guise, but it would be doubly rewarding to see Prokofiev get equal time in a production as perceptive on stage as it was in the Lyric's orchestra pit. There is authoritative precedent. During a rehearsal of *The Love for Three Oranges* Prokofiev protested from the orchestra pit. When the stage director demanded "Who is in charge here?" the composer said, "You—to carry out my wishes."

No one knows what became of Boris Anisfeld's settings for that long ago première. They were said to be enchanting, and possibly as fragile as a fairy tale, however sardonic. Lyric's lavish 1976 revival—in English this time—turned Gozzi's fable of the prince who couldn't laugh into a spectacle as elaborate as *Turandot*. Ornately designed by Ulisse Santicchi and fancifully staged by Giulio Chazalettes, with an Oriental air, elaborate uniforms, acrobats, amusing white horses, Italo Tajo as the cook entranced by a red ribbon, and a small cyclone to propel actors more usually blown about by wind gaily pumped up by a bellows.

There are times when a character, even a title, becomes a universal symbol. Samuel Beckett's *Waiting for Godot* holds the infinite loneliness of the human soul constricted in the im-

OPPOSITE PAGE, TOP AND BOTTOM: **THE LOVE OF THREE ORANGES**, 1976, A GENEROUS GIFT OF MR. JAMES C. HEMPHILL.

FOLLOWING SPREAD: **BORIS GODUNOV**, 1966, WITH NICOLAI GHIAUROV, IN THE TITLE ROLE, ON THE RIGHT.

mensity of space. Alban Berg's *Wozzeck* after Georg Buechner has become the prototype of all the thin-skinned and thick-witted who feel more than they comprehend, with in a larger sense the suggestion that disintegration of a human mind can be disintegration of a human race.

Wozzeck is a challenge to the highest talents, and Lyric's two productions, in English, with Bartoletti and with Geraint Evans a Golem figure in the title role, are worth further exploration into music that strips the skin from human suffering, exposing raw nerves and quivering entrails. With almost all operas, most of us can remember at least one deeply satisfying performance. With *Wozzeck*, for my part, no. But it is there, waiting.

The story is blunt as a sledge-hammer, the music is infinitely subtle. At the first performance in Salzburg in 1951, 37 years and two World Wars after *Wozzeck* was written, all the power lay in the orchestra pit. At a performance which drew musicians from all over the world, Karl Boehm and the Vienna Philharmonic let us hear Alban Berg—the tortures of doubt, the wild longings, the dull plodding of a hurt mind, the piercing conviction of compulsion to kill that blots out all other sound. If you shut your eyes, you knew all about *Wozzeck*.

Boehm let you hear it. A few years later in Stockholm, the late Goeran Gentele let you see

GERAINT EVANS AS **WOZZECK**, 1972.

it. His brilliant staging knew all about cruelty, stupidity, inhumanity, the unendurable. If Lyric could merge those marvelous conceptions we would all understand what Berg meant when he said, "From the time the curtain rises on *Wozzeck* until it falls, nobody should be impressed by anything more than the idea of the opera, which means more than only the fate of Wozzeck."

A major opera company is beyond price because it can make such an exploration.

In some operatic ventures, a crystal ball is imperative. Lyric waited until 1971 to launch its *Ring of the Nibelungen*, one opera each season through 1974. It was 1975 that Birgit Nilsson took off into the less taxable wild blue yonder. Lyric had her Brünnhilde if not her Elektra.

It was a notable *Ring*, Chicago's first in resident opera since the Campanini seasons of 1915–16 and 1916–17, earlier Egon Pollak engagements with Fremstad, Schumann-Heink, Whitehill, Maclennan, Dalmores and more.

Lyric's *Ring* had authentic Wagner from Ferdinand Leitner in the pit, and on stage productions designed by Ekkehard Gruebler and directed by Hans-Peter Lehmann which reflected both Wieland Wagner's Bayreuth and some of the more intimate humanity of Herbert von Karajan's productions. They must have been even more powerful than we thought at the time,

GERAINT EVANS AND ANJA SILJA IN **WOZZECK,** 1972.

TOP LEFT: JANIS MARTIN AND HERMAN ESSER, **DIE WALKÜRE,** 1972. TOP RIGHT: BENGT RUNDGREN,
FLORINDO ANDREOLLI, AND HANS SOTIN. RUNDGREN AND SOTIN APPEARED IN THE 1971 **RHEINGOLD**
AS THE GIANTS. BOTTOM: JEAN COX AND BIRGIT NILSSON, **SIEGFRIED,** 1973. THESE PRODUCTIONS ARE A
GENEROUS GIFT OF THE GRAMMA FISHER FOUNDATION.

OPPOSITE PAGE: BIRGIT NILSSON IN **SIEGFRIED,** 1973.

because the spell held over four seasons rather than the six days of Bayreuth lore.

Richard Wagner demanded miracles of stagecraft and sometimes even his inventive grandson Wieland threw in the sponge by turning out the lights so you had to imagine what was happening in the Festspielhaus dusk. Some conductors, and Wilhelm Furtwaengler was one of them, finally said they preferred to do Wagner in the concert hall.

Chicago had uncommonly stellar illustration of both styles when Georg Solti and the Chicago Symphony Orchestra presented a concert *Rheingold* in Orchestra Hall the April before the Lyric launched its *Ring* at the Opera House in November. I am not suggesting that Sir Georg prefers Wagner in concert. Just that he could not resist a superb Wagner orchestra with 12 soloists, six harps and all those Wagner horns. It was a remarkable performance with no less than Martti Talvela as Fasolt.

But the difference between a concert and an operatic *Rheingold* reminded me, for a very special reason, of Herbert von Karajan. When he was planning his Salzburg *Ring* he told me, "That struggle for power—it's the story of my life."

The thing was that in concert form and civilian dress, with that orchestra reminding you of the shrewdness as well as the beauty of Wagner, *Rheingold* in tailcoat version had a surprisingly contemporary aspect.

Wotan was the weary chairman of the board trying to save Valhalla for the family. Fasolt and Fafner were the builders determined to get their fee. Alberich was the greedy upstart getting all those proxies to wrest control. Loge was a combination corporation lawyer and public relations man. You immediately noticed that Wagner gave the most seductive music to Loge, who is selling a bill of goods.

On stage and in costume at the Lyric, *Rheingold* moved back into its Nordic mists. As Loge, Richard Holm had the cynical mockery, the precision, the tart tongue of the fire god, and in our time he would have been, say, an ideal diplomatist at the United Nations. Hubert Hofmann's Wotan had nobility, despite Wotan's notorious lack of it, Gustav Neidlinger's Alberich the blackness of malediction, Bengt Rundgren's Fasolt the unexpected yearning—he wanted Freia more than gold.

So the concert *Rheingold* was contemporary, the opera, timeless. So was the cycle, with Nilsson striding from Battle Cry to Immolation. It may have been the last time we were to hear her, and we all know the swan song can be the most poignant. She was never younger or more beautiful, especially than in *Siegfried*, and to hear her awakening on the rock was to know one of the true glories of Wagner, because it reaches for the whole joy of being alive.

The Lyric is oriented to Italian opera? No doubt. That was its stellar cradle. But Lyric has done nothing finer than *Siegfried*, the vernal opera of the cycle, a joyous opera, the point of the *Ring* where evil is at least temporarily vanquished, where the gods move into twilight and human love triumphs, it thinks, forever. Here is what Wagner wrote to Ludwig II when he resumed work on *Siegfried* after that long hiatus:

"Wonderful is the spot where . . . I shall resume the composition of the music. It is the loftiest scene of the most tragic of my heroes. Wotan, the all-powerful will to live, has resolved on his own self-destruction. Greater now in his renunciation than ever before in his striving, he feels omnipotent . . . He knows that he lives on in Siegfried. Wotan lives on in Siegfried as every artist does in his work.

RUDOLF NUREYEV, CENTER, LEADS THE POLOVETSIAN DANCES OF **PRINCE IGOR,** 1962, GIV

SET DESIGNS FOR **KHOVANSHCHINA,** 1969 AND 1976.

AND ILEANA COTRUBAS, 1975. THE PRODUCTION WAS A GENEROUS GIFT OF THE GRAMMA FISHER FOUNDATION.

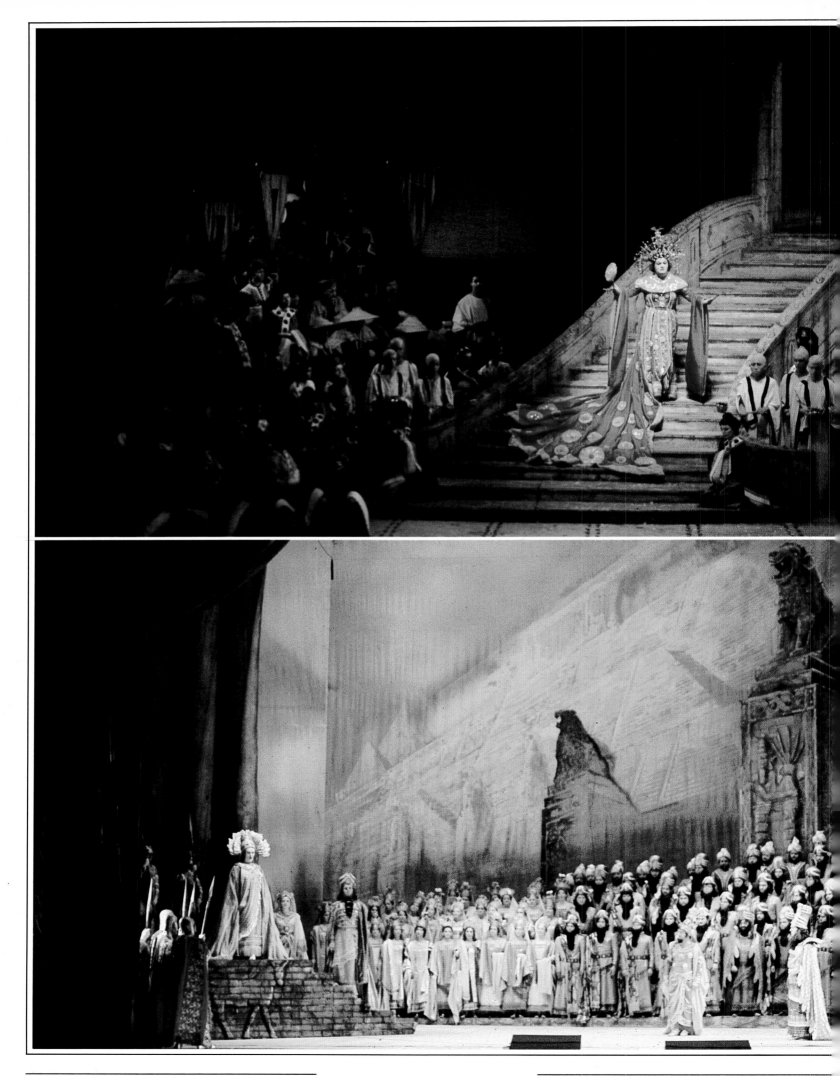

TOP LEFT AND RIGHT: BIRGIT NILSSON AS **TURANDOT,** 1970.

BOTTOM LEFT: **SEMIRAMIDE,** 1971, WITH JOAN SUTHERLAN

RO MALAS, AGOSTINO FERRIN AND MARILYN HORNE.

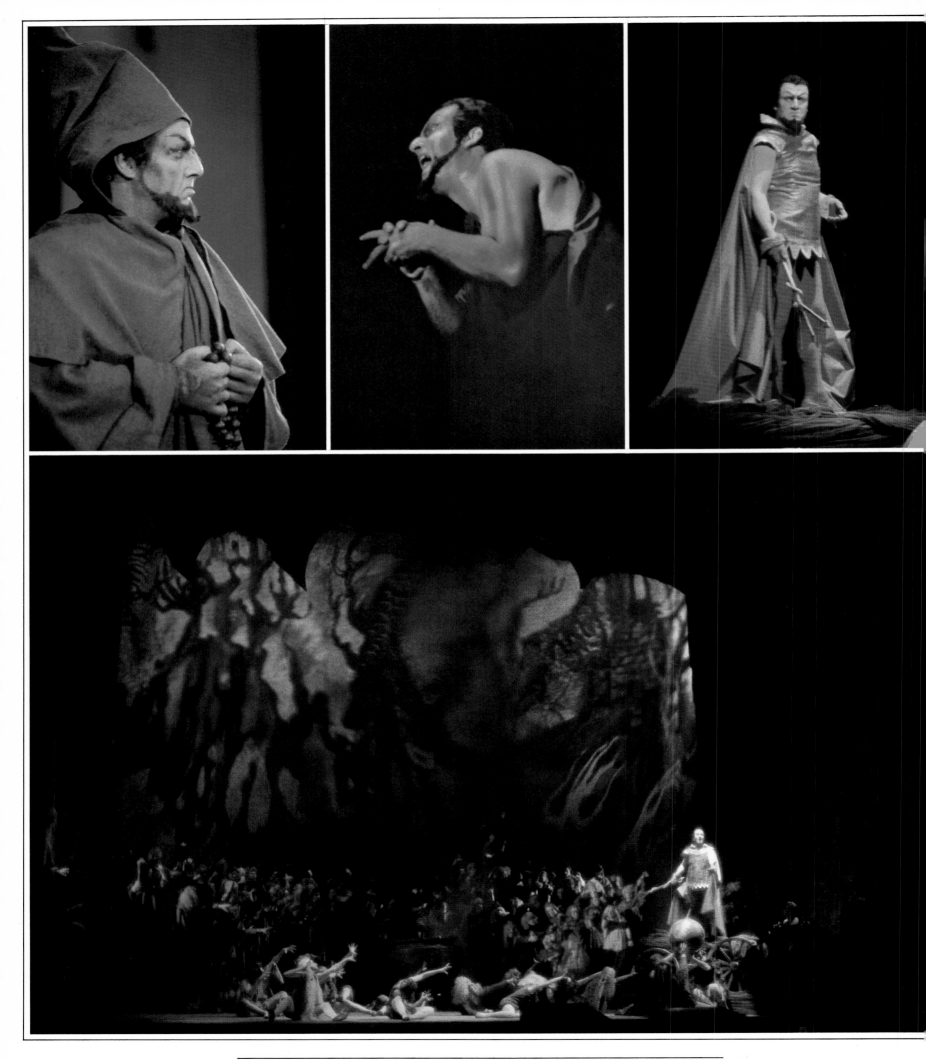

TOP LEFT TO RIGHT: NICOLAI GHIAUROV IN THE TITLE ROLE OF **MEFISTOFELE,** 1965. BOTTOM: THE BROCKEN SCENE, **MEFISTOFELE,** 1965, WITH GHIAUROV ON THE RIGHT.

TOP LEFT AND RIGHT: JON VICKERS IN **SAMSON ET DALILA,** 1965. BOTTOM: THE BACCHANAL OF
SAMSON ET DELILA, 1965.

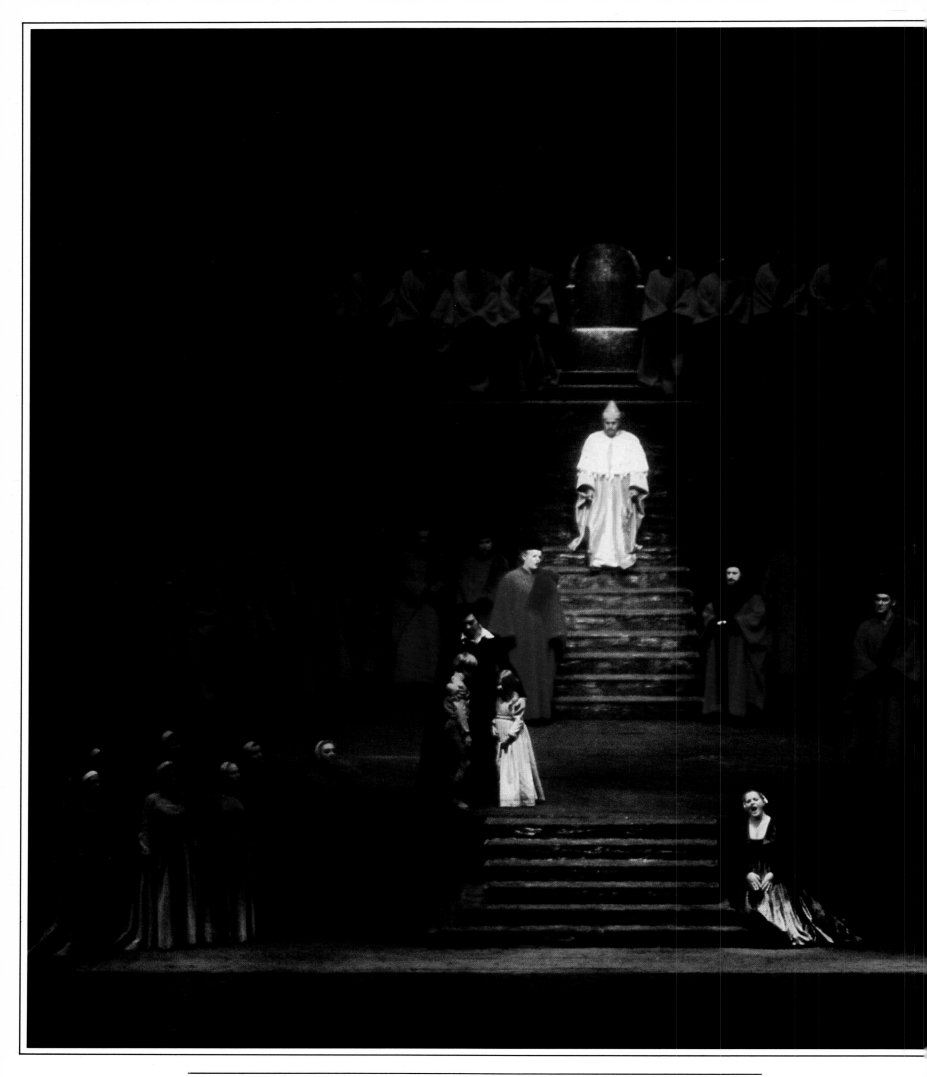

I DUE FOSCARI, 1972, WITH FRANCO TAGLIAVINI, LEFT, PIERO CAPPUCCILLI, CENTER, AND KATIA RICCIARELLI, RIGHT.

NICOLAI GHIAUROV AS **DON QUICHOTTE,** 1974.

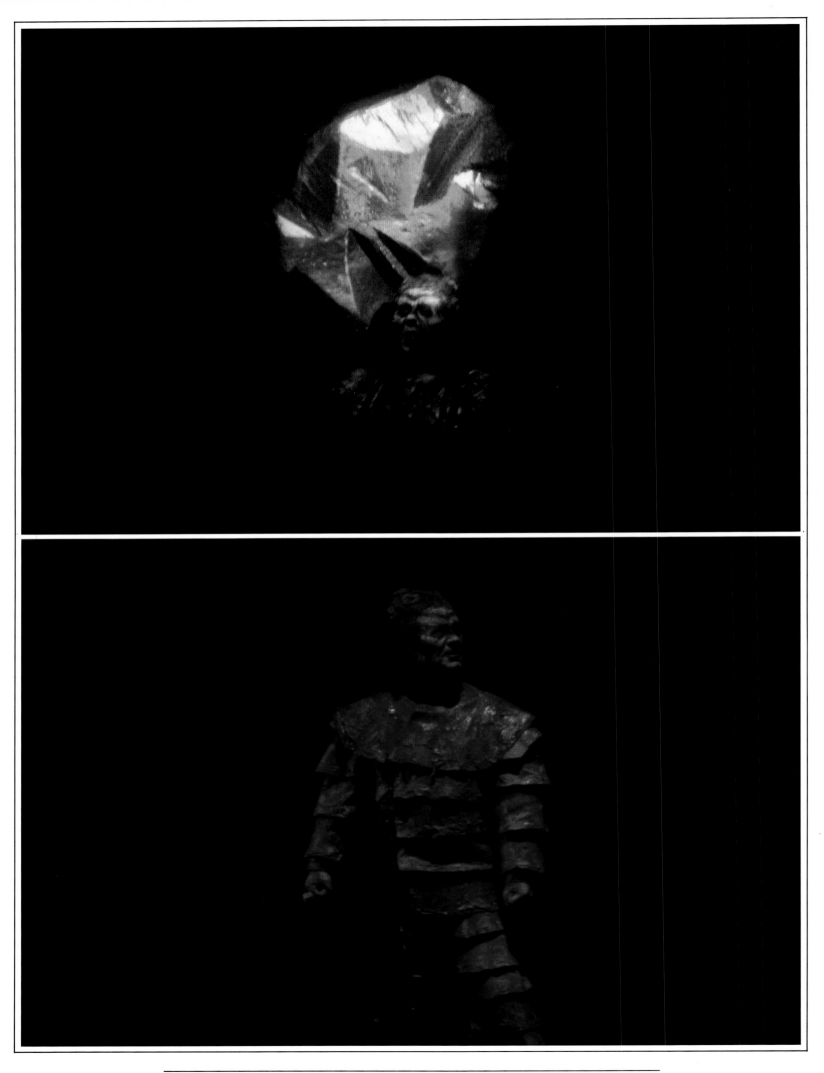

TOP: GUSTAV NEIDLINGER, **DAS RHEINGOLD,** 1971. BOTTOM: RICHARD HOLM, **DAS RHEINGOLD,** 1971.

TOP: BENGT RUNDGREN AND HANS SOTIN, **DAS RHEINGOLD,** 1971. BOTTOM: HUBERT HOFMANN, **DIE WALKÜRE,** 1972.

"With what consideration I shall awaken Brünnhilde from her long sleep. She slept while Siegfried grew to be a young man. How significant all this seems to me now. My last music was the forest bird's announcement that he could awaken Brünnhilde if he had not learned fear: he followed the bird, laughing, to the magic rock. That path, my royal friend, how long and hard it was for me. But if I am Wotan I shall succeed through Siegfried—he awakens the maiden, my work will live . . ."

It lived at the Opera House that *Siegfried* night so often a magical fairy tale, its hero naive and noble, brutal and gentle, who forges the sword, laughs in the forest, rescues Brünnhilde and becomes humanity's hope.

He was Jean Cox to Theo Adam's Wanderer, Gerhard Unger's Mime, Klaus Hirte's evil Alberich, Lili Chookasian's elemental Erda and, always, the promise of Brünnhilde to come.

Challenge is a wonderful thing. The Lyric orchestra played beyond itself at *Götterdämmerung*—again with Nilsson and Cox, Bengt Rundgren's magnificent Hagen, Donald McIntyre's potent Gunther. It was a performance of character, power and often climactic splendor. It opened new Lyric doors.

As for the door that closed, there was what may have been our last Nilsson Brünnhilde, the creature in the golden cloak with that voice vaulting in splendor. That voice had begun almost as stainless steel, a flung javelin, soaring, slashing and invincible. As the years went by it warmed in the sun. Later, it sometimes tired. Never tarnished. But you never knew when it would pour out in the passionate splendor that is the true inundation of the *Ring*. We are fortunate who knew Frida Leider, Kirsten Flagstad and Birgit Nilsson where they were born to sing—in opera.

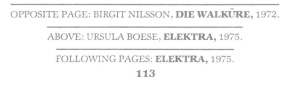

OPPOSITE PAGE: BIRGIT NILSSON, **DIE WALKÜRE,** 1972.

ABOVE: URSULA BOESE, **ELEKTRA,** 1975.

FOLLOWING PAGES: **ELEKTRA,** 1975.

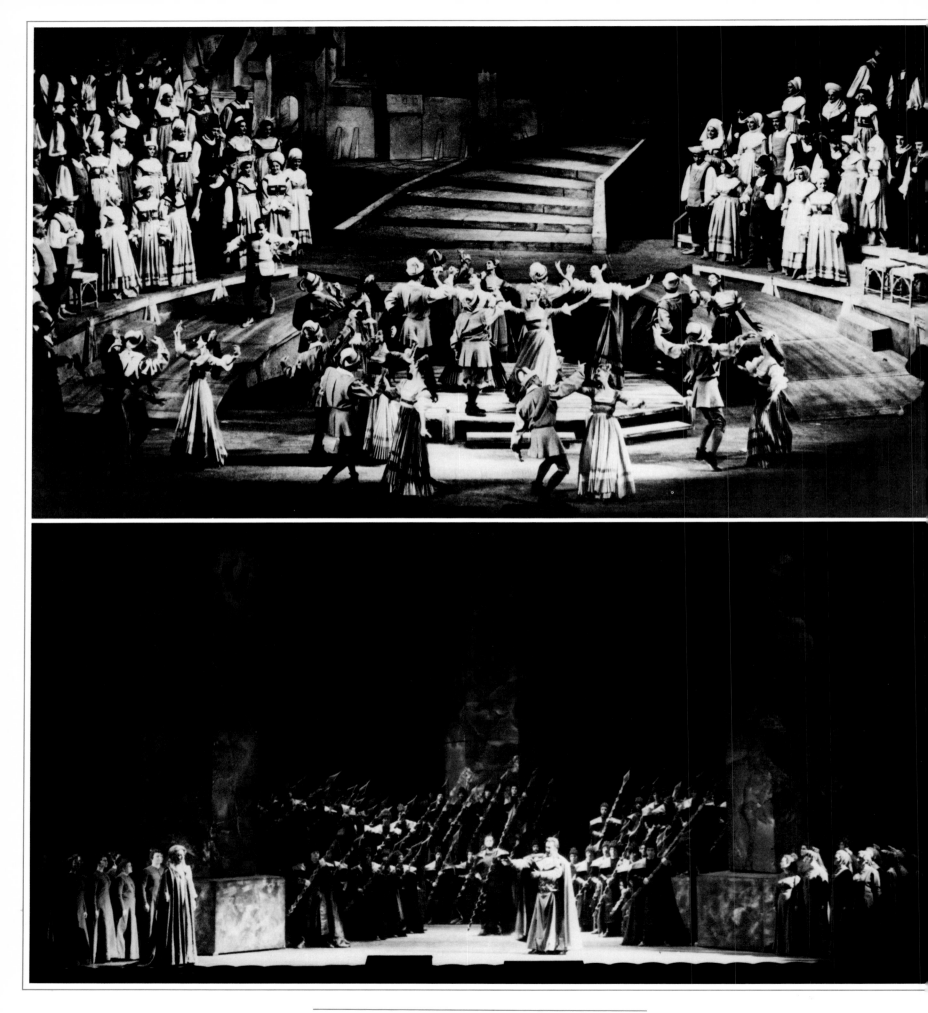

TOP: **DIE MEISTERSINGER,** 1977. BOTTOM: **GÖTTERDÄMMERUNG,**
1974. THE PRODUCTION IS A GENEROUS GIFT OF THE
GRAMMA FISHER FOUNDATION.

116

Where do you go from *Götterdämmerung?* May I quote myself the very next season of 1977: What is really good opera worth? Well, however rueful the admission, whatever it costs. If you heard the audience's exultant shout when the last curtain fell on *Die Meistersinger*— which the Lyric wisely waited 23 seasons to stage—you marked the account paid, plus that enormous intangible, credit.

To restore Wagner's great festival comedy to our stage was a bold gesture; to restore it so admirably was a priceless one. The opera house, like the theater and the concert hall, is the keeper of the keys of art's world treasure. Only a master key unlocks *Die Meistersinger*. That joyous shout at the end meant that the audience had been admitted. If not invariably to the holy of holies—a rare experience indeed—then to the great, glowing panorama of the up-surge of gifted youth in art, Richard Wagner's incandescent declaration of independence.

Meistersinger is so many things. A recreation of medieval Nuremberg of the proud guilds of artisans, mastersingers in their third century, here with the cobbler poet, Hans Sachs. A comedy of cross purposes, a parody of pedantry, a knightly love story, a boisterous brawl, the tenderest musings, the rue at a world gone mad, all this and more, counterpoised and coun-terpointed.

Wagner had no doubt about which came first, the words or the music. He wrote his play, an altogether remarkable play. Then his music surged into it, flooding, at times inundating, but never destroying it. The cresting to triumph is irresistible—and demanding. *Meistersinger* is insatiable, and Ferdinand Leitner had taken the orchestra a long way toward its enormous mobility, spectacular equilibrium and huge yet transparent tone.

The production and stage direction, basically sound, came from the Metropolitan to house an international cast. The Hans Sachs was Karl Ridderbusch, poet and peasant, dreamer and rough comedian, intolerant of fools, generous to talent, a voice suddenly holding all the shadows and textures of the fragrant dusk. William Johns the soaring heldentenor. Geraint Evans at best a dark, vain Beckmesser preening, Tom Fox's watchman a Don Quixote, Gwynne Howell's Pogner suggesting that Boris Godunov had wandered into Nuremberg.

A wonderful second act of outthrust gabled houses, a fusion of performance, sometimes rollicking, sometimes poetic. *Meistersinger* again. It had been away far too long.

What keeps your operatic strategist awake at night is the lurking suspicion that things are going too well. There is precedent.

In the very first Auditorium season of 1889 Francesco Tamagno was here to sing the *Otello* he had created at La Scala two years before. There was $9,000 in the till and Milford Adams, the manager, was smiling. Briefly. There was this report in the Tribune:

"Italian opera has the influenza. Sig. Tamagno is ill at the Leland. So is Mme Guido-Valda. So is Mme Pettigiani, and Mme Nordica is in bed at the Richelieu.

"Only Patti and myself are left," said Mr. Adams, "and I am not feeling any too well."

A committee headed by the ailing Mr. Adams called on Mme Patti, who was toasting her toes at the Richelieu and eating marshmallows. The conversation:

"You are well, are you not?"

"Perfectly."

"Then you will sing tonight?"

"For $4,000."

The committee withdrew, but not to cancel. Mme Albani was persuaded to switch from Desdemona to Valentine, and *Les Huguenots* went on, despite its demand for at least five stars. Tamagno's *Otello* came a few nights later when he had emerged triumphant from red flannel.

The Lyric's first *Elektra* without Birgit Nilsson was almost as unthinkable as Chicago's first *Otello* without its creator Tamagno. It was planned for her and built around her. But there it was, 1975, and she had taken off to a tax-haven Europe, presumably to stay. Lyric had a stunning production on loan from La Scala, but not a true protagonist until Ursula Schroeder-Feinen arrived as what Elektra must be, an implacable powerhouse.

It had from the start a strong conductor, Berislav Klobučar, interesting casting, often imaginative staging, and a rarely beautiful production designed by Rudolf Heinrich, who once gave *Salome* a strange little orchestra perched in silhouette high on the rim of Herod's terrace.

For *Elektra* Heinrich went back to ancient Mycenae—a great diagonal wall jutting from the high rock of the citadel palace, a wall washed in pale colors of ancient frescoes, flickering in the changing light. The bloody palace itself was a wash of Chinoiserie, its minions coolies with shaven heads, its Klytemnestra—a kind of Elizabeth I gone mad—losing her sparse, almost fright wig hair. Royal robes were of Chinese ceremonial splendor. Shorn of hers, Klytemnestra was a burned out shell.

It is often a problem, in the costly world of operatic production and the long ago loss of the luxury of infinite rehearsal, to know how much of a stage director's plan is realized. Nikolaus Lehnhoff's staging was rich in bold ideas that sometimes went overboard into the absurd. Apparently he had in mind the arrogant palace looking down in contempt on the near

LEFT: CAROL NEBLETT, **ELEKTRA**, 1975. RIGHT: MIGNON DUNN, **ELEKTRA**, 1975.

pigsty of Elektra's exile, a place of sacrificial fire in the torch of the maenad's dance, the action towering over a squirming, crawling world of minions and storm troopers and guards clanking chain whips. When it worked, it was riveting; when it failed, there was always the music.

Elektra's music is the fearful crest of Richard Strauss' soaring into *Schrechlichkeit,* a huge tone poem that frames, propels and inundates Sophocles' ancient Greece in terms of Hugo von Hofmannstahl. Music of such ferocity, demanding such virtuosity, that most of its legendary performances are heard in the great concert halls. But Klobučar's orchestra was massive, lyrical and in its Straussian way beautiful, an outpouring that did not drown the singers.

At best, Ursula Boese was a marvelous Klytemnestra of voice and imagination. Hofmannstahl wrote of the role's "sallow, bloated face," saying "She leans on her Confidante while a jaundiced, snake-like figure carries the train of her robe. She is entirely covered with precious stones and talismans . . . her fingers bristle with rings, her eyelids are unnaturally large and it seems to cost her an unspeakable effort to keep them from falling." Ursula Boese was a fascinating variation on the theme, "that tainted corpse, like garments that the moths have eaten." When not betrayed by whimsical stage direction, she was as remarkable as the setting.

Chrysothemis, often so unaccountably a blonde doll with curls, was in Carol Neblett a beautiful dark girl in a deep red robe, her troubled eyes searching, her voice soaring as if Strauss were a joy. Thomas Stewart was the strong Orestes, Frank Little as Aegisthus something out of *The Miraculous Mandarin.*

URSULA SCHROEDER-FEINEN AS **ELEKTRA,** 1975.

The pity is that such a performance cannot be held in repertory to ripen what was in this case such fascinating poison fruit. Even that one bold production was an extraordinary solution for an opera notoriously difficult to visualize because its supremacy lies not on the stage but in the orchestra pit.

You know how memory, or imagination, can trick you. About this time I was ruffling records and saying to myself, "Well, at least Lyric had Birgit Nilsson's Salome." She never sang it here, though my mind's eye has transferred her to the Opera House from some Metropolitan or European stage. A pity we lost her in the lustrous line of insatiable creatures demanding the Prophet's head.

Our first, of course, was Mary Garden in 1910, that first season of resident opera in the Auditorium, just five years after the Dresden première. Campanini conducted, and as Garden always sang *Salome* in Wilde's French text, the cast held Dalmores and Dufranne.

There was quite a non-operatic uproar. In 1910 the unofficial censors had no television to rouse their zeal. The Law and Order League declared *Salome* to be on a par with the red light district, and "Mary Garden as Salome a great degenerator of public morals." The opera company cravenly withdrew the opera after two performances, but took it on tour to Milwaukee, which apparently did not mind at all.

The best opera has always been wonderful theater. The most fascinating review of the Garden *Salome* was written by the Tribune's drama critic, Percy Hammond.

He invoked both Wilde and Huysmans, and drew this portrait on his own: "She is a fabulous she-thing, playing with love and death—loathsome, mysterious, poisonous, slaking her slimy passion in the blood of her victim. She is Salome according to the Wilde formulary, a monstrous oracle of bestiality."

That alone might very well shake up a Law and Order League. It was not until the season of 1921–22 when Garden was in charge that *Salome* was revived, this time with Polacco conducting and with a cast of Muratore, Dufranne and that supreme artist in smaller roles, José Mojica. I saw her *Salome* a few years later and knew exactly what James Huneker meant when he called her voice "a sonorous mirage."

Before Lyric's time and after Garden's, Chicago opera had Maria Jeritza in a scarlet wig, and in two blazing Rodzinski performances, both Marjorie Lawrence and the extraordinary Rose Pauly, whose voice had the taste of dried blood.

Lyric's first *Salome* was a disappointment. It was 1956 and Georg Solti's Lyric debut. There was no question about the validity of his Strauss but with the young company in its third season he lacked the virtuoso instrument eventually to be his in Orchestra Hall. Inge Borkh of the big, shining soprano turned out to be far less interesting on the opera stage than she had been in *Elektra* and *Salome* excerpts with Fritz Reiner and the Chicago Symphony Orchestra. She was blonde and hearty, with none of the strange perversity to make Salome as alluring as depraved. The true performance was Ramon Vinay's as Herod, a tortured man in a tipsy crown of flowers. The setting was the brooding beauty of older nights, held in a dusk of cypresses.

Felicia Weathers came in a Heinrich setting without the flaring little stage orchestra, and then there was a total change of Straussian pace with lissome Anja Silja in an adaptation of the Wieland Wagner *Salome* which seemed to be staged in the bottom of John the Baptist's cistern.

INGE BORKH AS **SALOME,** 1956.

FOLLOWING PAGES, LEFT: GRACE BUMBRY AS **SALOME,** 1978. RIGHT:
ANJA SILJA AS **SALOME,** 1971.

This was Wieland Wagner's first and as far as I know his last *Salome*, an unsuccessful experiment he might have rejected in subsequent seasons. It was a prosaic, pedestrian *Salome* cursed by the conviction that Salome is a nice, healthy girl who stands up and sings the terrifying closing scene as if it were an aria, that Herod is a piggish fellow who would be at home in a slaughter house, that Herodias is a red-wigged fishwife, and that it is much better to have Salome beheaded by the same scimitar that disposed of Jochanaan than to crush her on cue with the shields.

It was fairly typical of such readjustment of both Richard Strauss and Oscar Wilde that the golden haired Silja wore Aubrey Beardsley garb of tiny bra and low slung black lace Oriental tights. Oscar Wilde loathed the Beardsley illustrations. He said "They are too Japanese—my play is Byzantine."

When Sarah Bernhardt talked to Wilde about acting in the play—which she never did—she said it was heraldic, a fresco, that the word must fall like a pearl on a crystal disk. He immediately said he wanted yellow costumes against a violet sky, with braziers of perfume. That was before the miasma of Strauss' music with its hypnotic distillation of necrophilic lust. Wilde might have been astonished at what had happened to his *jeu d'esprit*.

What happened when Lyric had its finest *Salome* in 1978 was that the Wieland Wagner displacement, while still irritating, was less important. The mesmerizing things were Grace Bumbry's perverse little Judean princess and the orchestra with Berislav Klobučar capturing so much of the music's powerful sweep, its strange sweetness of fruit at the edge of the over-ripe.

The fortunate opera house is a showcase of collector's items. That is why you have the insatiable operagoer. It can happen; it just might.

Bumbry's Salome is like a small temple idol carved in teakwood come to life. She might actually be the 16 year-old at the court of Herod the Tetrarch, spoiled, imperious, implacable, tainted with bloodlust and yet, in a monstrous way, childlike. At the end, cuddling the head of John the Baptist with its flowing red scarf of blood as if it were some terrible, irreparably damaged doll.

Her voice, which Lotte Lehmann found in a master's class at Northwestern, has the Straussian subtleties and soaring, the childlike tendrils like tainted fruit, the seductiveness and yet the timbre to match the huge orchestra and cut through or over it on demand. She can sit quietly and potently, almost at the very edge of the stage, waiting, because she knows she will get what she wants. The jeweled bra and bikini under the seven veils the colors of flames? Right out of the famed Roman mosaics in the ancient villa near Sicily's Piazza Armerina.

Ragnar Ulfung was a corruptly powerful Herod—they said that Burrian, who created the role, almost decomposed before your eyes—and Frank Little understood the importance of Narraboth, the first to understand Salome (perhaps because he loves her) and to kill himself because of it.

This was a flaring, often mesmeric *Salome* holding the promise that it might go all the Straussian way the next time.

Opera is such vast territory. Take the distance, say, from *Don Pasquale* to *Falstaff* in the realm of preening beaux, or, in aspiration, from *Salome* to *Fidelio*. No one leaves Beethoven's only opera doubting that he is his brother's keeper. The intensity of the commitment probably varies with the headlines.

OPPOSITE PAGE: TOP LEFT: BIRGIT NILSSON AS **FIDELIO**, 1961. TOP CENTER: BORIS CHRISTOFF, **FIDELIO**, 1963. TOP RIGHT: GWYNETH JONES AS **FIDELIO**, 1975. BOTTOM: JON VICKERS, **FIDELIO**, 1961.

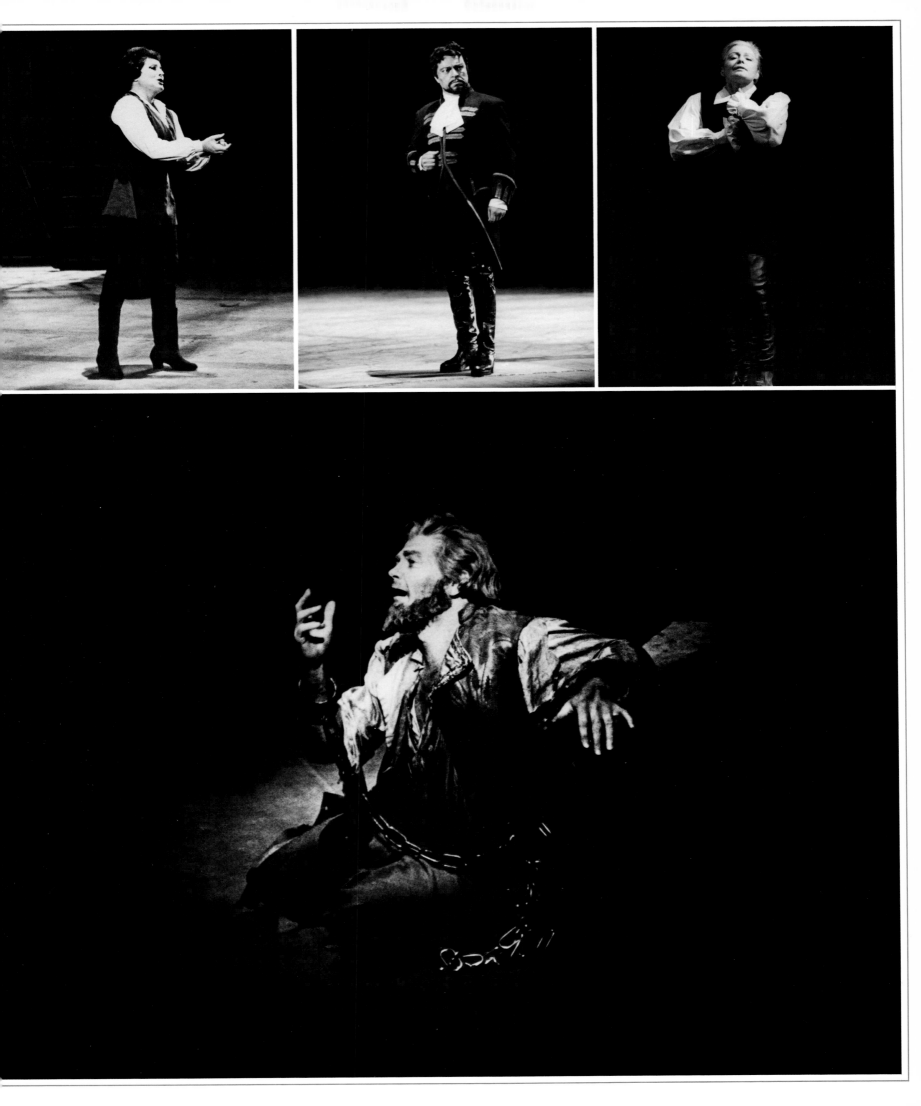

In Chicago's 1930s outburst of German opera, Frida Leider was the Leonore. Lotte Lehmann never sang it here except in concert with Stock, a great loss as *Fidelio* was to many her supreme achievement.

Everyone has his lodestar performance. Mine of *Fidelio* came at Salzburg in 1949 when Austria had risen from under the Nazi jackboot, still blinking at the light like the prisoners of Pizarro. Wilhelm Furtwaengler, the Vienna Philharmonic, Kirsten Flagstad and, as Pizarro, Paul Schoeffler, unmistakably Hitler. It was in the little Festspielhaus and so both intimate and immediate. When the third *Leonore* Overture released the tension before the closing scene, the audience went quite joyously mad.

It is an attribute of great music that in great performance you often seem never to have heard it before. Or, at least, not quite like that. Out of a great *Fidelio* pour Beethoven's fierce humanity, his two-fisted power, his infinite compassion, his limitless capacity for rage at injustice. There in the Festspielhaus when the trumpet call struck light into darkness you knew that the day of freedom will always come while brave men are willing to fight for it. Man is a hopeful animal, especially with Beethoven to remind him.

Audacity is a great asset, however risky. Lyric took its life in its hands with its 1961 *Fidelio*, especially after André Cluytens had to cancel and a new conductor, who turned out to be Peter Maag and quite competent, stepped in. Beethoven had his orchestral woes, but *Fidelio*, often accused of being a static opera, was vital and often powerful. Birgit Nilsson soared in warmth and brilliance, Jon Vickers made his opening cry against the darkness an indictment of all dungeons, Hans Hotter's evil Pizarro had the rusty, guttural voice of menace, Irmgard Seefried her unique generosity, William Wildermann's jailor a touch of poetry.

It was Chicago opera's first *Fidelio* since the 1930 opera days of Frida Leider, René Maison, Hans Hermann Nissen, Alexander Kipnis and Egon Pollak. For all that was lacking, it held the reminder: where there is a tyrant there will be a liberator, and where there is darkness, light.

Once revived, *Fidelio* was not shelved. Régine Crespin came as a Juno in man's guise, warmly and richly a woman with a voice almost always ample. Boris Christoff in magnificent voice sang what turned out to be his first Pizarro on any stage. Fritz Rieger, a knowing Beethoven man in the pit, looked like a happy lion with a white mane.

Still another *Fidelio*, always with Jon Vickers (except when Sebastian Feiersinger stepped in ably to give him a breather, in 1963) had Gwyneth Jones of the big, shining soprano, Franz Crass a powerful Rocco, and a surprise up its sleeve in Pizarro.

A great Lyric favorite almost from the start was Walter Berry of the joyous baritone, who sometimes obligingly sang *Fidelio's* Don Fernando. Suddenly he was cast as Pizarro, the archvillain who hid political prisoners chained in dank dungeons. What would he be like?

He was extraordinary. An angry little man in black with short bristled pompadour and a Beckmesser voice plus authority. The whole stage came instantly to life. It was a dangerous place where men were imperiled. It was Beethoven's *Fidelio* authentic and undiluted.

If Lyric's first venture into Beethoven was as rewarding as valiant, how about Wagner, which it boldly approached in 1956, at the age of three? But then you can't have forgotten the charmed life of the Lyric's *Walküre*.

Georg Solti was its brilliant conductor. Birgit Nilsson made her debut as Brünnhilde, her voice a huge, pliant column soaring into space. Paul Schoeffler was the Wotan, a stricken god both baleful and rakish, his voice as shadowed as resonant. Ludwig Suthaus was the heldentenor, a good one, William Wildermann the Hunding, dark, bleak and dangerous.

The spell, different but again potent, held for the 1960 *Walküre*, where the soaring steel of Nilsson's voice was warming to the luster of vermeil, and where the debut Siegmund was Jon Vickers, the most eloquent since Lauritz Melchior. Hans Hotter was the Wotan of poetry and power, Gre Brouwenstijn the Sieglinde, Christa Ludwig the superb Fricka—that lovely, warm voice with the edge a woman must have if she is to tell a god what to do.

A special quality of this *Walküre* was the intimacy made possible by rare collaboration of Lovro von Matačić and Christopher West as conductor and stage director—personages who seem sometimes never to have met.

Walküre can be an encounter between giants, viewed from afar. This was an absorbing, oddly accessible and often deeply moving adventure in lyric theater. It was a series of dialogues not dwarfed, but rather framed and projected by the vast loneliness of space—here the beautiful old Chicago Opera settings veiled in marvelously lighted clouds. Voices and orchestra were a lyrical sharing, which is really what opera is all about.

Opera is an international art and in the sense of hands across the sea—applauding hands—on the higher level of diplomacy. Interchange can be mutually enriching. The Vienna Staatsoper often is, and always should be, the house of Mozart and it was from Vienna the year before its dazzling Viennese *Figaro* that Lyric imported its enchanting *Così fan Tutte* of 1959, housed in settings and costumes borrowed from San Francisco.

The Lyric was born of a stellar *Don Giovanni* so expectation ran high for the quicksilver and so elusive *Così*. Would that intimate jest of masquerading by-play be lost in the big house? How nice to be so rich we could put it in the little Civic next door. Again, as the man said, the best theater is the one with the best performance. Especially when it has lured in debut no less than Elisabeth Schwarzkopf and Christa Ludwig.

OPPOSITE PAGE: JON VICKERS AND GRE BROUWENSTIJN, **DIE WALKÜRE,** 1960.

ABOVE: HANS HOTTER AND BIRGIT NILSSON, **DIE WALKÜRE,** 1960.

The problem, when you rushed back to your newspaper with deadlines looming, where to start to put things in perspective. With the cast, which added to the lustrous ladies Sylvia Stahlman, Walter Berry, Léopold Simoneau and Fernando Corena? With the orchestra, which played with spirit and equilibrium under Josef Krips' joyous direction? With the stage in its borrowed plumage so deftly set in motion by Adolf Rott's stage direction? Or with Mozart, who turned Lorenzo da Ponte's Neapolitan charade into one of the most enchanting operas that ever spilled melody like spring water after a long winter?

It all went together in a performance that neither froze into attitudes nor degenerated into horseplay—though its cavaliers picked up a trick from Chaliapin's Faustian Mephisto, who carried a sunflower into the garden scene—until Edith Mason's Marguerite tossed it out the stage door, to his audible anguish.

Lyric's *Così* was blithe enough without the broad stroke.

Its baroque decor (by George Jenkins) used a stage within a stage with private park, airy pavilion, and stage boxes for the seldom used but vitally important chorus. It let the play flow easily, and diverted the eye.

Così had the ideal Mozart ambience increasingly hard to create, a brilliant ensemble to display individual stars in a scintillant whole. Schwarzkopf's Fiordiligi was a total charmer, in radiant voice to parody, ever so slightly, the fearful leaps of *Come scoglio*, and the skill to sing it, along with the dazzling *Per pietà* of the horn obbligato.

Ludwig was the Dorabella of gamine gaiety and that luxurious voice then truly a mezzo-soprano. Walter Berry had the exuberance in leash that made his Papageno a delight, Simoneau spun Mozartean *mezza-voce* while resembling a Chinese mandarin, and Corena had the tongue-in-cheek amusement of that labyrinth of plot and counterplot. Despina was Sylvia Stahlman, a delight in and out of masquerade.

Opera in English? I have never been persuaded, though at times captivated by felicitous translation. But surely *Così* is as baffling as its title? Not necessarily. That November night at the Lyric you could have walked in without knowing a word of Italian or a line of the plot, and followed it all with amused ease. When the two men in disguise woo each other's fiancees the story tells itself, and Mozart makes it bewitching.

The 1966 importation of *Die Zauberflöte* in the Oscar Kokoschka production was less persuasive, despite the wealth of good people involved. That beguiling challenge remains in the Lyric's future.

If my records can be trusted, Chicago first heard *The Magic Flute* at old McVickers in 1865. The Metropolitan brought it to the Auditorium in 1902 with Sembrich, Gadski, Ternina, Homer, Fritzi Scheff as Papagena, Dippel, Campanari and Edouard de Reszke—a galaxy so costly the price went up from $3.50 to $5. (It was the next season at the Met that Scheff stopped the show, Sembrich walked out, and the opera ended without the closing ensemble.)

One of the alluring qualities of opera is the wine of production choice. Is this *Singspiel* a comedy, a noble work of art, or both? Whatever, it is a labyrinthine maze of knightly ordeal, comic pantomime, spoken dialogue, shining arias, and the general aura of the preposterous and the irresistible. I have known three vastly different performances of quality whose individual stamp was primarily that of the conductor.

OPPOSITE PAGE, TOP LEFT: ELISABETH SCHWARZKOPF, **COSI FAN TUTTE,** 1959. TOP CENTER: SCHWARZKOPF, **COSI FAN TUTTE,** 1961. TOP RIGHT: SCHWARZKOPF AND CHRISTA LUDWIG, **COSI FAN TUTTE,** 1959. CENTER: STANDING LEFT TO RIGHT: FERNANDO CORENA, LEOPOLD SIMONEAU, CAROL FOX, LOVRO VON MATAČIĆ, ELISABETH SCHWARZKOPF. SEATED: WALTER BERRY, SYLVIA STAHLMAN, CHRISTA LUDWIG, THE CAST OF THE 1961 **COSI FAN TUTTE.** CENTER RIGHT: JOSEPH KRIPS. BOTTOM LEFT: MARGARET PRICE, **LE NOZZE DI FIGARO,** 1975. BOTTOM RIGHT: MARGARET PRICE, GERAINT EVANS, AND ANN HOWELLS, **COSI FAN TUTTE, 1972.**

You may remember that when Chicago Opera was established at the Auditorium in 1910–11, the Metropolitan Opera agreed to stop its visits, though not the use of its artists. It was not until the spring of 1943, when we had no opera of our own, that the Metropolitan returned for an early spring visit at the Opera House. A jewel of that engagement was Bruno Walter's *The Magic Flute.*

It was in English, it was intimate, it had flame-tipped Mozart, and it was like a play with music. Ezio Pinza was Sarastro the magnificent, and one of the three ladies was Eleanor Steber.

My other two *Flutes* of Baccarat vintage were European. The first and always the most magnificent, Wilhelm Furtwaengler's at Salzburg in the Rocky Riding School carved from the flank of the Moenchberg. He had all the Vienna Staatsoper attributes for this Mozart probably nearest the German-speaking heart. Baroque fantasy with Masonic overtones with Oscar Fritz Schuh's fanciful staging, Caspar Neher's fairy tale costumes, the symbols of sun and moon, of darkness and light, the little toucan whose green wings had a red lining, the cozy dragon shedding sequins. The cast—Seefried, Dermota, Greindl the subterranean Sarastro, Erich Kunz the Papageno. The superb orchestra and chorus.

Most of all, Furtwaengler. It was above all human Mozart, filled with joy and sorrow, innocence and evil, generosity and greed, ennobled by the eternal striving to reach from darkness into light.

But the very next summer, 1952, this from my traveling scrapbook:

"Interesting how persuasive talent can make its point of view. One of the treasures of our time is Furtwaengler's *The Magic Flute* in Salzburg's Rocky Riding School, sublimely beautiful Mozart, warmly, lovingly, spaciously cast in the noble style.

"But here at the Edinburgh Festival the Hamburg Staatsoper with the Hamburg Philharmonic is playing the same opera as a joyously intimate comedy of fairy tale overtones. It is a matter of accent, tempo, detail, temperament, perhaps of dominant personality most of all. Furtwaengler is a mystic who penetrates the deepest mysteries of the score. Hamburg's performance is keyed to its most exuberant performance, which is Horst Guenter's as Papageno, set off by the mercurial Georg Solti in the pit."

On its chosen terms, this was a stellar production, intimately displayed in the little King's theater. Guenther Rennert staged it, with Lisa Della Casa the Pamina, Anneliese Rothenberger the feathery Papagena, Josef Metternich the magnificent Speaker. It was perhaps deliberate that Gottlob Frick's Sarastro was powerful rather then spiritual, for in this production the light was not the temple, but the sun.

Guenter was a great clumsy ox of a Papageno. The very point was that in seeming larger and more candid than life he also seemed not too stupid to follow the rules of knightly conduct, but a free spirit who found them slightly comical, or at least unnecessary. When such a Papageno takes over, the opera ends in the forest, its temple of the sun stately anticlimax.

What was Solti like 27 years ago? "He is a volatile man in the pit, who flings his head as well as his hands at the players, but it is pinpoint flinging, as his music has nerves without being nervous. His *Magic Flute* is swift, exact, yet joyously free within its compass in space. It simultaneously commands and serves the singers, as operatic conductors must."

There is wide and persuasive choice when Lyric next takes a speculative look at *The Magic Flute*. As when George Balanchine says he looks "to see what is in the icebox," decisions often are made on what is available.

Once upon a time—it was New Year's Eve 1927 at the Auditorium—Chicago Opera's festive *Fledermaus* more or less in English stirred unexpected laughter when Rosa Raisa, the Rosalinda, remarked, "I have an unfortunate passion for tenors." Her husband, the baritone Giacomo Rimini, was right there on stage as Dr. Falke.

Undeniably, opera fans have a passion for tenors, but they do not call it unfortunate. Remember the sigh of bliss that rose when Lyric announced more or less immediate contractual designs on, in alphabetical order, Jose Carreras, Carlo Cossutta, Placido Domingo, Alfredo Kraus, Luciano Pavarotti and Jon Vickers.

Perhaps this addiction has to do with the sense of danger in flight into stratospheric regions which also sets the balletomane shouting. But the operatic tenor is in other ways endangered. Composers over the centuries have assumed that he has, at least temporarily, a broken heart.

From Otello's sob to Nemorino's sigh, from Canio's jealous rage to Cavaradossi's lonely song to the stars, the great tenor triumphs in heartbreak. Though that special sound of sadness is more rare in sopranos, it was what made Callas unique in an operatic presence as haunting as dazzling. Primarily, though, it is a tenor prerogative.

Lyric's first tenor was a good omen. Léopold Simoneau was not only an unusual lyric tenor, his best role was Mozart's Don Ottavio where he spun *Il mio tesoro* from a silky skein the old John McCormack recording set as stellar standard. Giuseppe di Stefano was a total charmer whose ardor could fire up in molten glow, and who seemed, like Puccini, to fall in love with each heroine in turn. Perhaps the special word was blandishing. His Lyric roles were rich, and he enriched them.

Most of Lyric's stars were newcomers in that vocal renaissance after World War II. Because of Lyric one of the truly great ones came back. Jussi Bjoerling was a superb recitalist, and we had never lost that radiance. But he had not sung in Chicago opera in a decade when he joined Lyric in 1955.

Bjoerling's voice had a piercing sweetness, and yet a veil of mystery that shared Lauritz Melchior's gift for invoking legend. His debut *Trovatore* was with Callas, Bastianini and Ebe Stignani. His voice, for all its tenderness, flashed like a drawn sword. There are afficionados who claim that the crest of Callas' song was that heartstruck threnody in the dusk of grief, *D'amor sull'ali rosee*. That was when Bing came, contract in hand, and she smiled like a cat feasting on canaries. It turned out badly, but how was she to know?

Bjoerling, so long of world renown, may have shaken a commiserating head. Who knows? He kept on singing at that incredible peak of the matchless voice. His profligate Duke with Gobbi's subtly mesmeric Rigoletto. Riccardo in *Ballo* of the laughing barcarolle. A lambent *Tosca* with Tebaldi and Gobbi on a night of three brands of incandescence.

Without Lyric we would have lost all that.

The heroic tenor is a rare article; he always was. Lyric's first was Mario Del Monaco of the big, dark, impassioned outpouring, the Otello, the Canio, the man who helped restore *Andrea Chénier* as we had not heard it since the Martinelli nights at Ravinia. On one of those nights the

lights went out twice as Martinelli was soaring into the supercharger of the *Improvviso*, that declaration of revolutionary independence. Some of us suspected that Martinelli arranged the mechanical power failure, because he had none of his own, and he did love soaring.

In any case, it was 1956 when Lyric gave us that combustible Giordano tale of the French Revolution where the distance from patriot to victim was the flick of a tyrant's eye. There had been glorious Chicago performances in earlier days, when Claudia Muzio was always reported to have fainted after *La mamma morta*. Lyric had Eleanor Steber surprising us all with that outpouring of love in the face of death.

It was, as we happily took for granted in those nights, Tito Gobbi, the catlike singing actor, who was the tenor's equal antagonist and at the same time his foil. Gobbi as Gérard, gone from angry servant to head of the tribunal, really a kangaroo court, made the powerful aria *Nemico della patria* —an enemy of his country?—the sensitive probing of a generous heart.

Into this cauldron Del Monaco walked with the elegance of the grand manner and he sang the *Improvviso* as only a great tenor can sing it. In nobility of line, ease of style, and ringing beauty of tone. It was singing you might not match in a lifetime of opera.

Where to begin with Richard Tucker, whose big, dark beautiful voice vaulted like an arrow from Robin Hood's bow? He was Don Carlo when Gobbi and Christoff were joined by Giulietta Simionato in all her considerable glory as Eboli, and by a young Grand Inquisitor of granitic power, Ferruccio Mazzoli.

OPPOSITE PAGE, TOP LEFT: RICHARD TUCKER AND ETTORE BASTIANINI, **RIGOLETTO,** 1962. TOP RIGHT: TITO GOBBI AND TUCKER, **TOSCA,** 1964. BOTTOM LEFT: TUCKER, **UN BALLO IN MASCHERA,** 1963. BOTTOM RIGHT: CRISTINA DEUTEKOM AND TUCKER, **LUCIA DI LAMMERMOOR,** 1971.

ABOVE: **LA GIOCONDA,** 1959: LEFT TO RIGHT, IRENE KRAMARICH, EILEEN FARRELL, IRENE DALIS, JOSEPH GREINDL, AND GIUSEPPE TADDEI.

He was the man singing *Cielo e mar* beside the brigantine so soon to be set blazing, and few forgot that who heard the Lyric's early ventures into *La Gioconda*, where Maria Tallchief sometimes led the *Dance of the Hours*. Whenever he came, he was welcome, a serious artist with an opulent voice. Of course, his operatic home base was the Metropolitan. But as for what began it all, he would have told you that Henry Weber engaged a young cantor to sing Rodolfo in the Chicago Theater of the Air's *La Bohéme*. Where have you been all my life, demanded opera, and that took care of that.

It was always a pity that Callas never sang here with Franco Corelli. She said they were rather special together in Giordano's *Fedora*, and who is to doubt that? But there was a Lyric night when Corelli walked off with its less than best *Carmen*, a tall, handsome tenor with an urgent sense of drama and that proud, dark voice pouring heart and life into opera.

There was another, totally different Lyric tenor some of you may not even remember. The 1962 *Samson et Dalila* had seemed hopelessly jinxed when Giulietta Simionato and Jon Vickers canceled. But Rita Gorr, the Belgian mezzo, flew in to sing a spectacular Delilah of plangent beauty and innate musicality. Hans Kaart, the Dutch tenor, flew in to sing Samson.

It had been said that Kaart was about the size of Leo Slezak. Not quite. A big man who looked like a wrestler, and also an artist. He carried deep conviction in conquest and defeat. He made no false moves. His abysmal grief in the treadmill depths made the fury in the temple possible. His voice had heroic range and style.

But it turned out that his size was not the strong man's, rather the sick man's. Hans Kaart died soon after, much too young. It was opera's loss.

When Lyric opened its 21st season in 1975 it had the new pale gold curtain to replace the original ruined by fire, and an even more interesting replacement, a powerful new Otello. Carlo Cossutta (more recently a notable Canio) was a blackly imposing Moor in flowing white robes, with a clarion tenor rejoicing in the merciless tessitura. His foil was the subtly ironic Iago of Piero Cappuccilli, his support, Bartoletti in the pit.

ABOVE, LEFT: RENATO BRUSON, **UN BALLO IN MASCHERA,** 1976. CENTER: RENATA TEBALDI AND PLACIDO DOMINGO IN THE DRESS REHEARSAL OF **MANON LESCAUT,** 1968. RIGHT: DOMINGO AND VIORICA CORTEZ, **LES CONTES D'HOFFMANN,** 1976.

OPPOSITE PAGE: CARLO COSSUTTA AS **OTELLO,** 1975.

It was *L'Elisir d'Amore* that introduced Alfredo Kraus to Lyric as a tall lyric tenor of presence and style, happily at home in the bubbling production with Fernando Corena's engaging quack, Ezio Frigerio's knowing direction, and the brilliant Donizetti of Carlo Felice Cillario. He has sung many roles since, often with a crystalline elegance to remind you that a Spaniard from the Canary Islands lurks behind that adopted name.

Plácido Domingo, a brilliant tenor originally from Madrid, first came to Lyric as a welcome Des Grieux in *Manon Lescaut.* His return in the new production of *The Tales of Hoffmann* was a 1976 felicity on all counts. Offenbach's *Contes* had been turned into an opulent and wittily diverting *divertissement* with song, especially in the case of the tall, striking Spaniard.

Struck down on all sides by the wheel of misfortune, spun by the four aspects of his evil genius—in this case Norman Mittelmann—made the constant fool of love and even a dunce in rose colored glasses, Mr. Domingo was still the hero. Opera is like that when the unmistakable operatic timbre strikes the waiting ear—the real thing, plangent, ardent and beautiful.

Hoffmann had three delightful girls to woo—Ruth Welting as the doll, Viorica Cortez the Venetian Giulietta, Christiane Eda-Pierre as the poignant Antonia—with Elena Zilio in travesti as Nicklausse and Florindo Andreolli an expert droll. It was all spun of a piece with the chorus, the orchestra and the delight in spinning that is Bartoletti's.

A rare and special beguilement was the production itself. We live in an operatic age when many a designer and director walks the floor at night wondering what he can do to make a familiar opera "different." Sometimes he succeeds beyond his wildest dreams and hands us a nightmare. *Hoffmann* is such a delight, adventurous but authentic, amusing but accurate, and diverting to boot, that it is a true statement in the Lyric repertory, one of many generous gifts.

OPPOSITE PAGE: PLACIDO DOMINGO AND RUTH WELTING, **LES CONTES D'HOFFMANN,** 1976.

ABOVE: **UN BALLO IN MASCHERA,** 1976, WITH KATIA RICCIARELLI, LEFT, JOSE CARRERAS, CENTER, AND PATRICIA WISE, RIGHT.

Designed by Ezio Frigerio and staged by Virginio Puecher, this *Hoffmann* is a rare example of economy in style. Luther's tavern is like the inside of a great cask with elevators on either side. As the wheel of fortune turns you are inside the great concourse of a railway station, with snorting locomotive waiting to take Hoffmann on his journeys. It easily becomes Spalanzani's house with puppet theater, instruments played by disembodied hands, then Venice with a diamond of magical size, and cross tracks for gondolas—a masquerade and at the same time a sinister jest in shadowplay.

Lyric Theater. Lyric Opera's original name and always its greatest challenge. I once told Carol Fox what Peter Hall, director of Britain's National Theater and fascinated by staging opera, said about just that: "Opera at its best—which is almost never—is the most potent form of theater . . . if the dramatic skill came anywhere near the musical skill, we would have overwhelming opera."

"Yes, we would," said the keeper of our operatic keys. "Sometimes—we do."

You might not call *Hoffmann* overwhelming in the sense, say, of a great *Meistersinger*, a glorious *Don Giovanni*, but as a bewitchment in the night it was wonderful fun.

LA BOHEME, 1973. THE PRODUCTION IS A GENEROUS GIFT OF MR. JAMES C. HEMPHILL.

Assassination, said George Bernard Shaw, is the extreme form of censorship. Opera is strewn with the dismembered and dislocated shells of plots reckless enough to touch on assassinated royalty. Gustavus III of Sweden, a remarkable man who loved theater, really was assassinated in 1792 at a masked ball in Stockholm's opera house.

But when Verdi wrote *Un Ballo in Maschera* more than half a century later, the skittish censors really went into action. The king became Riccardo, Count of Warwick, the laughing conspirators and the sorceress Ulrica, blacks, and the locale was moved to Boston, which they probably thought was out there somewhere.

It seems to have been the tenor Mario—who like Garbo needed no other name—who set the Neapolitan stamp on *Ballo* in the Paris production, becoming a Spanish grandee who disguised himself as a fisherman for the barcarolle. The Metropolitan Opera, for one, moved the action back to Sweden. The Lyric's new production unaccountably chose Boston, a most peculiar Boston with stockade, cavaliers, Puritans and a few stray Indians.

Fortunately, it did not have a stray tenor. Where earlier productions had captured Richard Tucker and Franco Tagliavini, this new one introduced José Carreras, immediately an international opera favorite. Voice, presence and that rare operatic virtue, *dolce ardor.*

There was a new baritone, replacing the ailing Piero Cappuccilli, a big, brigandish Renato with an earring—Renato Bruson in opulent voice with overtones and undertones. There was the gifted Jesús López-Cobos in the pit, sometimes capturing *Ballo's* translucent aura of buoyancy, anguish, conspiratorial laughter and doom.

Then there was Pavarotti—Luciano, that is, though like Mario he really needs no elaboration. He is hard to describe because he is moving so fast that what he does today is augmented tomorrow. Beyond a doubt he is a man of lyric theater, an invaluable man, yet in some ways his supreme Lyric performance was that 1978 Lyric recital when, like Jussi Bjoerling of rich memory, he was an aristocrat working in the high style.

Here were technique, style, temperament devoted to a serious study of music, plus the mystery without which all of this would have been admirable, but not magnetizing, a voice. Quality, range, a fairly astonishing trill, but above all, quality. The sound that sets apart one voice in thousands, that reassures all of us that we can sing just like that—inside.

Pavarotti's debut Rodolfo was a little disappointing, as if Baryshnikov had done double cabrioles when we expected triple. Even then it was his Auditorium recital with *Nessun dorma* as encore that set the rafters ringing, not just with applause, but as the Auditorium can, with echoes of glories past.

Lucia with Joan Sutherland was richer operatic revelation in an intelligent production caught in an aura of that most romantic of resonant countries, Scotland. Sutherland had the ornamentation, the attack, the power. Pavarotti was a true tenor in quality and placement and the sense of phrasing with its fulfilled promise of the stratospheric.

The difference between them is that Miss Sutherland makes ornamentation compensate in part for a voice not essentially beautiful, while Pavarotti's voice is so beautiful that ornamentation, however brilliant, is an extra. It made you think of Bjoerling, Schipa, di Stefano, Gigli, even Caruso recordings in the special world of electrifying the opera house.

One other thing, perhaps implied in all that has gone before. There is a generosity about Pavarotti's art, a quality as difficult to define in a performer as it is impossible not to notice.

When he came in 1976 for his first Lyric Cavaradossi to Carol Neblett's Tosca and Cornell MacNeil's Scarpia—with that arch-Scarpia Tito Gobbi as stage director—there was the quality, the placement, the soaring, the discovery that Pavarotti at ease is a born actor. There was also the understanding of torture, the premonition of death, the instinctive courtesy of generosity, the cajolery Puccini wrote for lovers. There was López-Cobos in the orchestra pit, authoritative, yes, but also in true Puccini style, loving and cajoling. When that sort of thing happens at the opera you have triple pleasure—what is, what was, and what with luck can be.

Sometimes, the first stamp of the coin is indelible. It seems implausible that in its first season when it was more dream than reality Lyric had so rollicking a *Barbiere* that we measure all others by it. But 1954 was an era of singers, an avalanche of singers, just as a few years before pianists had reigned, and a little before that, violinists. No one knows what gets into the bewitched air.

It had been a long time since the stage held so rollicking a *Barber of Seville* deftly spun of gaiety and wit and the drollery of knowing slapstick. The lovely first act was the old Chicago Opera's square in Seville, the stars were Simionato, Gobbi, Rossi-Lemeni, Simoneau and Badioli, with Rescigno conducting and William Wymetal the stage director.

Giulietta Simionato had been the Adalgisa of the Callas *Norma*, and Rossi-Lemeni its Druidic high priest of epic grandeur. Here Simionato was a captivating Rosina, the luster of her voice cresting to a dazzle with Rossini. Rossi-Lemeni's Don Basilio was a gaunt buzzard in the high tradition of Chaliapin and Lazzari. Carlo Badioli was a Toby jug as the ideal Bartolo.

SET DESIGN FOR **LES CONTES D'HOFFMANN,** 1976. RIGHT INSERT: PLACIDO DOMINGO AND CHRISTIA

-PIERRE IN PERFORMANCE. THE PRODUCTION IS A GENEROUS GIFT OF MRS. THOMAS B. BURKE.

TOP LEFT: FIORENZA COSSOTTO AND LEONTYNE PRICE, **AIDA,** 1965. TOP RIGHT: MIRELLA FRENI, **LA BOHEME,** 1965. BOTTOM LEFT: TERESA BERGANZA, **L'INCORONAZIONE DI POPPEA,** 1966. BOTTOM RIGHT: FIORENZA COSSOTTO, **LA FAVORITA,** 1964.

TOP LEFT: ALFREDO KRAUS, **LES PECHEURS DE PERLES,** 1966. TOP RIGHT: FRANCO CORELLI, **CARMEN,**
1964. BOTTOM LEFT: TITO GOBBI, **TOSCA,** 1962. BOTTOM RIGHT: REGINE CRESPIN AS **TOSCA,** 1962.

THE AUTO-DA-FE SCENE, DON CARLO, 1974. GHIAUROV AND PILAR LORENGAR, CENTER. INSERT: HANS SOTIN.

TOP: RICHARD STILWELL, CENTER, IN **ORFEO ED EURYDICE**, 1975. BOTTOM: **DIE MEISTERSINGER,** 1977.

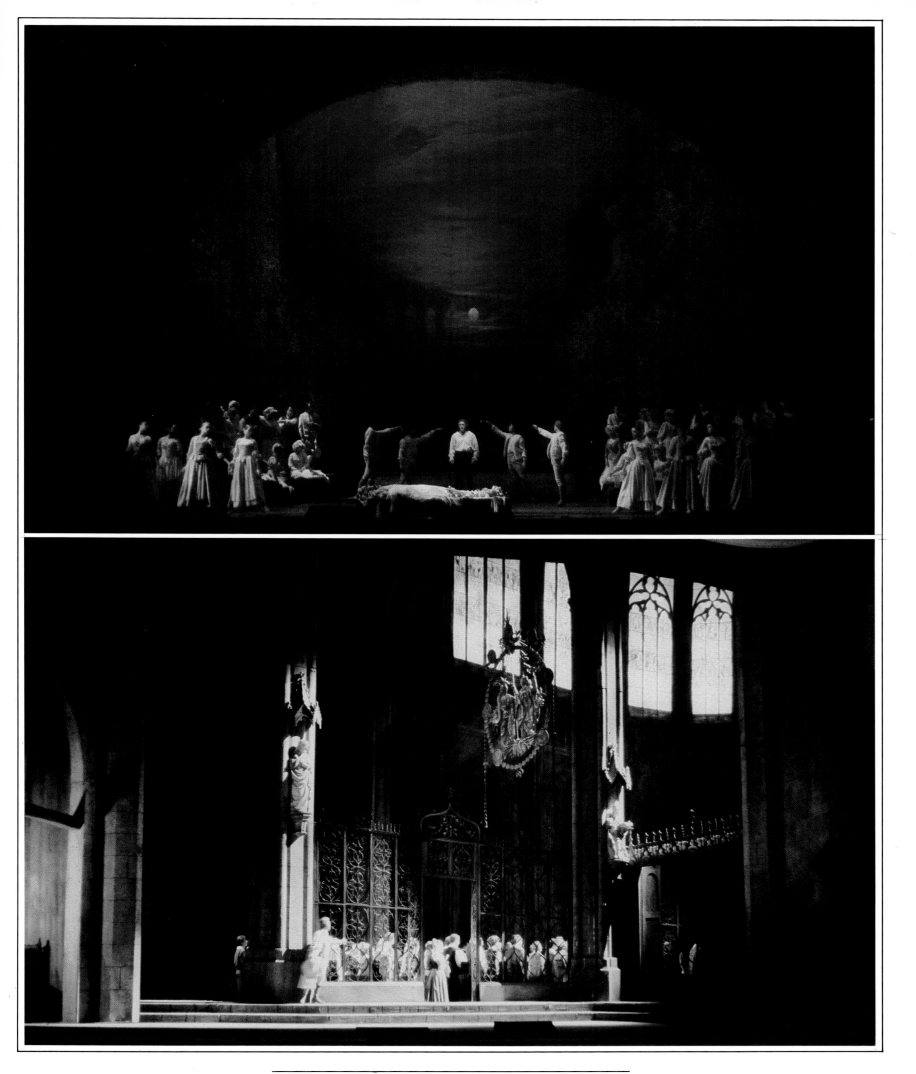

TOP: **ORFEO ED EURYDICE,** 1975. BOTTOM: **DIE MEISTERSINGER,** 1977.

TOP LEFT: GERAINT EVANS AS **DON PASQUALE,** 1978. TOP RIGHT: ALFREDO KRAUS, **DON PASQUALE,**
1978. THE PRODUCTION IS A GENEROUS GIFT OF MR. JAMES C. HEMPHILL. BELOW: GERAINT EVANS,
L'ELISIR D'AMORE, 1977.

TOP LEFT: CAROL NEBLETT AND LUCIANO PAVAROTTI, **TOSCA,** 1976. THE PRODUCTION IS A GENEROUS GIFT OF
MR. JAMES C. HEMPHILL. TOP RIGHT: PAVAROTTI, ***L'ELISIR D'AMORE,*** 1977. BOTTOM: PAVAROTTI, LEFT,
AND MARGHERITA RINALDI, CENTER, ***L'ELISIR D'AMORE.*** THE PRODUCTION IS A GENEROUS GIFT OF MRS. THOMAS B. BURKE.

LUCIA DI LAMMERMOOR, 1975, JOAN SUTHERLAND IN THE MAD SC

CRTS: LUCIANO PAVAROTTI AND JOAN SUTHERLAND.

Simoneau warmed to shining timbre and found the fun of Almaviva without losing the grandee in the masquerade.

The evening's debut opened a whole new chapter in Chicago opera when Tito Gobbi walked on stage as Figaro. Young, handsome, debonair, with a streak of wit, a touch of malice, a flair for movement. An accomplished singer who tossed off the *Largo* in tip-of-the-tongue brilliance, an actor with the appeal to shrink the big theater to conversational size.

Yet in 1961 the invaluable Gobbi had to cancel and there Lyric was, committed to *The Barber*. It more than worked, it was brilliant.

Sesto Bruscantini, straight out of Glyndebourne, was a striking Figaro of wit and style, Simionato was even more lustrous, Luigi Alva a first rate Almaviva, Fernando Corena the adroit Bartolo, and the new Basilio was Boris Christoff of huge voice, sly comedy and sulky melancholy. I always remember that Elsa Maxwell in brigand's cape and sombrero turned out to be Bernard Izzo.

Ezio Frigerio's staging knew about caste in 17th century Spain—vital for both Rossini and Mozart in the realm of Beaumarchais—and Cillario's conducting had a whiff of smoke with Rossini bubbles breaking below.

Does Rossini's Figaro have to be Italian? Not always. In 1971 Hermann Prey's crimson clad conspiratory was all quicksilver gaiety, bubbling Latin mischief, and that beautiful high baritone ranging the singer's richest realm, that of the high style.

The 1977 *Barber* circled back to the original ensemble effect, without the dazzling singers, but with good ones, and with Tito Gobbi for the first time fully transferring his high gifts as singing actor into the realm of stage director. It was especially interesting because Richard Stilwell, the tall, dashing Figaro of the good baritone, is scheduled to sing Lyric's *Don Giovanni* in 1980.

Maria Ewing's Rosina was felicitous once she got going, Luigi Alva was again Almaviva of the amused elegance, and two valuable newcomers sang the Dons. Paolo Montarsolo's music master was like a gaunt, haunted house with a fearful rattle upstairs, a melancholy droll. Claudio Desderi as Bartolo was plump, bespectacled and subtle, understanding that his fulminating aria is a highly skilled theme with comic variations. It was a *Barber* of expertise with a new conductor, Piero Bellugi, quietly in control.

In the life of every opera star is that role he just has to sing, or sing again. Tito Gobbi's in the wake of all that felicity of standard repertory was *Simon Boccanegra*, which has tantalized stellar baritones for more than a century, as they firmly believe it to be the baritone's *Boris*.

Not even Verdi—perhaps least of all Verdi—was satisfied with the 1857 premiere at the Fenice in Venice. But he did not desert it, either. In 1881 at La Scala, with Arrigo Boito's reworking of the Guitiérrez drama, *Boccanegra* had the first of many spectacular casts: Victor Maurel, Tamagno and Edouard de Reszke. The Metropolitan revived it in 1932 for Tibbett, Martinelli and Pinza, Serafin conducting. It was Serafin again in the pit when the Rome Opera restored it in 1949 for Tito Gobbi. It was 1959 when Lyric imported the Rome production and the stellar Gianandrea Gavazzeni to conduct the Gobbi *Boccanegra* with Richard Tucker and a new bass named Ferruccio Mazzoli to sing the aria everyone remembers, *Il lacerato spirito*.

The likeness to *Boris* is that Simon Boccanegra also usurps a throne, has a tender scene with his child, and dies in torment, though of poison, not struck down by madness. The cru-

PRECEDING PAGES, LEFT: **UN BALLO IN MASCHERA,** 1976, WITH KATIA RICCIARELLI, JOSE CARRERAS, AND PATRICIA WISE. THE PRODUCTION IS A GENEROUS GIFT OF MR. AND MRS. LEE A. FREEMAN AND MR. JAMES C. HEMPHILL.

RIGHT: LUCIANO PAVAROTTI AND JOAN SUTHERLAND, **LUCIA DI LAMMERMOOR,** 1975.

162

TOP LEFT: ALFREDO KRAUS AND MARIO ZANASI, **IL BARBIERE DI SIVIGLIA,** 1963. TOP RIGHT: GIULIETTA
SIMIONATO AND LUIGI ALVA, **IL BARBIERE DI SIVIGLIA,** 1961. BOTTOM LEFT: TERESA BERGANZA AS
LA CENERENTOLA, 1964. BOTTOM RIGHT: HERMANN PREY AS **IL BARBIERE DI SIVIGLIA,** 1971.
THIS PRODUCTION IS A GENEROUS GIFT OF THE GRAMMA FISHER FOUNDATION.

cial difference is that the Tsar of the Russias is a giant, the Doge of Venice a man. His scale is not heroic, so Gobbi's instinctive subtlety took command. He was singing then in that silkily shadowed baritone which could tell you by the single word *Figlia* what it meant to find his daughter, and with the mesmeric presence that by the grasp of a goblet told you it held death.

Early, incomplete but fascinating Verdi, and like all the early operas rich in promise of things to come. Boccanegra's finest scene, at the end of the first act, was added by Boito in 1881, a surging up in fury of the death rattle of Iago's *Credo* to come. Imagine the echo in the mind at the Scala's *Otello* première of 1887, with Maurel, the first Boccanegra, here the first Iago, again with Tamagno the tenor, and the great Italian conductor, Franco Faccio, in the pit.

Gobbi sang *Boccanegra* in three Lyric seasons, the second time with Tebaldi and Tucker, the third with Ilva Ligabue and Renato Cioni. He was stage director the third time, remembering Serafin's warning not to overlook the importance of Paolo the poisoner. The astute Serafin said a poor Paolo weakens *Boccanegra* as a poor Shuisky weakens *Boris*. This struck me as gospel because though I saw Chaliapin's *Boris* with a superior cast, the man I remember with him is the cringing, mortally dangerous Shuisky, who was José Mojica.

Without Gobbi, no more *Boccanegra*? Not at all. Lyric opened its 21st season with its own sumptuous production designed by Pier Luigi Pizzi, due this 25th season to house the new cast with Sherrill Milnes, Carlo Cossutta, William Stone as Paolo, and Margaret Price as Amelia.

In 1974, with the Verdi Congress in session, Piero Cappuccilli had the mesmerizing Verdi baritone, Martina Arroyo sang with a satiny sheen, and Carlo Cossutta was a near-heldentenor. But the dominant figure was Ruggiero Raimondi, the powerful young Italian bass. One of those big, black, voluminous voices with a commanding edge. Surely a *Boris.*

The simplest thing at *Boccanegra* is to forget the convoluted story, and just watch and listen. All that murmurous plotting for male voices and the mysterious choruses, with stellar embroideries. Watching the Pizzi stage is a pleasure. Fourteenth century Genoa wrapped in sea mists, all dark skies, blackish Romanesque and Gothic, noble arches, a wrought iron gate, a golden splash of the equestrian Saint George and the Dragon, the soaring scene of the council chamber suggesting the Sainte Chapelle in a thick fog. The costumes are somber, splashed with vivid jewel colors, the luster of Sargent satin.

In an era sometimes unduly persuaded that "less is more," opera can make luxurious watching.

Lyric's other excursions into early Verdi were valuable, but less lasting. *Nabucco* and the Venetian *I due Foscari* extended the operatic horizon.

Historically, *Nabucco* is of incalculable importance. It rescued Verdi from an abyss of tragedy—the loss of his young family which had all but paralyzed him—gave him his first triumph, and set off the splendors to come. Its haunting chorus of captive Jews, *Va, pensiero,* was Toscanini's and the Scala's choice in Verdi memorial. At Lyric's first *Nabucco* in 1963, with Gobbi in the title role, the chorus was sung in memory of Rosa Raisa, one of the great dramatic sopranos of all time and, by her choice, Chicago's own.

Nabucco is the Italian name of Nebuchadnezzar, and so much easier to spell. Primarily, the opera is reminder that Verdi always wrote music for voices on stage and in the pit, where Bartoletti was in Italian paradise. Gobbi often had the sound of his stellar Rigoletto and I for one regretted again the loss of a Verdi *King Lear.* Boris Christoff was a magnificent Old Testament zealot, and there was a young tenor who turned out to be Cossutta. It was opening night of the 10th season, with red roses pinned to every chair.

The story of an opera composer's life is the anguished, often fiercely angry, search for a libretto. Considering that *The Two Foscari* is historical drama by George Gordon, Lord Byron, written after he moved to Ravenna but was still haunted by Venice, it should be poetic and powerful. Especially as the Foscari lived in 14th century Venice and stamped it with their splendor. The Doge was forced to abdicate, and his son, accused of taking bribes, was banished to Crete and died in prison. Yet for all the wealth of Verdi song, the libretto turns powerful figures into marionettes, and lets the story sag.

Even so, the 1972 opening night when the curtain rose on the production borrowed from Rome, you caught your breath. A dusky, three-level stage glinting with spears and stabbed with scarlet, the patricians in judgment or the falsely accused younger Foscari, a Hamlet figure in black, the elder Foscari in vain white splendor, puppet of the Council of Ten.

When you looked more closely you saw that Pier Luigi Pizzi, the designer, had made them all puppets. Yet they were deadly dangerous men and the Doge, here indecisive, their puppet. There should have been blood, heart's blood, on that stage of Venetian pageantry. Would the uncut opera tell the whole story?

At Lyric, *I due Foscari* brought back the strikingly effective tenor Franco Tagliavini and the beautiful voice of Cappuccilli, and introduced Katia Ricciarelli, then a sumptuous young soprano in search of finesse and fire. It was another good night for Bartoletti the Florentine.

Interesting things have been done in the opera house to indulge a reigning prima donna. By 1957 with Callas gone and Tebaldi in voice all blandishing satin, Lyric staged *Adriana Lecouvreur*, Francesco Cilea's opera taken from the Scribe and Legouvé play for Sarah Bernhardt. Tebaldi wanted it, she sang it. So did Simionato, di Stefano and Gobbi, with Serafin himself in the pit. Great was the audience commotion, especially as it was the beloved Tebaldi's farewell for the season.

Bernhardt played *Adrienne* in tandem with something called *Frou-Frou*, which will give you an idea. She later wrote her own version, possibly because in the original she did not appear in the first act. At the New York première this prompted an indignant customer to demand his money back.

Adriana the opera is not so indiscreet. The time is 1730, the place the foyer of the Comédie-Française, and when all preparations are made for the grand entrance, in drifts Adriana Lecouvreur, star of stars, protesting that she is only a humble handmaiden of the arts. She has Alexandrines that melt into an aria and she gets to sing *Poveri fiori*, not knowing the sympathy is misplaced, as the violets will poison her.

It is a role for a diva and Tebaldi adored it while her audience adored Tebaldi. It was quite a scene to see her blow out three candles, with Serafin connivance. A pity no one can unhitch a limousine and pull it through the rejoicing streets.

When libretto-hunting Giacomo Puccini saw the Belasco production of *The Darling of the Gods*, and turned it into *Madama Butterfly*, which after fiasco turned into triumph, it was like hitting the top of the bestseller list. He even bought a motor boat for his retreat at Torre del Lago. He also began looking for other Belasco plays and was captivated by *The Girl of the Golden West*, the gold rush tale in which a handsome bandit and a sinister sheriff vie for sweet Minnie, who runs the Polka saloon like a Sunday school, except that she packs a gun. In earlier Chicago seasons, Minnie was a Raisa specialty of the house.

When Dimitri Mitropoulos came riding to rescue Lyric's *Fanciulla* in 1956 the revival was more than an affectionate joke. *The Girl* had always drawn from the top since its Metropolitan premiere with Caruso, Destinn, Amato and Toscanini. Lyric had Eleanor Steber at her creamiest, the powerhouse Del Monaco, and in Gobbi a Mephistophelean sheriff more Scarpia than *Gunsmoke*.

All this in the original *Fanciulla* staging. The new 1978 production, with Carol Neblett, Carlo Cossutta, Gian-Piero Mastromei and Bartoletti, came out of Broadway. This is not always a blessing, because some of the better theater directors quite misunderstand opera. Not Harold Prince and his collaborators, Eugene and Franne Lee and Ken Billington. They knew that what is unique about this gold Rush *Tosca* is its innocence, and that is what they captured without a taint of the fatuous. So out it poured, not all of it the best Puccini, but all Puccini with its folk tunes in blandishing flow.

There is a cloudy cyclorama of the low Sierras, the outside of the rickety saloon, bandits on the rocky slopes, dawn breaking, miners coming in to drink, to play faro, to greet the revered Minnie, the only girl in town. Do they trust her? She even keeps track of their gold dust. At one point Minnie and the bandit are waltzing almost in a dream, and the first act ends with a sigh. No horses, though. The Union Pacific Railroad, to prove Minnie quite a shot. Even more. A wealth of experts in smaller roles.

LILI CHOOKASIAN AND GERAINT EVANS, **FALSTAFF,** 1974.

Few operas are as elusive as *Falstaff*, Verdi's last and to many his masterwork, whose fat and fatuous non-hero he came to love so deeply that he turned him over to the stage reluctantly, saying, "Va, vecchio John." Old John went twice into immortality, Shakespeare's and Verdi's, ridiculous, deplorable, wonderful and lovable, forever luring actors and singers who seldom find the whole of the man.

Chicago has not had a great *Falstaff* since Giorgio Polacco's stellar production with Giacomo Rimini, a marvelous Sir John first given the role by Toscanini when he was so young and handsome the make-up man worked miracles. John Charles Thomas sang the role here vividly if sketchily, remarking afterward, "Good part. I must learn it sometime."

Lyric's two productions had their good qualities, but the real thing is still in the future. Tito Gobbi had made an interesting recording, but his Falstaff failed to command the big stage, even with Tebaldi and Simionato in the cast, the mighty Serafin in the pit.

The 1974 *Falstaff* must have been an enormous disappointment to Lyric, because a good production could have been so much better. Geraint Evans, an interesting stalwart without the fat Italian sound, yet working with authority in a cast with Ilva Ligabue, Luigi Alva, Lili Chookasian and Thomas Stewart. The production was Franco Zeffirelli's from Rome, a 15th century realm of half-timbered houses, mullioned casements, and the great gnarled oaks of Windsor Park.

But the orchestra with Peter Maag was at best efficient, without the love and laughter that flood *Falstaff*, and something dire had happened to Zeffirelli's stage direction. Most of it was capering slapstick demeaning the stage. Now and then, aside from the stars, you glimpsed what it might have been. Luigi Roni magnetic as Pistol. The little skip of joy Norman Paige gave as Dr. Cajus when he thought he would get the girl. The droll curtain call after the scene in Ford's house. No Falstaff—just the clothes hamper eloquently empty.

Falstaff is still in the Lyric wings, waiting.

Opera in the jet age is a different world. Once upon a time singers were in residence for the Auditorium season, often living at the Congress, the two then connected by a tunnel leading straight to Peacock Alley and what some men claimed to be the best shoeshine in Chicago. At Ravinia singers scattered happily over the North Shore, and one woman said she picked a flower a day from her garden, because it was next to the Tito Schipa house and he just might be singing.

Today for a star may be Lyric Monday, La Scala Wednesday. A stellar replacement is often a matter of frantic cabling rather than a neighborly telephone call. But miracles do happen. The 1961 night of the gifted Eberhard Waechter's *Don Giovanni* with Simoneau, Seefried and Berry when Elisabeth Schwarzkopf, the Elvira, had to cancel. In came the beautiful Lisa Della Casa, pride of the Munich Staatsoper and points international, in brilliant performance.

Two nights later Schwarzkopf had recovered, fully and perhaps plus. Remember that Schwarzkopf is a blue eyed blonde. On she swept, a beautiful virago, a proud, frightened woman, wearing a black wig, gold earrings and a green mantilla, totally dazzling.

The whole thing proved Waechter an even better actor than we had thought. His haughty Don spurned both women.

How to get so far without mentioning the less patrician Don, the one named José, who is spurned by the woman? Just that while *Carmen* may be the most popular of all operas, it is also one of the most difficult. Lyric's Carmens have been Giulietta Simionato, Jean Madeira of the burnt umber mezzo, Grace Bumbry and Viorica Cortez, all with things to offer though at the time with less than the whole. In sometimes puzzling productions the tenors held their own, giving life to the performances.

The ardent Giuseppe di Stefano was in vaulting voice in those early Lyric days, and he had a piratical Spanish flair. Franco Corelli in 1964 was the great Don José, tall, dark, handsome, with the sense of drama, the beautiful, all but molten tenor pouring heart and life into opera. I sat there wishing he could have had the Verona Arena production he mesmerized one summer night when Rosa Raisa and I sat there, rejoicing.

The 1973 *Carmen* had two notable Lyric firsts, the debuts of the young Spanish conductor Jesús López-Cobos and of James King as Don José. López-Cobos took hold instantly with verve and style, reminding you, had you forgotten, just what marvelous music Bizet wrote, all audacity and brooding tenderness arching the ominous undertow. King was no village bumpkin but a fairly dangerous customer of dark and brooding temperament and, of course, being a heldentenor, the voice to command. When he was on stage, he was the one I watched.

It was a coup to have Antonio Gades as stellar dancer and choreographer—at Spoleto's *Carmen* he had danced a superb farruca—but he was diminished in an unfortunate production. This probably hurt the Lyric's pride, but of course not its boxoffice. *Carmen* as usual, sold out.

Carmen, *Don Quichotte*, Offenbach's *Hoffmann*—you may think of them as French exceptions in the Lyric repertory. It is surprising to look back and discover how wrong you are.

Lyric's first try after *Carmen* was bold but all wrong and so woefully disappointing. In 1959 Leontyne Price ventured into *Thaïs* with Georges Prêtre conducting and with Vladimir Rosing, often so brilliant in earlier days, as stage director. Michel Roux came from Paris to appear as the monk who confuses sacred and profane love, and Léopold Simoneau was the young sybarite luckier at the gaming table than in love. There was a late and noisy audience, and what sounded like several bass drums and cymbals clattered to the orchestra floor when least needed. There were problems.

Miss Price was trying out the role, rather as John Charles Thomas had once glanced over Falstaff. She was a strikingly decorative courtesan with that gleaming lyric soprano of dusky shadows that sometimes rejoiced in the special subtleties of French sound.

But *Thaïs* in its great days of Chicago Opera fame had Mary Garden, who knew all about standing still and making you imagine wonders. José Mojica as the Nicias, the most gorgeous young pagan who ever turned monk to devote himself to the poor. The Athanael might be Renaud or Vanni-Marcoux, Dufranne, Journet or Baklanoff, even, surprisingly, Titta Ruffo.

It is hard to know if such powerful artists could magnetize *Thaïs* today, or if it is just a Massenet period piece. Period pieces shifted into revealing light have a way of seeming never to have been faded.

Ambroise Thomas' *Mignon*, which turns Goethe's *Kennst du das Land?* into *Connais-tu le pays?*, was a 1957 revival in salute to Giulietta Simionato, who reciprocated in two languages. In general, French, with Anna Moffo to sing the Polonaise and Gavazzeni to conduct, but Italian when she encountered the tenor, Alvinio Misciano, who had learned the role in that language.

OPPOSITE PAGE: **DON GIOVANNI,** 1961. TOP LEFT: LEOPOLD SIMONEAU, TERESA STICH-RANDALL, LISA DELLA CASA, IRMGARD SEEFRIED, WALTER BERRY AND RENATO CESARI. TOP RIGHT: SIMONEAU, STICH-RANDALL, EBERHARD WÄCHTER AND DELLA CASA. CENTER LEFT: WÄCHTER AND SEEFRIED. MID-CENTER: WÄCHTER AND BERRY. CENTER RIGHT: DELLA CASA AND BERRY. BOTTOM LEFT: WÄCHTER, BERRY, CESARI AND SEEFRIED. BOTTOM RIGHT: BERRY AND DELLA CASA.

CARMEN. TOP LEFT: GIULIETTA SIMIONATO, 1954. CENTER: JEAN MADEIRA AND GIUSEPPE DI STEFANO, 1959. THE PRODUCTION WAS A GENEROUS GIFT OF MRS. D. ECKHART WILLIAMS. TOP RIGHT: JAMES KING, 1973. BOTTOM, LEFT-RIGHT: GRACE BUMBRY AND FRANCO CORELLI, 1964.

(These things happen. The old Chicago Opera sang *La Juive* in Italian. Ravinia sang it in French. When Rosa Raisa sang it with Martinelli on the North Shore, she had not had time to change languages. So Louis Eckstein, Ravinia's tactful Maecenas, asked the reviewers please not to notice. With two such voices a tower of Babel would have been a delight. However, there was a problem. At one point José Mojica as the young prince confessed to Raisa, *"Je suis Chrétien,"* whereupon she cried in horror, *"Cristiano!"* Raisa had a voice as huge as beautiful. The little pavilion seated about 1400. Even for music critics often believed to be deaf, it was a problem.)

Less arbitrary gear shifting takes place in *La Fille du Régiment,* which is, after all, Donizetti, despite its Opéra-Comique premiere. Toti Dal Monte used to sing it with Chicago Opera, in Italian, always walking down front to do her own conducting in precarious places.

Lyric's version was not its own, but the Metropolitan's indiscretion done at the whim of Joan Sutherland and her husband, the conductor Richard Bonynge. It was a slapstick fiesta of toy grenadiers, rataplan drums, and the tall lady clowning in coloratura. Miss Sutherland turned the daughter of the regiment (once Lily Pons' miniature charmer) into a motherly hoyden who at one point tore up the music and flung it at the orchestra. The non-singing duchesses gave us Regina Resnik and a last glimpse of Jennie Tourel. Spiro Malas strode through the uproar as a sergeant absolutely first class.

Mr. Bonynge, often maligned as the soprano's conductor husband is apt to be, was entirely competent and often lyrical. He had no hope of capturing the Donizetti bubble of gaiety when the opera was guffawing at the top of its lungs.

When it came to the Donizetti bubble, early Lyric style, there was that *L'Elisir d'Amore* of 1962. Robert O'Hearn's fairy tale production, again borrowed from the Metropolitan, Ezio Frigerio's staging both exuberant and restrained, the serenity and laughing charm of Carlo Felice Cillario's conducting. In the cast, Fernando Corena's consummate quack, Mario Zanasi a handsome droll as Belcore, Mariella Adani a coloratura comedienne jewel cut. Plus.

The plus that October night was the debut of Alfredo Kraus. Why should an enraptured listener shout *Olé!* to a man named Kraus? Just that though he came from Italian opera houses, Alfredo Kraus was born a Trujillo in the Canary Islands. That night he looked like a

OPPOSITE PAGE: ALFREDO KRAUS, **MANON**, 1973. THE PRODUCTION IS A GENEROUS GIFT OF MR. JAMES C. HEMPHILL.

ABOVE, LEFT: REGINA RESNIK AND JOAN SUTHERLAND, **LA FILLE DU REGIMENT**, 1973. RIGHT: ALFREDO KRAUS, **LA FILLE DU REGIMENT**, 1973.

179

young Pinza, he spun out pure *bel canto*, and he knew that even when Nemorino is a tipsy bumpkin he remains the hero. Kraus was a joy in *opera buffa*, and we thought he would go on from there. But a restraint, perhaps the quality that made him change his romantic name, cooled things a bit. He turned out to be, among other things, Lyric's man for French opera.

Bizet's *Les Pêcheurs de Perles*, which he sang with Christiane Eda-Pierre, remained an occasional opera about pearl fishers, temple priestess and funeral pyre in Ceylon, unable to survive the most stellar casting. Ravel's *L'Heure Espagnole*, which he shared with Teresa Berganza, came back in double bill with Orff's *Carmina Burana*, haunted by what turned out to be the picturesque shadow of the once great dancer, Harald Kreutzberg.

It was as Goethe's *Werther*, by courtesy of Jules Massenet, that Alfredo Kraus took over as French tenor, with Tatiana Troyanos as Charlotte, and a good baritone from Paris, Jean Angot, as the luckless husband. Jean Fournet was the conductor, the staging was Lotfi Mansouri's, and Lorenzo Ghiglia's 18th century Germany understood the bourgeois era called Biedermeier.

Everyone quotes Thackeray's jest, which is not entirely beside the point:

> "Charlotte, having seen his body
> Borne before her on a shutter,
> Like a well-conducted person,
> Went on cutting bread and butter."

Even though some stage directors have been guilty of giving the children pre-buttered and no doubt pre-sliced bread, there is no doubt that Charlotte is a well-conducted person whose gentility causes the emotional Werther to blow his brains out. Charlotte needs understanding.

Ghiglia's room in her house reflected her taste, background, her very position in society, and at the same time held her captive. It was no place for a beautiful woman to realize that she had married the wrong man. A room as authentic as Massenet's music—full of echoes, but music whose *Pourquoi me réveiller?* reminds you that Massenet wrote *Manon*—does wonders for *Werther*.

Mary Garden used to sing the opera here, and Lyric's was the first revival in more than 40 years. Troyanos was a true Charlotte, with a warm smile, a warmer mezzo soprano, and a stunning actress, wearing a Directoire gown.

That 1971 night of Lyric's first *Werther* Alfredo Kraus lived up to all his promise. A strikingly handsome poet who reveled in the French style, he knew the difference between pathos and bathos, he sang superbly, and he knew about that operatic risk, the death fall.

The next production, even with Yvonne Minton as Charlotte, was no match for that first stamp of Lyric's *Werther* coin, which lived in the opera's crucial realm of the era, the restrictions, the life style. Every opera worth staging has such authenticity, waiting to be restored.

If *Werther* was an occasional Mary Garden opera, *Pelléas et Mélisande* was her unique property. She created Mélisande at the Opéra-Comique in the spring of 1902, introduced it to New York at the Manhattan in 1908, and to Chicago at the Auditorium in 1910. Our first resident opera opened with *Aida*, but Pelléas came next. For 22 years it was a unique bewitchment of Chicago's nights at the opera. Percy Hammond wrote long ago that while as an exhibition Garden's Salome outshone her Mélisande, as acting there was no comparison. He spoke of instinct, intuition, genius, of Maeterlinck's "fragile marionette." She was all of that, and Debussy's too, a dream creature in the cascade of blonde hair no one who saw it ever forgot.

OPPOSITE PAGE, TOP: **LA FANCIULLA DEL WEST,** 1978. THE PRODUCTION IS A GENEROUS GIFT OF THE GRAMMA FISHER FOUNDATION. BOTTOM: **MANON LESCAUT,** 1977. THE PRODUCTION IS A GENEROUS GIFT OF MR. JAMES C. HEMPHILL.

Reviving *Pelléas* is risky in Chicago, even now. Lyric in 1972 caught the lovely, dream-struck quality which knew that dreams hold violence. Desmond Heeley's production from the Metropolitan, Paul-Emile Deiber's direction, Jeannette Pilou, Richard Stilwell, Franz Petri and Raffaele Ariè in major roles, Fournet conducting.

Comparatively, Lyric's *Manon* in 1973 went only part of the way, but that was the stellar part with Teresa Zylis Gara as Manon, Kraus as Des Grieux, plus Michael Lepore's chorus and the understanding skill of Jean Fournet in the orchestra pit.

The production, painted in a mist, might be rescued with sensitive lighting. As opera, it simply lacked the wealth of character actors in demanding and grateful roles. As audience, it had for one, Christa Ludwig, who had just married the stage director, Paul-Emile Deiber of the Comédie Française. Perhaps he lacked casting resources and rehearsal time. I expected more from the man I once saw play *Cyrano de Bergerac* in brilliant Paris performance designed by Christian Berard.

The 1968 Stravinsky double bill was at least half French, and totally a conversation piece, expecially the stunning Giacomo Manzù decor for *Oedipus Rex*. Its companion was *Le Rossignol* with the creamy Carla Fracci dancing the real nightingale sung by Christiane Eda-Pierre.

Both productions are hybrids in the opera world—opera-ballet, opera-oratorio—and challenging to stage. *Rossignol* is at heart compassionate and gentle, its music intoxicating on a stellar night. Here, though the performance ran smoothly without interruption, often in Chagall colors, its design and direction chose comedy, even burlesque. The mechanical nightingale was a clowned cock of the walk. Hans Christian Andersen's haunting story was lost, though not by Stravinsky.

LEFT: TATIANA TROYANOS, **WERTHER,** 1971. RIGHT: LEONTYNE PRICE,
CENTER AS **THAÏS,** 1959.

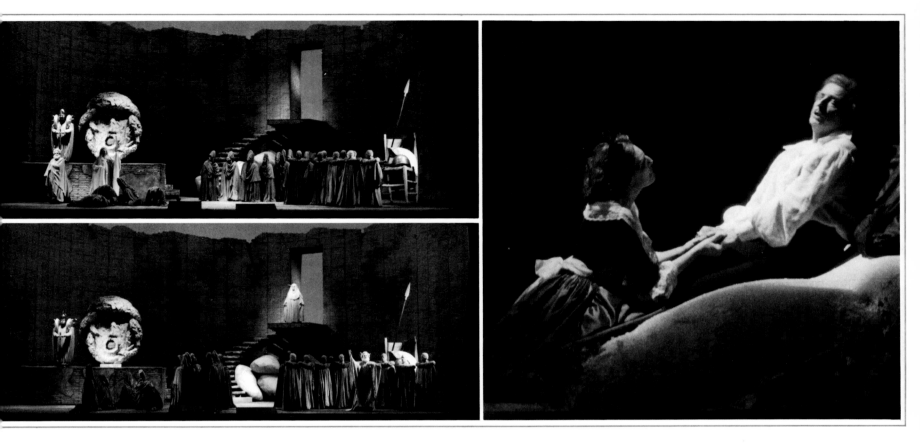

Once in Vienna, when Jean Cocteau was narrating his text to *Oedipus Rex* he had to cajole the slightly huffy Viennese audience because they were showing the concert version, not the elaborate Paris production. He said, "As the world well knows, Paris is the city of the eyes, but Vienna is the city of the ears." Vienna purred.

Lyric's production, borrowed from Rome, had the eyes. Manzù built a semicircle of crumbling wall against the Athenian sky. At the rear, a curve of stone steps. At right, a golden helmet and spear for a god, possibly Apollo or Zeus, plainly meant to dwarf Oedipus.

But what you saw first was the great stone head at the left, the ambiguous head with the open, twisting mouth, almost a fountain, surely the Delphic oracle. A sculptor's head, monumental, alive, dangerous.

The singing chorus was in the pit. The mime chorus had the color and draperies of wet clay, the veiled, enigmatic faces of that oddly frightening disguise, the sheer, pulled-over stocking. Tiresias was as tall, beautiful, frail and white as bleached bone. When men told of the oracle they stood before the huge head with the twisted mouth open.

A wonderful stage, but shorn of the full power of the story and the music. Its theatrical strength came from the narrator, here William Marshall, an imposing black actor, who used e. e. cummings' English translation. His was a spontaneous outpouring in a black voice of passionate conviction which had played both Oedipus and Othello.

Productions with so much to give are never failures, rather experiments in imaginative restoration, knowing that with luck there is always a next time.

In the alluring world of the double bill, or even the triple as in Puccini's *Trittico*, *Gianni Schicchi* remains a favorite. Lyric staged a grim and powerful *Il Tabarro* in 1955 for Tito

Gobbi, with Carlo Bergonzi a welcome tenor. *Schicchi*, a Gobbi favorite, came later, and in 1970 was teamed with Bartok's *Duke Bluebeard's Castle.*

Bluebeard's Castle remains an enigma tantalizing production. In opera, in concert, sometimes on stage with dancers miming the action, it never loses and seldom fully shares its spell. Its realm is the universal world of the ambivalence of lovers. As the man holds power, he pursues; as the woman increasingly takes over power, he retreats. And vice versa. It is a singular, powerful, poignant music drama, darkly mirroring the way of the world with lovers.

Lyric's most powerful asset was Bartoletti's orchestra, darkly beautiful and menacing. Virginio Puecher's stage design, a room in the castle with steep spiral staircase, seemed under water or perhaps made of mirrors reflecting water. There was a gallows, and just one door, centered. As each key opened its mystery the stage wall on either side opened to reveal and reflect the silver, jewels, gardens and skeletons of the slaughter house, each in its turn to be stained with blood.

Stage direction was comparatively commonplace, the English translation elusive. Janis Martin was the tall, lost Judith with a beautiful voice of almost metallic penetration. Douglas Campbell was the narrator, declaiming. The one man I ever heard who dominated and revealed *Bluebeard's Castle* was George London, whose haunting, cavernous voice and presence also made him the unique Flying Dutchman.

Just when and where was Gianni Schicchi, that preposterous rogue, born into immortality? In the 30th canto of the *Inferno* Dante says, pointing him out to Virgil, "That sprite of air is Schicchi; in like mood of random mischief vents he still his spite . . ."

That "mood of random mischief" is a happier key to the opera than helter-skelter exaggeration. The first Schicchi, Galeffi, was described as a young Titta Ruffo. In earlier Chicago Opera days two favorites were Giacomo Rimini and Vanni-Marcoux. Tito Gobbi has done it for Lyric in two styles—as the best singing actor in the business, and as a bedraggled red rooster of a minor Falstaff. As the caprice strikes him. In the 1970 production he had some felicitous company and an enchanting production.

Lorenzo Ghiglia took us to the Florence of Giotto and Fra Angelico da Fiesole, among others, in gleaming pastels, elegant simplicity, a panorama of the Duomo, the campanile and the baptistry, just possibly the most beautiful view in the world.

What a setting for lyrical chicanery of all but *commedia dell'arte* characters so greedy they went right on risking an old Florentine custom even now not quite vanished from other lands—chopping off the culprit's right hand.

They say at Bayreuth that Wagner's operas are projections of images and dreams to be seen with the mind's eye, and that from the darkness of the theater the audience must be transferred to the heart of the dream, where it finds realization and fulfillment. Theoretically, this is gospel. In reality it depends on what and whose mind's eye. I remember a Wolfgang Wagner *Der Fliegende Holländer* whose ghostly Dutchman wore a seashell cloak, and whose ghost ship had scarlet sails sagging as if filled with blood. But when Simon Estes, a black baritone with a beautiful voice, was invited to Bayreuth to sing the Dutchman, he found himself a slave in chains.

Lyric's *Dutchman* in 1959 was a remarkable first try for so young a company venturing into early Wagner as mystically elusive as it is imaginatively bold. The major advantage was

Lovro von Matačić, who swept the orchestra headlong into the storms as if he tasted sea salt, and swung it into the dances from the tip of his baton. Birgit Nilsson was a glorious Senta when she soared, Josef Greindl's Daland was Bayreuth's best, and the new Dutchman was the Yugoslav Tomislav Neralic, an almost Golem-like figure whose blackish baritone had a rusty, disused sound—a valid point of view for the outcast who forever sails the lonely seas. The conventional borrowed production left vaulting imagination to the music.

Tannhäuser—well *Tannhäuser*. The 1963 production had Grace Bumbry a voluptuous Venus, a tenor singing in a bunch of keys while searching for the master, Oskar Danon a competent conductor without stellar resources, and a most peculiar Rolf Gerard production from the Metropolitan.

Like the settings, the staging seemed to be about some other opera. The Venusberg ballet of nymphs and satyrs was crowded out by a swirl of red rock, and lack of space may have been why Venus and Tannhäuser were not present for the festivities. They were brought in later in a contraption rather like Carabosse's carriage, without the mice. There is truly something to be said for the lend-lease system of sharing opera productions. It is such a relief to send some of them back where they came from.

I did not mention the Elisabeth that fateful night, because it would be totally unfair to a remarkable soprano, Régine Crespin, who had been fatally miscast. Only the year before she had come to Lyric to substitute for the ailing Renata Tebaldi in a *Tosca* that struck verismo

OPPOSITE PAGE, TOP LEFT: ANJA SILJA, **DER FLIEGENDE HOLLANDER,** 1969. TOP CENTER: BIRGIT NILSSON, **DER FLIEGENDE HOLLANDER,** 1959. TOP RIGHT: THOMAS STEWART AS **DER FLIEGENDE HOLLANDER,** 1969. BOTTOM LEFT: DAVID WARD AND JANIS MARTIN, **BLUEBEARD'S CASTLE,** 1970. BOTTOM RIGHT: TITO GOBBI AND REGINE CRESPIN, **TOSCA,** 1962.

ABOVE: PETER VAN GINKEL, **PARADISE LOST,** 1978.

fire. Gobbi's matchless Scarpia, the poetic tenor Giuseppe Zampieri, Carlo Felice Cillario capturing Puccini's lyric cajolery, and a Tosca to remind us that the role came from Paris by way of Sarah Bernhardt.

The Crespin Tosca was a big, beautiful woman with a sumptuous soprano, alluring and worldly. Hers was a lovely Puccini voice missing no cadence of cajolery, no flick of jealousy, an actress so deeply in the role that *Vissi d'arte* was not an aria she stopped to sing, but a crucial moment in Tosca's encounter with Scarpia at the Farnese palace. Her special blandishment went on to other roles and other operas, notably a stellar *Ballo* with Richard Tucker and Grace Bumbry pouring out opulent voices in the high style.

Had you forgotten that Tebaldi made her 1955 Lyric debut in *Aida*, with Astrid Varnay, Doro Antonioli and Tito Gobbi? Or that it was Callas, allegedly her bitter rival, who told Lyric to engage her? *Aida* in a second season. Of course it was too early, but it worked. Everyone was in shining young voice and the youngest person present was 76 year-old Tullio Serafin stepping for the first time into the Lyric pit. He had been at work more than 50 years in the high places of the world, a master conductor who cherished a score and plainly loved singing.

Opera companies are always being importuned to stage new works, whether or not they are being written. Lyric's first season had Vittorio Giannini's *The Taming of the Shrew*, an amusing frolic. But the 1961 Ford Foundation grant of Giannini's *The Harvest* was a disaster. Oddly, the grant did not pay for all of it. Just the difference between a box-office failure and a box-office success, which is not the way a major opera house does its bookkeeping.

Leoš Janaček's *Jenůfa*, an opera about a kind of Czech Santuzza, apparently does not like salt water. It did not survive the crossing to the Metropolitan in 1924, even with Jeritza, Matzenauer and Bodanzky. Lyric's 1959 version in English stirred more controversy than admiration. Perhaps Ernest Newman was right when he lamented, "Apparently in these Central European countries you do everything to these (dance) rhythms. You shave yourself to a krakoviak, cut a man's throat to a mazurka, and bury him to a czardas."

It must be tempting, if you sit in the driver's seat and know that the one thing you can count on is that it will cost more, to settle for the most attractive possible productions of standard repertory. That is how the opera house not only survives, as Faulkner said of the human race, but prevails. But now and then there must be a bold gesture. Lyric took it by commissioning Krzysztof Penderecki to write a Bicentennial opera. He chose Milton's *Paradise Lost* as libretto, in adaptation by Christopher Fry. In 1976 they were still working. It was November 29, 1978 when *Paradise Lost* had its world premiere at the Civic Opera House, ending Lyric's 24th season, then moving on to complete an historic circle.

From its very first performances, Lyric had the richest and warmest collaboration of artists from Milan's La Scala, approximately 200 years its senior. In January 1979, despite the delaying tactics of our monumental snowstorm, Lyric's *Paradise Lost*, complete with chorus, flew to Milan for eight performances at La Scala, with a possibly unprecedented plus. Pope John Paul II asked for a concert performance at the Vatican.

That took place at the Sala Nervi February 7, precisely 25 years after Lyric's second *Don Giovanni* calling card performance, which prompted Chicago to invite it to stay. In another forging of a circle, Carol Fox was accompanied by Tito Gobbi, one of Lyric's first and most cherished artists.

MAESTRO BRUNO BARTOLETTI AND KRZYSZTOF PENDERECKI, COMPOSER OF **PARADISE LOST,** WHICH
HAD ITS WORLD PREMIERE ON NOVEMBER 29, 1978, LYRIC OPERA OF CHICAGO.

Immediately, European opera houses began to announce their own *Paradise Lost* productions. Lyric's was a major challenge for the most part boldly met.

For Milton's vast conception of the Jehovan God, the rebellion and fall of angels, the temptation and fall of Eve, then Adam, and so all mankind, Ezio Frigerio created a stunning, darkly glimmering stage, and Penderecki cast a reverberant web of sound—conservative, even romantic, in 20th century terms—illustrative, allusive, reminiscent, often magnificent for orchestra and chorus.

In Chicago, the high points were Bruno Bartoletti's orchestra, sighing, swooping, storming, rattling the Serpent's warning, and Robert Page's brilliant chorus, caged four meshed tiers high on either proscenium side, a chorus hissing and slithering, fiercely attacking, murmuring, turning celestial.

John Butler's choreography was striking, especially for Adam and Eve as dancers—Dennis Wayne and Nancy Thuesen—beautifully, almost nakedly in blinding white—and for Cain and Abel, who were Wayne and Edward Tuell. There were theater marvels in Frigerio's conception. His stage a blackly vertical tunnel, its brazen roof rising and descending as the action changed, its trapped, watching, almost invisible chorus like a fantasy of terror by Hieronymous Bosch. Pestilence, famine and flood hovered in a cloud of *Dies Irae*.

Comparatively, the solo voices were challenged rather than fulfilled. Stage direction, changed at the last moment at the composer's request, meandered. *Paradise Lost* that first night was truly a major work in progress. Given a composer of Penderecki's authority, it is a potential powerhouse.

All that is part of what Lyric, on the threshold of its 25th season, has given us. A wealth of opera, which at its best is a glorious fusion of music, theater, ballet, stage direction and design, the revelation of lighting, each art complementing, contrasting, intensifying the others. It is a concentration of theater forces, a heightening of emotional impact, often an irresistible force. It can be a molten outpouring of high drama, a glittering interplay of high comedy, a dazzle of bravura song, a stripping of the skin from quivering nerves—see *Wozzeck*—a labyrinthine maze of the psychopathic, the psychotic, the miasmic.

It is also scandalously expensive to produce, though Lyric has doggedly kept its prices down, even in the face of Salzburg's $120 top. I have always secretly longed for an opera house all curving tiers of boxes, with red roses on the shelves in the dimming light, as at La Scala. I wish our river were gentle, so we could go by gondola as Malibran did in Venice. In the line of solvency, opera might wish for the old gaming concessions, with faro going full tilt in the boxes, interrupted now and then when players were warned of an impending aria. Or maybe a door lottery, the grand prize a ticket to everything, always.

The real point is, does opera cost too much? Not if it is good. A city is more than tall buildings, crowded streets and, in our case, a magnificent lakefront. A great city is a rewarding, exciting place to live. Without Lyric, Chicago would be underprivileged.

The greatest pity of all would be to think of opera as a solemn occasion. Opera can be a lot of things, but stuffy it is not. There once was a bravura critic who blew a lot of dust off the pedantic. He was James Huneker of whom Henry Mencken said, "Because of him, art is no longer a device for improving the mind. It is wholly a magnificent adventure."

That is really what it is all about.

OPPOSITE PAGE: DENNIS WAYNE AND NANCY THUESEN, **PARADISE LOST**, 1978.

LYRIC OPERA PRESIDENTS

CAROL FOX
1954-55

THOMAS I. UNDERWOOD
1956-57

LEONARD SPACEK
1957-58

ALFRED C. STEPAN, JR.
1959-61

J. W. VAN GORKOM
1962-63

DAGGETT HARVEY
1964-1968

EDWARD F. BLETTNER
1969-1971

T. M. THOMPSON
1972-1975

WILLIAM S. NORTH
1976

WILLIAM O. BEERS
1977-79

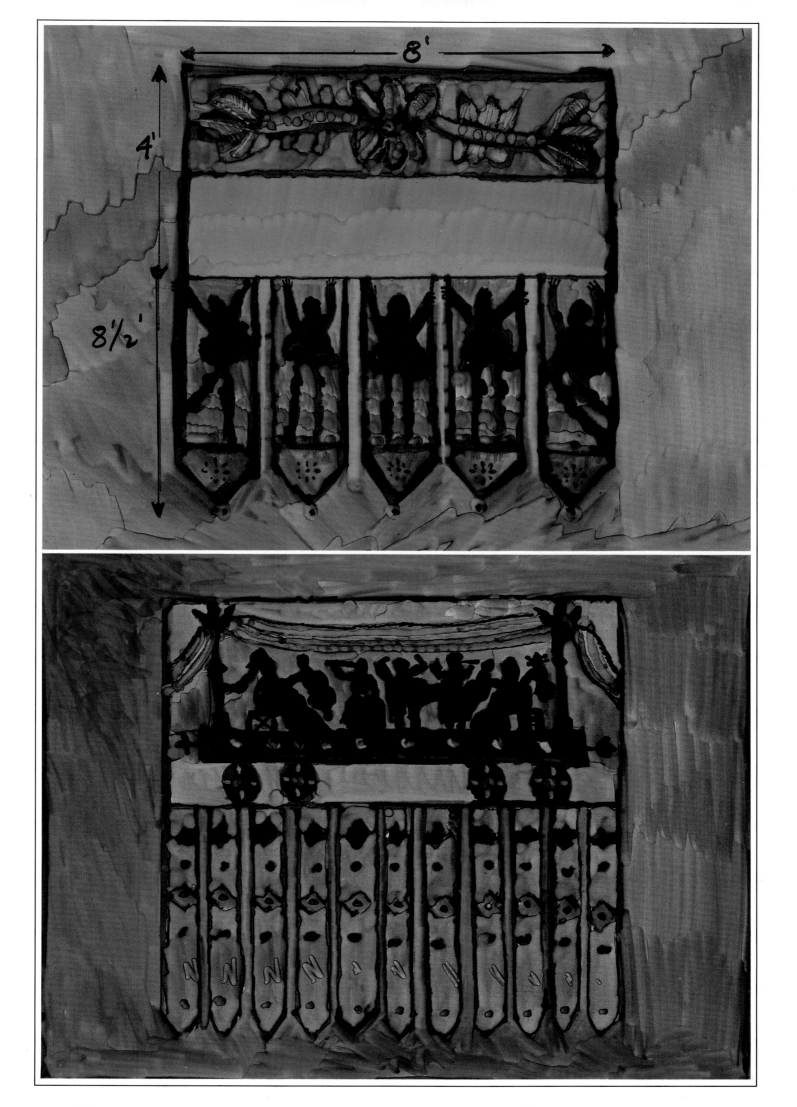

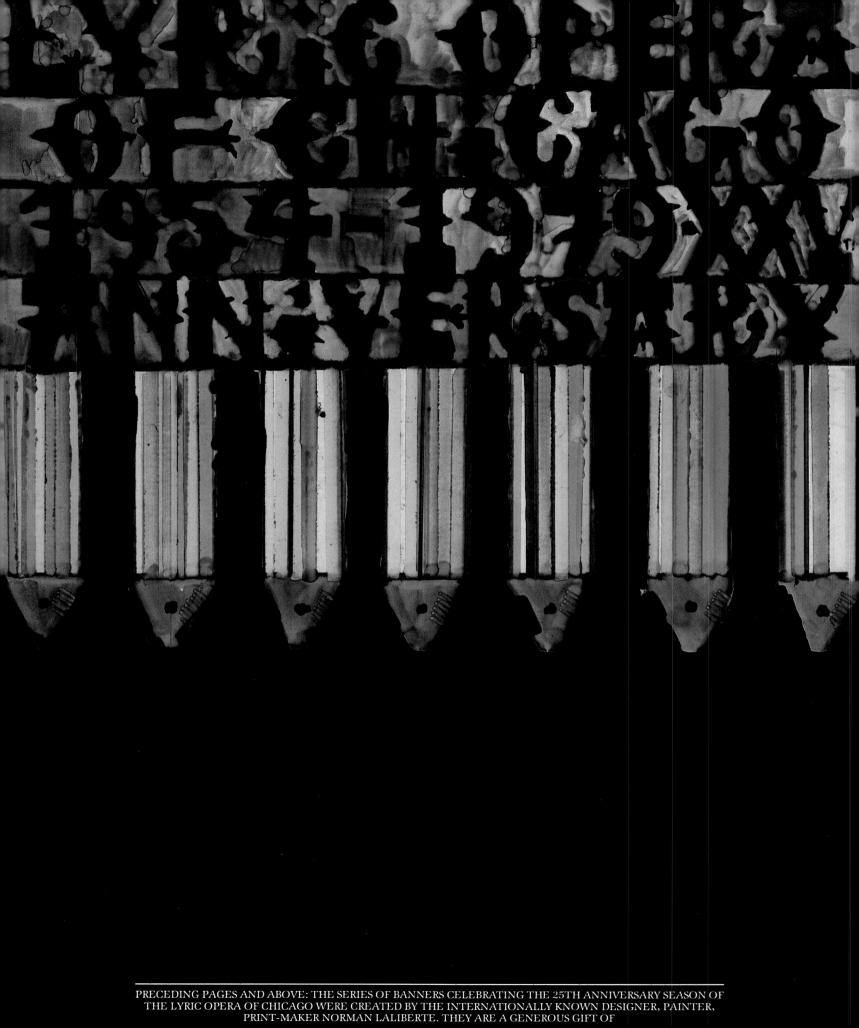

RECOLLECTIONS BY CAROL FOX

When I was asked to pen my thoughts on 25 years as general manager of Lyric Opera I felt my editors had gone mad. I had two options. I could write the most detailed, precise, minute history of the company—commenting on each and every planning session, rehearsal, performance. But that would require notes from the diary that I never kept. Or I could skim the surface of these 25 years and recall the highlights, the debuts, the triumphs, the premieres, and the "most memorable operatic nights of my life." I resisted that option on the grounds that I would overlook someone, something, some performance and in doing so I would unconsciously hurt by omission.

So bear with me—this is what Lyric Opera of Chicago—Lyric Theatre—has been for me. And why I have loved this life as General Manager.

It all began with *Don Giovanni*.

In all honesty I don't remember those calling card performances of *Don Giovanni* that well. It seems to me that since those two performances in February of 1954 we have done so many things so much better. But those performances obviously showed a spark of something that had not been in Chicago for many years. *Don Giovanni* might have come up to the expectations of others but it didn't come up to mine. It didn't fulfill my dream of producing total opera—it was only a vocal triumph. We couldn't afford to add the visual. We were all nervous about those performances. We wanted to start out with four weeks of performances but the opera house management didn't believe we had the money or the talent for something that ambitious. They agreed to rent us the building for one night.

And this I remember well: "But what if the audience doesn't like it?" we cried. It was the author of this book, Claudia Cassidy, who replied, "If you can do 'Don Giovanni' well, then you can do any opera."

Still uneasy I then worried because the advance mail orders were only from Lake Shore Drive, Lake Forest, the socially arrived. I didn't find any orders from young people, from musicians. Again Miss Cassidy reassured me, "They'll find you."

One performance sold out, a second was added, and the critics and audiences were gracious. But I wanted more—I wanted that "season" of opera in repertoire.

That fall of 1954 it was eight operas on the schedule. In the early sixties we had grown to ten productions per season. Now we do seven. As we grew in maturity, stature, calibre, and quality we were forced to retreat to the seven opera season as we know it today. That is a regret—a big regret. With two performances each of the eight operas in the early years we could present the same singers in three and four operas a season. It was exciting to watch them and compare them and contrast them from one role to another. Maria Callas did three roles each of those first two seasons. That was fun for her, for our audiences, and for us. And with two performances of each opera we didn't have to keep the singers in the city—thus limiting other engagements for them each season—that long. In the "old" days we rehearsed longer hours, fewer days, and had fewer performances.

Now we have grown in depth—we sell eight or nine performances of each opera. We rehearse for several weeks. It is a broader season, it has balance. But it is different.

My favorite opera is *Der Rosenkavalier*. And to every poor newspaper feature writer desperately polling with the question, "If you were on a desert island and could have only one record, what would it be?" I have always answered, *Der Rosenkavalier*. I love the Viennese interpretation of the work. I can always conjure up in my mind the sound of those waltzes. Christa Ludwig did it for us with Walter Berry and then later for a few performances with Hans Sotin. It's special to me and those productions are special to me.

From the Italian repertoire I guess I am most partial to *Don Carlo*—it still sounds in my head—in 1957 with Jussi Bjoerling and Tito Gobbi in the duet in the first scene. That whole year was very special—Bjoerling, Tucker, Di Stefano, Del Monaco—it was a tenor lover's fantasy season. Del Monaco woke me up with a telephone call one night that season. He was to sing the next night. He had a temperature of 105. Should he sing? I said no, the doctors said no. He did sing and broke the temperature on stage in the middle of the performance.

There are very special memories of dinner parties in the Garden Room of the old Morrison Hotel. They were fund-raising dinners and the artists came and sang. Ludwig and Berry in their famous "Meow" duet! Never to be repeated, and for me, never to be forgotten. Too soon we outgrew that hotel and those nights. The camaraderie, the fun, the opera talk, and the impromptu singing. Growth and success have cheated us out of those evenings.

And for that same poor feature writer (the individual changes from year to year, but never the question) who asks annually: "If you had it all to do again, would you?" Of course. I'd try not to batter my mind and body so much, but of course I would do it all over again and probably the same way. I know of no more gratifying sport than the production of grand opera. It's a challenge, seasonal, monthly, and daily.

And the greatest challenge is with the artists: to keep them at a distance, to get them to do our bidding, to keep the spirit of the artistic promise. From 1954 to today one of the greatest challenges has been to match the artists with the role, to convince them to try a new role, and to pull in the reins when they want to do a role that isn't right for them. Callas knew what was

right for her and wanted the chance to prove it. She wanted to experiment and she had the self-understanding and self-knowledge to know what was right. Many other artists have too many fantasies about what is right for them. For me the challenge has been to spark the perfect match: singer and role. I thrive on that.

Today I almost dread the actual performances. The size, the economics, the logistics demand that I pull out at the dress rehearsal. There is nothing left after that for me to do or that I can do. My excitement stops at the dress rehearsal. Another regret.

I dream of the day when we have our own house, our own warehouse, our own space for a ballet company—practice rooms, rehearsal rooms, storage facilities. We have to shut down stage rehearsals now for orchestra rehearsals. We are the only major opera company in America without our own space or without space that we can control year round. A very personal regret.

I have very high hopes and very big dreams for our Lyric Opera School of Chicago. From my days as a student I watched with envy the Cadets of La Scala, the Piccola Scala. I wanted to start our own American school. A unique place like none other in America. And ours is unique. We give young singers the chance to study and perform with a major opera and ballet company. I have great hopes for opera in America and know that we can't continue to always go to Europe to advance a career. We must give young singers and dancers the opportunity for training, experience. Instead of beating the bushes in the provinces of Europe we must let them beat the provinces within our companies and programs here in America.

They tell me it is "Lyric at 25" and while I am not senile and not that old—I have lost track. The seasons, the years, the performances, the work seem to blend into one larger than life memory. For your patience with this series of digressions and recollections I am most grateful. For your support in bringing us through these 25 years I am most grateful. And for your encouragement in the next 25 years I will continue to be most grateful. —CAROL FOX

CAROL FOX MEETS POPE JOHN PAUL II AT THE VATICAN FOLLOWING THE PERFORMANCE OF **PARADISE LOST** ON FEBRUARY 8, 1979.

1954

'Calling Card' Performances

DON GIOVANNI   MOZART
February 5 and 7 / In Italian

LUIGI SGARRO   *The Commendatore*
ELEANOR STEBER   *Donna Anna*
LEOPOLD SIMONEAU   *Don Ottavio*
NICOLA ROSSI-LEMENI   *Don Giovanni*
JOHN BROWNLEE   *Leporello*
IRENE JORDAN   *Donna Elvira*
BIDU SAYÃO   *Zerlina*
LORENZO ALVARY   *Masetto*

Conductor   NICOLA RESCIGNO
Stage Director   WILLIAM WYMETAL
Chorus Director   JOHN HALLORAN
Ballet Mistress   EDNA Mc RAE

FALL SEASON / *November 1 – 20*

NORMA   BELLINI
November 1 and 5 / In Italian

***MIRTO PICCHI   *Pollione*
NICOLA ROSSI-LEMENI   *Oroveso*
***MARIA MENEGHINI-CALLAS   *Norma*
GIULIETTA SIMIONATO   *Adalgisa*
GLORIA LIND   *Clotilda*
LAWRENCE WHITE   *Flavio*

Conductor   NICOLA RESCIGNO
Stage Director   WILLIAM WYMETAL
Chorus Master   MICHAEL LEPORE

THE TAMING OF THE SHREW
GIANNINI
November 3 and 13 / In English
First full-scale staging of this work.
First Chicago performances

THOMAS STEWART   *Baptista*
IRENE JORDAN   *Katharina*
GLORIA LIND   *Bianca*
HUGH THOMPSON   *Petrucchio*
LAWRENCE WHITE   *Lucentio*
JOHN TYERS   *Tranio*
ANDREW FOLDI   *Biondello*
DONALD GRAMM   *Hortensio*
JOSEPH MORDINO   *Gremio and a Pedant*
ALGERD BRAZIS   *Vincentio*
ANDREW McKINLEY   *Grumio*
MILES NEKOLNY   *Curtis*

Conductor   NICOLA RESCIGNO
Stage Director   REXFORD HARROWER
Decor re-designed by   GERALD L. RITHOLZ
Costumes re-designed by   RUTH MORLEY

IL BARBIERE DI SIVIGLIA
ROSSINI
November 6 and 10 / In Italian

LEOPOLD SIMONEAU   *Count Almaviva*
***CARLO BADIOLI   *Doctor Bartolo*
NICOLA ROSSI-LEMENI   *Basilio*
TITO GOBBI   *Figaro*
ALGERD BRAZIS   *Fiorello*
GIULIETTA SIMIONATO   *Rosina*
MARY KRESTE   *Berta*

Conductor   NICOLA RESCIGNO
Stage Director   WILLIAM WYMETAL
Chorus Master   MICHAEL LEPORE

LA BOHEME   PUCCINI
November 6 (Mat.) and 13 / In Italian

GIACINTO PRANDELLI   *Rodolfo*
***GIAN GIACOMO GUELFI   *Marcello*
LORENZO ALVARY   *Colline*
JOHN TYERS   *Schaunard*
CARLO BADIOLI   *Benoit and Alcindoro*
GLORIA LIND   *Musetta*
ROSANNA CARTERI   *Mimi*

Conductor   JONEL PERLEA
Stage Director   WILLIAM WYMETAL
Chorus Master   MICHAEL LEPORE

LA TRAVIATA   VERDI
November 8 and 12 / In Italian

LEOPOLD SIMONEAU   *Alfredo*
TITO GOBBI   *Giorgio Germont*
VIRGINIO ASSANDRI   *Gastone*
ALGERD BRAZIS   *Baron Douphol*
MILES NEKOLNY   *Marchese d'Obigny*
ANDREW FOLDI   *Doctor Grenvil*
MARIA MENEGHINI-CALLAS   *Violetta*
GLORIA LIND   *Flora Bervoix*
MARY KRESTE   *Annina*

Solo Dancers   PATRICIA WILDE (Nov. 8),
    BARBARA STEELE (Nov. 12),
    KENNETH JOHNSON

Conductor   NICOLA RESCIGNO
Stage Director   WILLIAM WYMETAL
Chorus Master   MICHAEL LEPORE
Choreographer   RUTH PAGE

LUCIA DI LAMMERMOOR
DONIZETTI *November 15 and 17 / In Italian*

GIAN GIACOMO GUELFI   *Lord Henry Ashton*
MARIA MENEGHINI-CALLAS   *Lucia*
GIUSEPPE DI STEFANO   *Edgar of Ravenswood*
LAWRENCE WHITE   *Lord Arthur Bucklaw*
THOMAS STEWART   *Raymond*
MARY KRESTE   *Alisa*
VIRGINIO ASSANDRI   *Norman*

Solo Dancers   BARBARA STEELE, KENNETH
    JOHNSON

Conductor   NICOLA RESCIGNO
Stage Director   WILLIAM WYMETAL
Chorus Master   MICHAEL LEPORE
Choreographer   RUTH PAGE

CARMEN   BIZET
November 16 and 20 (Mat.) / In French

MIRTO PICCHI   *Don José*
GIAN GIACOMO GUELFI   *Escamillo*
CARLO BADIOLI   *El Dancairo*
VIRGINIO ASSANDRI   *El Remendado*
ANDREW FOLDI   *Zuniga*
ALGERD BRAZIS   *Morales*
IRENE JORDAN   *Micaela*
GLORIA LIND   *Frasquita*
MARY KRESTE   *Mercedes*
GIULIETTA SIMIONATO   *Carmen*

Conductor   NICOLA RESCIGNO
Stage Director   WILLIAM WYMETAL
Chorus Master   MICHAEL LEPORE

TOSCA   PUCCINI
November 18 and 20 / In Italian

ELEANOR STEBER   *Floria Tosca*
GIUSEPPE DI STEFANO   *Mario Cavaradossi*
TITO GOBBI   *Baron Scarpia*
THOMAS STEWART   *Cesare Angelotti*
CARLO BADIOLI   *A Sacristan*
VIRGINIO ASSANDRI   *Spoletta*
ANDREW FOLDI   *Sciarrone*
ALGERD BRAZIS   *Jailer*
BILLY MASON   *A Young Shepherd*

Conductor   NICOLA RESCIGNO
Stage Director   WILLIAM WYMETAL
Chorus Master   MICHAEL LEPORE

1955

October 31 – December 3

I PURITANI   BELLINI
October 31 and November 2 / In Italian
Production by courtesy of Camillo Parravicini,
Rome. First Chicago performances

WILLIAM WILDERMANN   *Lord Walter*
    Walton
NICOLA ROSSI-LEMENI   *Sir George Walton*
GIUSEPPE DI STEFANO   *Lord Arthur Talbot*
ETTORE BASTIANINI   *Sir Richard Forth*
***MARIANO CARUSO   *Sir Bruno Robertson*
EUNICE ALBERTS   *Henrietta*
MARIA MENEGHINI-CALLAS   *Elvira*

Solo Dancers   *CAROL LAWRENCE, KENNETH
    JOHNSON

Conductor   NICOLA RESCIGNO
***Stage Director*   ALDO MIRABELLA VASSALLO
Chorus Master   MICHAEL LEPORE
Choreographer   RUTH PAGE
Decor   CAMILLO PARRAVICINI
Costumes   BERARDI

AIDA   VERDI
November 1 and 4 / In Italian

RENATA TEBALDI   *Aida*
ASTRID VARNAY   *Amneris*
TITO GOBBI   *Amonasro*
***DORO ANTONIOLI   *Radames*
WILLIAM WILDERMANN   *Ramfis*
KENNETH SMITH   *King of Egypt*
MARIANO CARUSO   *Messenger*
MARILU ADAMS   *Priestess*

Solo Dancers   BARBARA STEELE, KENNETH
    JOHNSON, RONALD FRAZIER

Conductor   TULLIO SERAFIN
Stage Director   WILLIAM WYMETAL
Chorus Master   MICHAEL LEPORE
Choreographer   RUTH PAGE

*Lyric Opera Debut   **American Opera Debut   ***American Debut   ‡American Debut, by courtesy of the Metropolitan Opera   ‡Lyric Opera School

200

IL TROVATORE VERDI
November 5 and 8 / In Italian

ETTORE BASTIANINI *Count Di Luna (Nov. 5)*
ROBERT WEEDE *Count Di Luna (Nov. 8)*
WILLIAM WILDERMANN *Ferrando*
JUSSI BJOERLING *Manrico*
MARIANO CARUSO *Ruiz*
JONAS VAZNELIS *An Old Gypsy*
MARIA MENEGHINI-CALLAS *Leonora*
EUNICE ALBERTS *Inez*
**EBE STIGNANI *Azucena (Nov. 5)*
CLARAMAE TURNER *Azucena (Nov. 8)*

Conductor NICOLA RESCIGNO
Stage Director ALDO MIRABELLA VASSALLO
Chorus Master MICHAEL LEPORE

LA BOHEME PUCCINI
November 7 and 9 / In Italian

GIUSEPPE DI STEFANO *Rodolfo*
TITO GOBBI *Marcello*
NICOLA ROSSI-LEMENI *Colline*
RICHARD TORIGI *Schaunard*
ANDREW FOLDI *Benoit*
LLOYD HARRIS *Alcindoro*
MARIO MARIANI *Parpignol*
JOHN RUDAWSKI *Custom-House Sergeant*
GLORIA LIND *Musetta*
RENATA TEBALDI *Mimi*
ALFIO ZAGNOLI *Guard*

Conductor TULLIO SERAFIN
Stage Director ALDO MIRABELLA VASSALLO
Chorus Master MICHAEL LEPORE
Children's Chorus ZERLINE MUHLMAN
                    METZGER

MADAMA BUTTERFLY PUCCINI
November 11, 14 and 17 / In Italian

MARIA MENEGHINI-CALLAS *Madama*
                        Butterfly
EUNICE ALBERTS *Suzuki*
MARILU ADAMS *Kate Pinkerton*
GIUSEPPE DI STEFANO *B. F. Pinkerton*
ROBERT WEEDE *Sharpless*
MARIANO CARUSO *Goro*
LLOYD HARRIS *Prince Yamadori*
KENNETH SMITH *The Bonze*
ANDREW FOLDI *Imperial Commissioner*
MILES NEKOLNY *Official Registrar*

Conductor NICOLA RESCIGNO
Stage Director HITZI KOYKE
Chorus Master MICHAEL LEPORE

LEFT TO RIGHT: MR. AND MRS. JUSSI BJOERLING, MARIA CALLAS, RUDOLF BING, GIUSEPPE DI STEFANO, 1955.

RIGOLETTO VERDI
November 12 and 25 / In Italian

JUSSI BJOERLING *Duke of Mantua*
TITO GOBBI *Rigoletto*
ANDREW FOLDI *Count Ceprano*
KENNETH SMITH *Count Monterone*
WILLIAM WILDERMANN *Sparafucile*
MARIANO CARUSO *Matteo Borsa*
LLOYD HARRIS *Cavaliere Marullo*
MARILU ADAMS *Countess Ceprano*
**TERESA STICH-RANDALL *Gilda*
ARDIS KRAINIK *Giovanna*
MIGNON DUNN *Maddalena*
SHIRLEY JOHNSON *Page*

Solo Dancers JANE BOCKMAN, KENNETH
                JOHNSON

Conductor NICOLA RESCIGNO
Stage Director WILLIAM WYMETAL
Chorus Master MICHAEL LEPORE
Choreographer RUTH PAGE

FAUST GOUNOD
November 15 and 18 / In French

JUSSI BJOERLING *Faust*
NICOLA ROSSI-LEMENI *Méphistophélès*
ROSANNA CARTERI *Marguerite*
ROBERT WEEDE *Valentin*
MIGNON DUNN *Siebel*
MILES NEKOLNY *Wagner*
EUNICE ALBERTS *Marte Schwerlein*

Solo Dancers CAROL LAWRENCE, KENNETH
                JOHNSON

Conductor TULLIO SERAFIN
Stage Director WILLIAM WYMETAL
Chorus Master MICHAEL LEPORE
Choreographer RUTH PAGE

TRIPLE BILL / *November 16 and 19*

IL TABARRO PUCCINI
In Italian

TITO GOBBI *Michele*
***CARLO BERGONZI *Luigi*
MARIANO CARUSO *Il Tinca*
WILLIAM WILDERMANN *Il Talpa*
GERTRUDE RIBLA *Giorgetta*
CLARAMAE TURNER *Frugola*
LAWRENCE WHITE *Vendor of Songs*
ARDIS KRAINIK *A Lover*
RAYMOND PACINELLI *A Lover and Off-Stage*
                   Voice
SHIRLEY JOHNSON *Off-Stage Voice*

Conductor NICOLA RESCIGNO
Stage Director VLADIMIR ROSING
Chorus Master MICHAEL LEPORE

IL BALLO DELLE INGRATE
MONTEVERDI — Masque
In Italian
First fully-staged American performances

Singers
EBE STIGNANI *Venus*
TERESA STICH-RANDALL *Amore*

KENNETH SMITH *Pluto*

Dancers
VERA ZORINA *Venus*
JANE BOCKMAN *Amore*
RONALD FRAZIER *Pluto*
BARBARA STEELE *Ungrateful Soul*
CAROL LAWRENCE *Sposa*
KENNETH JOHNSON *Sposo*

Conductor NICOLA RESCIGNO
Production Director RICHARD BALDRIDGE
Chorus Master MICHAEL LEPORE
Choreographer RUTH PAGE
Re-designed by GERALD RITHOLZ
Costumes ROBERT FLETCHER

THE MERRY WIDOW LEHAR,
arranged and orchestrated by
May and Van Grove
*Ballet adaptation by Ruth Page and Hassard
Short*

ALICIA MARKOVA *Sonia*
**OLEG BRIANSKY *Prince Danilo*
BENTLEY STONE *Baron Popoff*
SONIA AROVA *Baroness Popoff*
KENNETH JOHNSON *Vicomte de Jolidon*
JOSEPH KAMINSKI *Nish*
BARBARA STEELE *Zozo*
CAROL LAWRENCE *Frou-Frou*

Conductor NICOLA RESCIGNO
Choreographer RUTH PAGE
Production Supervised by HASSARD SHORT
Scenery and Costumes ROLF GERARD, executed
                        by KARINSKA

A PARTY AT THE ITALIAN VILLAGE, CHICAGO 1955.
CAROL FOX, LEFT.

TRIPLE BILL / *November 21 and 26*

CAVALLERIA RUSTICANA
MASCAGNI / *In Italian*

GIUSEPPE DI STEFANO *Turiddu (Nov. 21)*
CARLO BERGONZI *Turiddu (Nov. 26)*
CESARE BARDELLI *Alfio*
MIGNON DUNN *Lola*
EUNICE ALBERTS *Mamma Lucia*
EBE STIGNANI *Santuzza*

Conductor NICOLA RESCIGNO
Stage Director WILLIAM WYMETAL
Chorus Master MICHAEL LEPORE

*Lyric Opera Debut **American Opera Debut ***American Debut ‡American Debut, by courtesy of the Metropolitan Opera ‡Lyric Opera School

LORD BYRON'S LOVE LETTER
DE BANFIELD / *In English*
New production, donated in part by The
American Opera Society
First Chicago performances

GERTRUDE RIBLA *Spinster*
ASTRID VARNAY *Grandmother*
CLARAMAE TURNER *Matron from Milwaukee*
LLOYD HARRIS *Mr. Tutweiler*

Solo Dancers CAROL LAWRENCE, KENNETH
JOHNSON

Conductor NICOLA RESCIGNO
Stage Director RICHARD BALDRIDGE
Choreographer RUTH PAGE
Designed by GERALD RITHOLZ

REVANCHE
Based on Verdi's Il Trovatore, arranged and
orchestrated by Van Grove
Ballet by Ruth Page with the collaboration of
Nicholas Remisoff
(On November 21 the Merry Widow was
performed instead of Revanche. See cast above)

ALICIA MARKOVA *Leonora*
SONIA AROVA *Azucena*
OLEG BRIANSKY *Manrico*
CAROL LAWRENCE *The Nurse*
ETTA BURO *Azucena's Mother*
BENTLEY STONE *Count Di Luna*
BARBARA STEELE *Inez*
KENNETH JOHNSON *Jester*
JOSEPH KAMINSKI *Count Di Luna (Prologue)*
ELLEVA DAVIDSON *His Son*

Conductor NICOLA RESCIGNO
Choreographer RUTH PAGE
Scenery and costumes ANTONI CLAVE,
executed by KARINSKA

L'ELISIR D'AMORE   DONIZETTI
November 22 and 30 / In Italian

LEOPOLD SIMONEAU *Nemorino*
ROSANNA CARTERI *Adina*
HUGH THOMPSON *Belcore*
NICOLA ROSSI-LEMENI *Dulcamara*
GLORIA LIND *Giannetta*

Conductor TULLIO SERAFIN
Stage Director VLADIMIR ROSING
Chorus Master MICHAEL LEPORE

L'AMORE DEI TRE RE
MONTEMEZZI
November 28 and December 2 / In Italian

NICOLA ROSSI-LEMENI *Archibaldo*
ROBERT WEEDE *Manfredo*
CARLO BERGONZI *Avito*
MARIANO CARUSO *Flaminio*
DOROTHY KIRSTEN *Fiora*
PATRICIA FRAHER *L'Ancella*
RAYMOND PACINELLI *Un Giovanotto*
PRUDENCIJA BICKUS *Una Giovanetta*
EUNICE ALBERTS *La Vecchia*
LAWRENCE WHITE *Backstage Voice*

Conductor TULLIO SERAFIN

Stage Director VLADIMIR ROSING
Chorus Master MICHAEL LEPORE

UN BALLO IN MASCHERA   VERDI
November 29 and December 3 / In Italian

JUSSI BJOERLING *Riccardo*
***ANITA CERQUETTI *Amelia*
TITO GOBBI *Renato*
WILLIAM WILDERMANN *Samuele*
ANDREW FOLDI *Tomaso*
LLOYD HARRIS *Silvano*
PEGGY BONINI *Oscar*
CLARAMAE TURNER *Ulrica*
MARIANO CARUSO *Primo Judice*

Conductor NICOLA RESCIGNO
Stage Director WILLIAM WYMETAL
Chorus Master MICHAEL LEPORE
Choreographer RUTH PAGE

1956

October 10 – November 17

LA FANCIULLA DEL WEST
PUCCINI
October 10 and 13 / In Italian

ELEANOR STEBER *Minnie*
TITO GOBBI *Jack Rance*
MARIO DEL MONACO *Dick Johnson*
MARIANO CARUSO *Nick*
WILLIAM WILDERMANN *Ashby*
HENRI NOEL *Sonora*
RALPH NIELSEN *Trin*
BERNARD IZZO *Sid*
MILES NEKOLNY *Handsome*
JOHN CARMEN ROSSI *Harry*
ALAN SMITH *Joe*
ANDREW FOLDI *Happy*
LLOYD HARRIS *Larkens*
ARLINGTON ROLLMAN *Billy Jackrabbit*
EUNICE ALBERTS *Wowkle*
LEON LISHNER *Jake Wallace*
ARLINGTON ROLLMAN *José Castro*
WILHELM SILBER *A Courier*

Conductor DIMITRI MITROPOULOS
Stage Director ALDO MIRABELLA VASSALLO
Chorus Master MICHAEL LEPORE

DIMITRI MITROPOULOS

ANDREA CHENIER   GIORDANO
October 16 and 19 / In Italian

BERNARD IZZO *A Major-Domo*
TITO GOBBI *Charles Gérard*
ELEANOR STEBER *Madeleine de Coigny*
EVELYN REYNOLDS *Contesse de Coigny*
GLORIA LIND *Bersi (Oct. 16)*
SHIRLEY WINSTON *Bersi (Oct. 19)*
MILES NEKOLNY *Fléville*
JOHN CARMEN ROSSI *The Abbé*
MARIO DEL MONACO *Andrea Chénier*
LLOYD HARRIS *Mathieu*
MARIANO CARUSO *Incredibile*
HENRI NOEL *Roucher*
EUNICE ALBERTS *Madelon*
BERNARD IZZO *Dumas*
ANDREW FOLDI *Fouquier-Tinville*
LEON LISHNER *Schmidt*

Solo Dancers BARBARA STEELE,
KENNETH JOHNSON

Conductor EMERSON BUCKLEY
Stage Director ALDO MIRABELLA VASSALLO
Chorus Master MICHAEL LEPORE
Choreographer RUTH PAGE

SALOME   STRAUSS
October 17 and November 3 / In German

RAMON VINAY *Herod*
MARTHA LIPTON *Herodias*
INGE BORKH *Salome*
ALEXANDER WELITSCH *Jokanaan*
JOHN ALEXANDER *Narraboth*
EUNICE ALBERTS *A Page*
MARIANO CARUSO, ALAN SMITH, JOHN
CARMEN ROSSI, WILHELM SILBER, HENRI
NOEL *Five Jews*
ANDREW FOLDI, RALPH NIELSEN
Two Nazarenes
ARLINGTON ROLLMAN, LLOYD HARRIS
Two Soldiers
MILES NEKOLNY *A Cappadocian*
EVELYN REYNOLDS *A Slave*

**Conductor* GEORG SOLTI
Stage Director WILLIAM WYMETAL

DIE WALKÜRE   WAGNER
October 20 and 22 / In German

LUDWIG SUTHAUS *Siegmund*
WILLIAM WILDERMANN *Hunding*
PAUL SCHOEFFLER *Wotan*
INGE BORKH *Sieglinde*
BIRGIT NILSSON *Brünnhilde*
CLARAMAE TURNER *Fricka*
Valkyries:
VIRGINIA PARKER *Gerhilde*
GLORIA LIND *Ortlinde*
EVELYN REYNOLDS *Waltraute*
PATRICIA FRAHER *Schwertleite*
JANE McGOWAN *Helmwige*
AUDREY PAUL *Siegrune*
EUNICE ALBERTS *Grimgerde*
ARDIS KRAINIK *Rossweisse*

Conductor GEORG SOLTI
Stage Director WILLIAM WYMETAL

IL TROVATORE   VERDI
October 23 and 27 / In Italian

ETTORE BASTIANINI   *Count Di Luna*
HERVA NELLI   *Leonora (Oct. 23)*
GERTRUDE RIBLA   *Leonora (Oct. 27)*
JUSSI BJOERLING   *Manrico*
MARIANO CARUSO   *Ruiz*
JONAS VAZNELIS   *An Old Gypsy*
WILLIAM WILDERMANN   *Ferrando*
VIRGINIA PARKER   *Inez*
CLARAMAE TURNER   *Azucena*
VIRGIL ABNER   *A Messenger*

***Conductor*   BRUNO BARTOLETTI
Stage Director   ALDO MIRABELLA VASSALLO
Chorus Master   MICHAEL LEPORE
Choreographer   RUTH PAGE

LA TRAVIATA   VERDI
October 26 and 31 / In Italian
Production by courtesy of the Teatro
Massimo, Palermo

LEOPOLD SIMONEAU   *Alfredo Germont*
ETTORE BASTIANINI   *Giorgio Germont*
MARIANO CARUSO   *Gastone de Letorères*
HENRI NOEL   *Baron Douphol*
MILES NEKOLNY   *Marchese d'Obigny*
ANDREW FOLDI   *Doctor Grenvil*
VIRGIL ABNER   *Giuseppe*
ELEANOR STEBER   *Violetta Valéry*
VIRGINIA PARKER   *Flora Bervoix*
ARDIS KRAINIK   *Annina*
LLOYD HARRIS   *A Commissionario*

Solo Dancers   BARBARA STEELE,
KENNETH JOHNSON

Conductor   BRUNO BARTOLETTI
Stage Director   ALDO MIRABELLA VASSALLO
Chorus Master   MICHAEL LEPORE
Choreographer   RUTH PAGE

DON GIOVANNI   MOZART
October 29 and November 13 / In Italian

PAUL SCHOEFFLER   *The Commendatore*
ELEANOR STEBER   *Donna Anna*
LEOPOLD SIMONEAU   *Don Ottavio*
NICOLA ROSSI-LEMENI   *Don Giovanni*
FERNANDO CORENA   *Leporello*
GLORIA LIND   *Donna Elvira (Nov. 13)*
EVA LIKOVA   *Donna Elvira (Oct. 29)*
DOLORES WILSON   *Zerlina*
ANDREW FOLDI   *Masetto*

Conductor   GEORG SOLTI
Stage Director   WILLIAM WYMETAL
Chorus Master   MICHAEL LEPORE
Choreographer   RUTH PAGE

TOSCA   PUCCINI
October 30, November 2 and 5 / In Italian

RENATA TEBALDI   *Floria Tosca*
JUSSI BJOERLING   *Mario Cavaradossi*
TITO GOBBI   *Baron Scarpia*
ARLINGTON ROLLMAN   *Cesare Angelotti*
CARLO BADIOLI   *A Sacristan*
MARIANO CARUSO   *Spoletta*
ANDREW FOLDI   *Sciarrone*

LLOYD HARRIS   *Jailer*
BILLY MASON   *A Young Shepherd*

Conductor   BRUNO BARTOLETTI
(Oct. 30, Nov. 5)
LEO KOPP (Nov. 2)
Stage Director   ALDO MIRABELLA VASSALLO
Chorus Master   MICHAEL LEPORE
Children's Chorus   ZERLINE MUHLMAN
METZGER

LA FORZA DEL DESTINO   VERDI
November 8 and 12/ In Italian

RENATA TEBALDI   *Donna Leonora*
GIULIETTA SIMIONATO   *Preziozilla*
RICHARD TUCKER   *Don Alvaro*
ETTORE BASTIANINI   *Don Carlo di Vargas*
NICOLA ROSSI-LEMENI   *Padre Guardiano*
LLOYD HARRIS   *Marchese di Calatrava*
CARLO BADIOLI   *Fra Melitone*
ARDIS KRAINIK   *Curra*
LLOYD HARRIS   *The Mayor of Hornachuelos*
MARIANO CARUSO   *Trabucco*
BERNARD IZZO   *A Surgeon*

Solo Dancers   BARBARA STEELE, KENNETH
JOHNSON, JANE BOCKMAN

Conductor   GEORG SOLTI
Stage Director   ALDO MIRABELLA VASSALLO
Chorus Master   MICHAEL LEPORE
Choreographer   RUTH PAGE

IL BARBIERE DI SIVIGLIA
ROSSINI
November 9, 15 and 17 / In Italian

LEOPOLD SIMONEAU   *Count Almaviva*
CARLO BADIOLI   *Doctor Bartolo*
NICOLA ROSSI-LEMENI   *Don Basilio*
TITO GOBBI   *Figaro*
MILES NEKOLNY   *Fiorello*
LLOYD HARRIS   *Ambrogio*
GIULIETTA SIMIONATO   *Rosina*
EUNICE ALBERTS   *Berta*
MILES NEKOLNY   *Sergeant*

Conductor   EMERSON BUCKLEY
Stage Director   WILLIAM WYMETAL
Chorus Master   MICHAEL LEPORE

GALA CONCERT
November 10

Singers
RENATA TEBALDI
GIULIETTA SIMIONATO
RICHARD TUCKER
ETTORE BASTIANINI
MIRASLAV CANGALOVICH

Conductors   GEORG SOLTI,
EMERSON BUCKLEY

LA BOHEME   PUCCINI
November 14 and 16 / In Italian

JUSSI BJOERLING   *Rodolfo (Nov. 16)*
BARRY MORELL   *Rodolfo (Nov. 14)*
ETTORE BASTIANINI   *Marcello*
***MIRASLAV CANGALOVICH   *Colline*

HENRI NOEL   *Schaunard*
CARLO BADIOLI   *Benoit and Alcindoro*
GUGLIELMO CASPI   *Parpignol*
ALFIO ZAGNOLI   *Custom-House Sergeant*
DOLORES WILSON   *Musetta*
RENATA TEBALDI   *Mimi*
JONAS VAZNELIS   *Guard*

Conductor   BRUNO BARTOLETTI
Stage Director   WILLIAM WYMETAL
Chorus Master   MICHAEL LEPORE
Children's Chorus   ZERLINE MUHLMAN
METZGER

1957

October 11 – November 30

OTELLO   VERDI
October 11, 14 and 18 / In Italian

MARIO DEL MONACO   *Otello*
TITO GOBBI   *Iago*
LESLIE CHABAY   *Cassio*
ANDREA VELIS   *Roderigo*
WILLIAM WILDERMANN   *Lodovico*
LLOYD HARRIS   *Montano*
MILES NEKOLNY   *Herald*
RENATA TEBALDI   *Desdemona (Oct. 11 and 18)*
ANNA MARIE KOEHN   *Desdemona (Oct. 14)*
IRENE KRAMARICH   *Emilia*

Conductor   TULLIO SERAFIN
Stage Director   ALDO MIRABELLA VASSALLO
Chorus Master   MICHAEL LEPORE

LA BOHEME   PUCCINI
October 16, November 4 / In Italian

JUSSI BJOERLING   *Rodolfo*
***ALDO PROTTI   *Marcello*
KENNETH SMITH   *Colline*
HENRI NOEL   *Schaunard*
CARLO BADIOLI   *Benoit and Alcindoro*
JONAS VAZNELIS   *Custom-House Sergeant*
EVA LIKOVA   *Musetta*
***ANNA MOFFO   *Mimi*

***Conductor*   GIANANDREA GAVAZZENI
Stage Director   ALDO MIRABELLA VASSALLO
Chorus Master   MICHAEL LEPORE
Children's Chorus   ZERLINE MUHLMAN
METZGER

MIGNON   THOMAS
October 19 and 28 / In French

GIULIETTA SIMIONATO   *Mignon*
ANNA MOFFO   *Philine*
ROSALIND NADELL   *Frédéric*
***ALVINIO MISCIANO   *Wilhelm Meister*
MARIANO CARUSO   *Laerte*
WILLIAM WILDERMANN   *Lothario*
ANDREW FOLDI   *Jarno*

Solo Dancer   BARBARA STEELE

Conductor   GIANANDREA GAVAZZENI
Stage Director   RICHARD BALDRIDGE
Chorus Master   MICHAEL LEPORE
Choreographer   RUTH PAGE

MANON LESCAUT PUCCINI
October 21 and 25, November 9 / In Italian

RENATA TEBALDI *Manon Lescaut*
CORNELL MacNEIL *Lescaut*
JUSSI BJOERLING *Chevalier des Grieux*
CARLO BADIOLI *Geronte de Ravoir*
LESLIE CHABAY *Edmondo*
ANDREA VELIS *Music Master and Lamplighter*
ROSALIND NADELL *Musician*
ANDREW FOLDI *Naval Captain*
LLOYD HARRIS *Innkeeper and Sergeant*

Conductor TULLIO SERAFIN
Stage Director ALDO MIRABELLA VASSALLO
Chorus Master MICHAEL LEPORE
Choreographer RUTH PAGE

DOUBLE BILL / *October 23 and 26*

CAVALLERIA RUSTICANA
MASCAGNI / *In Italian*

BRIAN SULLIVAN *Turiddu*
CORNELL MacNEIL *Alfio*
ROSALIND NADELL *Lola*
IRENE KRAMARICH *Mamma Lucia (Oct. 23)*
PATRICIA FRAHER *Mamma Lucia (Oct. 26)*
GIULIETTA SIMIONATO *Santuzza*

Conductor LEO KOPP
Stage Director VLADIMIR ROSING
Chorus Master MICHAEL LEPORE

I PAGLIACCI LEONCAVALLO
In Italian

MARIO DEL MONACO *Canio*
EVA LIKOVA *Nedda*
TITO GOBBI *Tonio*
MARIANO CARUSO *Beppe*
CORNELL MacNEIL *Silvio*

Conductor BRUNO BARTOLETTI
Stage Director VLADIMIR ROSING
Chorus Master MICHAEL LEPORE

ANDREA CHENIER GIORDANO
October 30, November 2 / In Italian

BERNARD IZZO *Major-Domo and Dumas*
TITO GOBBI *Charles Gérard*
RENATA TEBALDI *Madeleine de Coigny*
ARDIS KRAINIK *Countess de Coigny*
ROSALIND NADELL *Bersi*
MILES NEKOLNY *Fléville*
ANDREA VELIS *The Abbé*
MARIO DEL MONACO *Andrea Chénier*
CARLO BADIOLI *Mathieu*
MARIANO CARUSO *Incredibile*
HENRI NOEL *Roucher*
IRENE KRAMARICH *Madelon*
ANDREW FOLDI *Fouquier-Tinville*
LLOYD HARRIS *Schmidt*

Solo Dancers BARBARA STEELE,
          KENNETH JOHNSON

Conductor GIANANDREA GAVAZZENI
Stage Director ALDO MIRABELLA VASSALLO
Chorus Master MICHAEL LEPORE
Choreographer RUTH PAGE

LA GIOCONDA PONCHIELLI
November 1 and 6 / In Italian

EILEEN FARRELL *La Gioconda*
IRENE KRAMARICH *La Cieca*
WILLIAM WILDERMANN *Duke Alvise*
GIULIETTA SIMIONATO *Laura*
RICHARD TUCKER *Enzo Grimaldo (Nov. 1)*
GIUSEPPE DI STEFANO *Enzo Grimaldo (Nov. 6)*
ALDO PROTTI *Barnaba*
LLOYD HARRIS *Zuane*
MARIANO CARUSO *Isepo*
KENNETH SMITH *A Monk*
JONAS VAZNELIS *Un Cantore*

Solo Dancers KENNETH JOHNSON,
          MARIA TALLCHIEF (Nov. 1),
          DOREEN TEMPEST (Nov. 6)

Conductor TULLIO SERAFIN
Stage Director ALDO MIRABELLA VASSALLO
Chorus Master MICHAEL LEPORE
Choreographer RUTH PAGE

LE NOZZE DI FIGARO MOZART
Nov. 8 and 11 / In Italian
New Production

TITO GOBBI *Count Almaviva*
***WALTER BERRY *Figaro*
CARLO BADIOLI *Doctor Bartolo*
MARIANO CARUSO *Don Basilio*
GIULIETTA SIMIONATO *Cherubino*
ANDREW FOLDI *Antonio*
ANDREA VELIS *Don Curzio*
ELEANOR STEBER *Countess Almaviva*
ANNA MOFFO *Susanna*
ROSALIND NADELL *Marcellina*
JEANNE DIAMOND *Barbarina*

Conductor GEORG SOLTI
***Stage Director* HANS HARTLEB
Chorus Master MICHAEL LEPORE
Choreographer RUTH PAGE
Scenic Design GERALD L. RITHOLZ

ADRIANA LECOUVREUR CILEA
November 13 and 16 / In Italian
First Chicago performances

GIUSEPPE DI STEFANO *Maurizio*
CARLO BADIOLI *Prince De Bouillon*
MARIANO CARUSO *Abbé de Chazeuil*
TITO GOBBI *Michonnet*
KENNETH SMITH *Quinault*
ANDREA VELIS *Poisson*
RENATA TEBALDI *Adriana Lecouvreur*
GIULIETTA SIMIONATO *Princess de Bouillon*
JEANNE DIAMOND *Mlle. Jouvenot*
ARDIS KRAINIK *Mlle. Dangeville*

Solo Dancers KENNETH JOHNSON, PATRICK
          CUMMINGS, PATRICIA
          KLEKOVIC, DOLORES LIPINSKI,
          ETTA BURO

Conductor TULLIO SERAFIN
Stage Director ALDO MIRABELLA VASSALLO
Chorus Master MICHAEL LEPORE
Choreographer RUTH PAGE
Re-designed by GERALD L. RITHOLZ

UN BALLO IN MASCHERA VERDI
November 15 and 18 / In Italian

JUSSI BJOERLING *Riccardo*
ANITA CERQUETTI *Amelia*
ALDO PROTTI *Renato*
WILLIAM WILDERMANN *Samuele*
ANDREW FOLDI *Tomaso*
LLOYD HARRIS *Silvano*
SYLVIA STAHLMAN *Oscar*
CLARAMAE TURNER *Ulrica*
MARIANO CARUSO *Judge, Servant*

Conductor GEORG SOLTI
Stage Director ALDO MIRABELLA VASSALLO
Chorus Master MICHAEL LEPORE
Choreographer RUTH PAGE

TOSCA PUCCINI
November 20 and 29 / In Italian

ELEANOR STEBER *Floria Tosca*
GIUSEPPE DI STEFANO *Mario Cavaradossi (Nov. 20)*
JUSSI BJOERLING *Mario Cavaradossi (Nov. 29)*
TITO GOBBI *Baron Scarpia*
KENNETH SMITH *Cesare Angelotti*
MARIANO CARUSO *Spoletta*
ANDREW FOLDI *Sciarrone*
LLOYD HARRIS *A Jailer*
PATRICIA FRAHER *Shepherd Boy (Nov. 29)*
BILLY MASON *Shepherd Boy (Nov. 20)*
CARLO BADIOLI *The Sacristan*

Conductor BRUNO BARTOLETTI
Stage Director ALDO MIRABELLA VASSALLO
Chorus Master MICHAEL LEPORE
Children's Chorus ZERLINE MUHLMAN
          METZGER

DON CARLO VERDI
November 22, 25 and 30 / In Italian
New Production
First Chicago performances

ANITA CERQUETTI *Elisabetta di Valois*
NELL RANKIN *Principessa Eboli*
BRIAN SULLIVAN *Don Carlo (Nov. 22 and 25)*
JUSSI BJOERLING *Don Carlo (Nov. 30)*
TITO GOBBI *Rodrigo*
BORIS CHRISTOFF *Filippo II*
WILLIAM WILDERMANN *Grand Inquisitor*
KENNETH SMITH *A Monk*
JEANNE DIAMOND *Tebaldo*
MARIANO CARUSO *Count Lerma*
ANDREA VELIS *The Royal Herald*
SYLVIA STAHLMAN *A Heavenly Voice*

Conductor GEORG SOLTI
Stage Director HANS HARTLEB
Chorus Master MICHAEL LEPORE
Scenic design and costumes ROBERT FLETCHER

LUCIA DI LAMMERMOOR
DONIZETTI
November 23 and 27 / In Italian

ALDO PROTTI *Lord Enrico Ashton*
ANNA MOFFO *Lucia*
GIUSEPPE DI STEFANO *Edgardo (Nov. 23)*
BRIAN SULLIVAN *Edgardo (Nov. 27)*
KENNETH SMITH *Raimondo*

ARDIS KRAINIK   *Alisa*
MARIANO CARUSO   *Normanno*
LESLIE CHABAY   *Lord Arturo Bucklaw*

Solo Dancers   PATRICIA KLEKOVIC, ORRIN
KAYAN

Conductor   BRUNO BARTOLETTI
Stage Director   VLADIMIR ROSING
Chorus Master   MICHAEL LEPORE
Choreographer   RUTH PAGE

LYRIC OPERA STAGE PARTY, 1957. CENTER, CAROL FOX.

1958

October 10 – November 29

FALSTAFF   VERDI

October 10 and 17 / In Italian
Broadcast over CBS-WBBM AM and FM,
sponsored by Chicago Title and Trust Company

TITO GOBBI   *Sir John Falstaff*
ALVINIO MISCIANO   *Fenton*
CORNELL MacNEIL   *Ford*
MARIANO CARUSO   *Dr. Cajus*
LUIGI VELLUCCI   *Bardolph*
KENNETH SMITH   *Pistol*
RENATA TEBALDI   *Alice Ford*
ANNA MOFFO   *Nanetta*
ANNAMARIA CANALI   *Mistress Page*
GIULIETTA SIMIONATO   *Dame Quickly*

Conductor   TULLIO SERAFIN
Stage Director   CARLO PICCINATO
Chorus Master   MICHAEL LEPORE
Choreographer   RUTH PAGE

MADAMA BUTTERFLY   PUCCINI

October 13 and 15 / In Italian

RENATA TEBALDI   *Madama Butterfly*
ANNAMARIA CANALI   *Suzuki*
JEANNE DIAMOND   *Kate Pinkerton*
GIUSEPPE DI STEFANO   *B. F. Pinkerton*
CORNELL MacNEIL   *Sharpless*
MARIANO CARUSO   *Goro*
HENRI NOEL   *Prince Yamadori*
KENNETH SMITH   *The Bonze*
LLOYD HARRIS   *The Imperial Commissioner*

BERNARD IZZO   *The Official Registrar*

**Conductor*   KIRIL KONDRASHIN
Stage Director   CARLO PICCINATO
Chorus Master   MICHAEL LEPORE

TURANDOT   PUCCINI

October 18, 22 and 27 / In Italian
Stage settings through the courtesy of the
San Francisco Opera

BIRGIT NILSSON   *Princess Turandot*
JOSEPH QUINLIN   *The Emperor Altoum*
WILLIAM WILDERMANN   *Timur*
GIUSEPPE DI STEFANO   *Calaf*
ANNA MOFFO   *Liu*
RICHARD TORIGI   *Ping*
MARIANO CARUSO   *Pang*
LUIGI VELLUCCI   *Pong*
HENRI NOEL   *A Mandarin*

Conductor   TULLIO SERAFIN
Stage Director   VLADIMIR ROSING
Chorus Master   MICHAEL LEPORE
Designed by   HARRY HORNER
Children's Chorus   ST. GERTRUDE
BOYS' CHOIR

IL TROVATORE   VERDI

October 20, 24 and 29 / In Italian

ETTORE BASTIANINI   *Count Di Luna*
WILLIAM WILDERMANN   *Ferrando*
JUSSI BJOERLING   *Manrico*
LUIGI VELLUCCI   *Ruiz*
JONAS VAZNELIS   *An Old Gypsy*
ELINOR ROSS   *Leonora*
ANNAMARIA CANALI   *Inez*
GIULIETTA SIMIONATO   *Azucena*
JEFFREY WOLFE   *Messenger*

Conductor   LEE SCHAENEN
Stage Director   CARLO PICCINATO
Chorus Master   MICHAEL LEPORE

DOUBLE BILL / *October 25,*
31 and November 3

GIANNI SCHICCHI   PUCCINI

In Italian

TITO GOBBI   *Gianni Schicchi*
ANNA MOFFO   *Lauretta*
ANNAMARIA CANALI   *Zita*
ALVINIO MISCIANO   *Rinuccio*
MARIANO CARUSO   *Gherard*
JEANNE DIAMOND   *Nella*
SALVATORE DI MASI   *Gherardino*
CHESTER WATSON   *Betto Di Signa*
WILLIAM WILDERMANN   *Simone*
HENRI NOEL   *Marco*
SOPHIA STEFFAN   *La Ciesca*
ANDREW FOLDI   *Maestro Spinnelloccio*
BERNARD IZZO   *Ser Amantio Di Nicolao*
JONAS VAZNELIS   *Pinellino*
ROBERT SMITH   *Guccio*

Conductor   TULLIO SERAFIN
Stage Director   CARLO PICCINATO

I PAGLIACCI   LEONCAVALLO

In Italian

CORNELL MacNEIL   *Prologue*
GIUSEPPE DI STEFANO   *Canio*
EVA LIKOVA   *Nedda*
TITO GOBBI   *Tonio*
MARIANO CARUSO   *Beppe*
CORNELL MacNEIL   *Silvio*

Conductor   TULLIO SERAFIN
Stage Director   VLADIMIR ROSING
Chorus Master   MICHAEL LEPORE

TRISTAN UND ISOLDE   WAGNER

November 1, 7 and 10 / In German

KARL LIEBL   *Tristan*
WILLIAM WILDERMANN   *King Marke*
BIRGIT NILSSON   *Isolde*
WALTER CASSEL   *Kurwenal*
MARIANO CARUSO   *Melot*
GRACE HOFFMAN   *Brangaene*
LUIGI VELLUCCI   *A Shepherd*
JOSEPH QUINLIN   *A Sailor*
HENRI NOEL   *A Helmsman*

Conductor   ARTUR RODZINSKI
Stage Director   WILLIAM WYMETAL
Chorus Master   MICHAEL LEPORE

LA TRAVIATA   VERDI

November 5, 8 and 14 / In Italian

LEOPOLD SIMONEAU   *Alfredo*
ETTORE BASTIANINI   *Giorgio Germont*
MARIANO CARUSO   *Gastone de Letorières*
HENRI NOEL   *Baron Douphol*
BERNARD IZZO   *Marchese d'Obigny*
ANDREW FOLDI   *Doctor Grenvil*
JOSEPH QUINLIN   *Giuseppe*
ELEANOR STEBER   *Violetta Valéry*
TAMARA BERING   *Flora Bervoix*
ARDIS KRAINIK   *Annina*

Solo Dancers   BARBARA STEELE, KENNETH
JOHNSON

Conductor   TULLIO SERAFIN
Stage Director   CARLO PICCINATO
Chorus Master   MICHAEL LEPORE
Choreographer   RUTH PAGE

IL BARBIERE DI SIVIGLIA
ROSSINI

November 12 and 21 / In Italian

ALVINIO MISCIANO   *Count Almaviva*
FERNANDO CORENA   *Doctor Bartolo*
PAOLO MONTARSOLO   *Basilio*
TITO GOBBI   *Figaro*
HENRI NOEL   *Fiorello*
GIULIETTA SIMIONATO   *Rosina*
ANNAMARIA CANALI   *Berta*
LLOYD HARRIS   *Sergeant*

Conductor   LEE SCHAENEN
Stage Director   CARLO PICCINATO
Chorus Master   MICHAEL LEPORE

RIGOLETTO VERDI
November 15 and 19 / In Italian

JUSSI BJOERLING *The Duke of Mantua*
TITO GOBBI *Rigoletto (Nov. 15)*
CORNELL MacNEIL *Rigoletto (Nov. 19)*
BERNARD IZZO *Count Ceprano*
KENNETH SMITH *Count Monterone*
WILLIAM WILDERMANN *Sparafucile*
LUIGI VELLUCCI *Matteo Borsa*
HENRI NOEL *Cavaliere Marullo*
TAMARA BERING *Countess Ceprano*
ANNA MOFFO *Gilda*
ARDIS KRAINIK *Giovanna*
SOPHIA STEFFAN *Maddalena*
JEANNE DIAMOND *A Page*

Conductor GEORGES SEBASTIAN
Stage Director CARLO PICCINATO
Chorus Master MICHAEL LEPORE
Choreographer RUTH PAGE

BORIS GODUNOV
MUSSORGSKY,
RIMSKY-KORSAKOV
version
November 17, 22 and 28 / In Russian

BORIS CHRISTOFF *Boris Godunov*
SOPHIA STEFFAN *Feodor*
JEANNE DIAMOND *Xenia*
TAMARA BERING *The Old Nurse*
MARIANO CARUSO *Prince Shuiski*
CHESTER WATSON *Andrey Tchelkalov*
WILLIAM WILDERMANN *Pimen*
BRIAN SULLIVAN *The Pretender Dimitri*
GRACE HOFFMAN *Marina Mnishek*
***MARCO STEFANONI *Varlaam*
JOSEPH QUINLIN *Missail*
ANNAMARIA CANALI *The Hostess of the Inn*
ALGERD BRAZIS *Nikitich*
LUIGI VELLUCCI *The Idiot*
BERNARD IZZO, KAY CHARLES GRAVES
  Two Jesuits
ANDREW FOLDI *A Guard*
REINERT LINDLAND *A Boyar*
JEFFREY WOLFE *Krushchov*
JONAS VAZNELIS *Mitiukh*

Solo Dancers DOLORES LIPINSKI, PATRICIA
  KLEKOVIC, ORRIN KAYAN,
  WILLIAM MALONEY

Conductor GEORGES SEBASTIAN
Stage Director VLADIMIR ROSING
Chorus Master MICHAEL LEPORE
Choreographer RUTH PAGE
Children's Chorus ST. GERTRUDE BOYS'
  CHOIR

AIDA VERDI
November 24, 26 and 29 / In Italian

LEONIE RYSANEK *Aida*
GIULIETTA SIMIONATO *Amneris*
TITO GOBBI *Amonasro*
JUSSI BJOERLING *Radames*
WILLIAM WILDERMANN *Ramphis*
KENNETH SMITH *King of Egypt*
LUIGI VELLUCCI *Messenger*
SOPHIA STEFFAN *Priestess*

Solo Dancers BARBARA STEELE, KENNETH
  JOHNSON, PATRICK CUMMINGS

Conductor GEORGES SEBASTIAN
Stage Director CARLO PICCINATO
Chorus Master MICHAEL LEPORE
Choreographer RUTH PAGE

1959

October 12 – November 28

CARMEN BIZET
October 12, 16, 21 and 24 / In French
New Production —gift of Mrs.
D. Eckhart Williams

GIUSEPPE DI STEFANO *Don Jose*
***ERNEST BLANC *Escamillo*
LUIGI VELLUCCI *El Dancairo*
MARIANO CARUSO *El Remendado*
PETER HARROWER *Zuniga*
BERNARD IZZO *Morales*
DOROTHY WARENSKJOLD *Micaela*
IRENE CALLAWAY *Frasquita*
CECILIA WARD *Mercedes*
JEAN MADEIRA *Carmen*

Solo Dancers LUIS OLIVARES,
  JOSELA VELASCO,
  KENNETH JOHNSON,
  BARBARA STEELE,
  PATRICIA KLEKOVIC

***Conductor* LOVRO VON MATACIC
***Stage Director* MARGHERITA WALLMAN
Chorus Master MICHAEL LEPORE
Choreographer RUTH PAGE
After the design of PIERO ZUFFI
Children's Chorus ST. GERTRUDE BOYS' CHOIR

LA CENERENTOLA ROSSINI
October 14, 17 and 19 / In Italian
Stage setting through the courtesy
of the Rome Opera

NICOLA MONTI *Don Ramiro*
DONALD GRAMM *Dandini*
FERNANDO CORENA *Don Magnifico*
IRENE CALLAWAY *Clorinda*
CORINNA VOZZA *Thisbe*
***ANNA MARIA ROTA *Angelina (Cinderella)*
ANDREW FOLDI *Alidoro*

Conductor GIANANDREA GAVAZZENI
Stage Director CARLO MAESTRINI
Chorus Master MICHAEL LEPORE

SIMON BOCCANEGRA VERDI
October 23, 26 and 29 / In Italian
Stage setting through the courtesy
of the Rome Opera
First Chicago performances

MARGHERITA ROBERTI *Amelia Grimaldi*
RICHARD TUCKER *Gabriele Adorno*
TITO GOBBI *Simon Boccanegra*
***FERRUCCIO MAZZOLI *Jacopo Fiesco*
PHILIP MAERO *Paolo Albiani*
PETER HARROWER *Pietro*
MARIANO CARUSO *Captain of the Guard*
ARDIS KRAINIK *Amelia's Servant*

Conductor GIANANDREA GAVAZZENI
Stage Director CARLO MAESTRINI
Chorus Master MICHAEL LEPORE

TURANDOT PUCCINI
October 28 and 30 / In Italian
Stage setting through the courtesy
of the San Francisco Opera

BIRGIT NILSSON *Princess Turandot*
RALPH NIELSEN *The Emperor Altoum*
FERRUCCIO MAZZOLI *Timur*
GIUSEPPE DI STEFANO *Calaf*
LEONTYNE PRICE *Liu*
FERNANDO CORENA *Ping*
MARIANO CARUSO *Pang*
LUIGI VELLUCCI *Pong*
BERNARD IZZO *A Mandarin*

Conductor GIANANDREA GAVAZZENI
Stage Director VLADIMIR ROSING
Chorus Master MICHAEL LEPORE
Designed by HARRY HORNER
Children's Chorus ST. GERTRUDE
  BOYS' CHOIR

JENŮFA JANÁČEK
November 2 and 6 / In English
Production through the courtesy of the
Royal Opera, Covent Garden, London
First Chicago performances

***GRE BROUWENSTIJN *Jenůfa*
IRENE KRAMARICH *Grandmother Buryja*
RICHARD CASSILLY *Laca Klemeň*
SUSAN WINCHESTER *Jano*
PHILIP MAERO *Foreman*
***SYLVIA FISHER *Kostelnička Buryja*
ROBERT CHARLEBOIS *Števa Buryja*
IRENE CALLAWAY *Barena*
ARDIS KRAINIK *A Maid*
ANDREW FOLDI *Mayor*
EVELYN REYNOLDS *His Wife*
CORINNA VOZZA *Karolka*
ANN IRVING *An Aunt*

Solo Dancer KAROLY BARTA

Conductor LOVRO VON MATAČIĆ
***Stage Director* CHISTOPHER WEST
Chorus Master MICHAEL LEPORE
Choreographer RUTH PAGE
Scenery and costumes designed by JAN BRAZDA

UN BALLO IN MASCHERA VERDI
November 4 and 7 / In Italian

GIUSEPPE DI STEFANO *Riccardo*
BIRGIT NILSSON *Amelia*
TITO GOBBI *Renato*
PETER HARROWER *Samuele*
ANDREW FOLDI *Tomaso*
BERNARD IZZO *Silvano*
SYLVIA STAHLMAN *Oscar*
IRENE KRAMARICH *Ulrica*
MARIANO CARUSO *Judge, Servant*

Conductor BRUNO BARTOLETTI
Stage Director CARLO MAESTRINI
Chorus Master MICHAEL LEPORE
Choreographer RUTH PAGE

COSI FAN TUTTE MOZART

November 9, 11 and 14 / In Italian
Stage setting through the courtesy of the
San Francisco Opera

ELISABETH SCHWARZKOPF *Fiordiligi*
+CHRISTA LUDWIG *Dorabella*
LEOPOLD SIMONEAU *Ferrando*
WALTER BERRY *Guglielmo*
FERNANDO CORENA *Don Alfonso*
SYLVIA STAHLMAN *Despina*

Conductor JOSEF KRIPS (Nov. 9), LOVRO VON
MATAČIĆ (Nov. 11 and 14)
***Stage Director ADOLF ROTT
Chorus Master MICHAEL LEPORE
Designed by GEORGE JENKINS

DER FLIEGENDE HOLLÄNDER
WAGNER

November 13, 16 and 21 / In German
Stage setting through the courtesy of the
Rome Opera

JOSEF GREINDL *Daland*
BIRGIT NILSSON *Senta*
EUGENE TOBIN *Eric*
MARY MacKENZIE *Mary*
CESARE CURZI *Daland's Steersman*
***TOMISLAV NERALIC *The Flying Dutchman*

Conductor LOVRO VON MATAČIĆ
Stage Director ADOLF ROTT
Chorus Master MICHAEL LEPORE
Backstage chorus CHICAGO LITHUANIAN
MALE CHORUS

LA GIOCONDA PONCHIELLI

November 18, 20 and 28 / In Italian

EILEEN FARRELL *La Gioconda*
IRENE KRAMARICH *La Cieca*
JOSEPH GREINDL *Duke Alvise*
IRENE DALIS *Laura*
RICHARD TUCKER *Enzo Grimaldo*
GIUSEPPE TADDEI *Barnaba*
BERNARD IZZO *Zuane*
MARIANO CARUSO *Isepo*
ANDREW FOLDI *A Monk*
JONAS VAZNELIS *Un Cantore*

Solo Dancers PATRICIA KLEKOVIC,
KENNETH JOHNSON

Conductor BRUNO BARTOLETTI
Stage Director CARLO MAESTRINI
Chorus Master MICHAEL LEPORE
Choreographer RUTH PAGE

THÄIS MASSENET

November 23, 25 and 27 / In French

***MICHEL ROUX *Athanaël*
LEOPOLD SIMONEAU *Nicias*
FERNANDO CORENA *Palémon*
KAY CHARLES GRAVES *Servant of Nicias*
LEONTYNE PRICE *Thaïs*
IRENE CALLAWAY *Crobyle*
ARDIS KRAINIK *Myrtale*
IRENE KRAMARICH *Albine*

Solo Dancers KENNETH JOHNSON, BARBARA

STEELE, JANE BOCKMAN,
PATRICIA KLEKOVIC, DOLORES
LIPINSKI

***Conductor GEORGES PRÊTRE
Stage Director VLADIMIR ROSING
Chorus Master MICHAEL LEPORE
Choreographer RUTH PAGE

1960

October 14 – December 3

DON CARLO VERDI

October 14, 21 and 24 / In Italian
Broadcast over CBS-WBBM AM and FM,
sponsored by TIME, the Weekly News Magazine

MARGHERITA ROBERTI *Elisabetta Di Valois*
GIULIETTA SIMIONATO *Principessa Eboli*
RICHARD TUCKER *Don Carlo*
TITO GOBBI *Rodrigo*
BORIS CHRISTOFF *Filippo II*
FERRUCCIO MAZZOLI *The Grand Inquisitor*
FRANCO VENTRIGLIA *A Monk*
JEANNE DIAMOND *Tebaldo*
MARIANO CARUSO *Count Lerma*
SHIRLEY JOHNSON *A Heavenly Voice*

***Conductor ANTONINO VOTTO
Stage Director CHRISTOPHER WEST
Chorus Master MICHAEL LEPORE
Scenic design and costumes ROBERT FLETCHER

AIDA VERDI

October 17, 19, 22 and 28 / In Italian

MARGHERITA ROBERTI *Aida (Oct. 17 and 19)*
LEONTYNE PRICE *Aida (Oct. 22 and 28)*
GIULIETTA SIMIONATO *Amneris*
ROBERT MERRILL *Amonasro*
CARLO BERGONZI *Radames (Oct. 17 and 19)*
***LUIGI OTTOLINI *Radames (Oct. 22 and 28)*
FERRUCCIO MAZZOLI *Ramphis*
FRANCO VENTRIGLIA *King of Egypt*
MARIANO CARUSO *Messenger.*
DORIS YARICK *Priestess*

Solo Dancers IRINA BOROWSKA (Oct. 17, 19
and 28), KENNETH JOHNSON,
PATRICIA KLEKOVIC (Oct. 22),
ORRIN KAYAN

Conductor ANTONINO VOTTO
Stage Director CARLO MAESTRINI
Chorus Master MICHAEL LEPORE
Choreographer RUTH PAGE
Scenic production re-designed
GERALD L. RITHOLZ

LE NOZZE DI FIGARO MOZART

Oct. 26, 29 and 31 / In Italian

***EBERHARD WAECHTER *Count Almaviva*
WALTER BERRY *Figaro*
FERNANDO CORENA *Doctor Bartolo*
MARIANO CARUSO *Don Basilio*
CHRISTA LUDWIG *Cherubino*
CHESTER WATSON *Antonio*
ROBERT SCHMORR *Don Curzio*
ELISABETH SCHWARZKOPF
Countess Almaviva

RITA STREICH *Susanna*
MARTHA LIPTON *Marcellina*
JEANNE DIAMOND *Barbarina*
GLADYS VACEK *Peasant Girl*
CHARLOTTE GACKLE *Peasant Girl*

Solo Dancers PATRICIA KLEKOVIC,
KENNETH JOHNSON

Conductor JOSEF KRIPS
Stage Director CHRISTOPHER WEST
Chorus Master MICHAEL LEPORE
Choreographer RUTH PAGE
Scenic production GERALD L. RITHOLZ

LA BOHEME PUCCINI

November 2, 5 and 7 / In Italian

RICHARD TUCKER *Rodolfo*
***RENATO CESARI *Marcello*
FERRUCCIO MAZZOLI *Colline*
HENRI NOEL *Schaunard*
FERNANDO CORENA *Benoit and Alcindoro*
JEFFREY WOLFE *Parpignol*
JONAS VAZNELIS *Custom-House Sergeant*
DORIS YARICK *Musetta*
***RENATA SCOTTO *Mimi*
ROBERT SMITH *Guard*

Conductor GIANANDREA GAVAZZENI
Stage Director CARLO MAESTRINI
Chorus Master MICHAEL LEPORE
Children's Chorus CHILDREN'S CHOIR, FIRST
UNITARIAN CHURCH

CARMEN BIZET

November 4, 9 and 12 / In French
Gift of Mrs. D. Eckhart Williams

GIUSEPPE DI STEFANO *Don José (Nov. 4*
and 9)
RICHARD CASSILLY *Don José (Nov. 12)*
ROBERT MERRILL *Escamillo*
ROBERT SCHMORR *El Dancairo*
MARIANO CARUSO *El Remendado*
FRANCO VENTRIGLIA *Zuniga*
BERNARD IZZO *Morales*
RENATA SCOTTO *Micaela*
DORIS YARICK *Frasquita*
KAY GRIFFEL *Mercedes*
JEAN MADEIRA *Carmen*

Solo Dancers LUIS OLIVARES, NILA AMPARO,
KENNETH JOHNSON, PATRICIA
KLEKOVIC, JANE BOCKMAN

Conductor LOVRO VON MATAČIĆ
Production by MARGHERITA WALLMAN
Realized by CARLO MAESTRINI
Chorus Master MICHAEL LEPORE
Choreographer RUTH PAGE
Children's Chorus CHILDREN'S CHOIR, FIRST
UNITARIAN CHURCH
Scenery and costumes after design of
PIERO ZUFFI

TOSCA PUCCINI

November 11, 14 and 19 / In Italian

RENATA TEBALDI *Floria Tosca*
GIUSEPPE DI STEFANO *Mario Cavaradossi*
TITO GOBBI *Baron Scarpia*
FRANCO VENTRIGLIA *Cesare Angelotti*

GERHARD PECHNER *A Sacristan*
MARIANO CARUSO *Spoletta*
BERNARD IZZO *Sciarrone*
KAY CHARLES GRAVES *A Jailer*
KAY GRIFFEL *A Shepherd Boy*

Conductor GIANANDREA GAVAZZENI
Stage Director CARLO MAESTRINI
Chorus Master MICHAEL LEPORE
Children's Chorus CHILDREN'S CHOIR, FIRST
UNITARIAN CHURCH

DIE WALKÜRE WAGNER
November 16, 18 and 21 / In German

JON VICKERS *Siegmund*
WILLIAM WILDERMANN *Hunding*
HANS HOTTER *Wotan*
GRE BROUWENSTIJN *Sieglinde*
BIRGIT NILSSON *Brunnhilde*
CHRISTA LUDWIG *Fricka*
Valkyries:
ALICE RILEY *Gerhilde*
DORIS YARICK *Ortlinde*
EMALEE THOMPSON *Waltraute*
MARY MacKENZIE *Schwertleite*
PRUDENCIJA BICKUS *Helmwige*
KAY GRIFFEL *Siegrune*
PATRICIA SAGE *Grimgerde*
SHARON NAWROCKI *Rossweisse*

Conductor LOVRO VON MATAČIC
Stage Director CHRISTOPHER WEST

FEDORA GIORDANO
November 23 and 25 / In Italian

RENATA TEBALDI *Princess Fedora Romanov*
GIUSEPPE DI STEFANO *Count Loris Ipanov*
TITO GOBBI *De Siriex*
JEANETTE SCOVOTTI *Countess Olga Sukarev*
FRANCO VENTRIGLIA *Grech*
CHESTER WATSON *Cirillo*
SUSAN WINCHESTER *Dmitri*
KAY GRIFFEL *A Little Savoyard*
MARIANO CARUSO *Désiré*
ROBERT SCHMORR *Baron Rouvel*
KAY CHARLES GRAVES *Lorek*
BERNARD IZZO *Borov*
ROBERT SMITH *Nicola*
JEFFREY WOLFE *Sergio*
SHELDON SHKOLNIK *Boleslao Lazinski,*
a pianist

Conductor LOVRO VON MATAČIC
Stage Director CARLO MAESTRINI
Chorus Master MICHAEL LEPORE
Choreographer RUTH PAGE
Scenic Production re-designed by
GERALD L. RITHOLZ

MADAMA BUTTERFLY PUCCINI
Nov. 26, 28 and Dec. 2 / In Italian

LEONTYNE PRICE *Madama Butterfly*
MILDRED MILLER *Suzuki*
KAY GRIFFEL *Kate Pinkerton*
RICHARD CASSILLY *B. F. Pinkerton*
RENATO CESARI *Sharpless*
MARIANO CARUSO *Goro*
BERNARD IZZO *Prince Yamadori*

CHESTER WATSON *The Bonze*
ROBERT SMITH *The Imperial Commissioner*
JONAS VAZNELIS *The Official Registrar*

Conductor GIANANDREA GAVAZZENI
Stage Director CHRISTOPHER WEST
Chorus Master MICHAEL LEPORE

SIMON BOCCANEGRA VERDI
November 30, December 3 / In Italian
Stage settings by the courtesy of the Rome Opera

RENATA TEBALDI *Amelia Grimaldi*
RICHARD TUCKER *Gabriele Adorno*
TITO GOBBI *Simon Boccanegra*
FERRUCCIO MAZZOLI *Jacopo Fiesco*
RENATO CESARI *Paolo Albiani*
CHESTER WATSON *Pietro*
MARIANO CARUSO *Captain of the Guard*
SHARON NAWROCKI *Amelia's Servant*

Conductor GIANANDREA GAVAZZENI
Stage Director CARLO MAESTRINI
Chorus Master MICHAEL LEPORE

1961

October 14 – December 1

LUCIA DI LAMMERMOOR
DONIZETTI
October 14, 16 and 18 / In Italian
Broadcast over CBS-WBBM AM and FM,
as a public service
Production courtesy of the Teatro Massimo,
Palermo, Italy

MARIO ZANASI *Lord Enrico Ashton*
JOAN SUTHERLAND *Lucia*
RICHARD TUCKER *Edgardo (Oct. 14 and 16)*
CARLO BERGONZI *Edgardo (Oct. 18)*
****PIERO DE PALMA *Lord Arturo Bucklaw*
WILLIAM WILDERMANN *Raimondo*
MARGERY MacKAY *Alisa*
MARIANO CARUSO *Normanno*

Conductor ANTONINO VOTTO
Stage Director FRANCO ZEFFIRELLI
Chorus Master MICHAEL LEPORE
Choreographer RUTH PAGE
Costumes and scenery designed by FRANCO
ZEFFIRELLI

FRANCO ZEFFIRELLI

ANDREA CHENIER GIORDANO
October 20, 25 and 28 / In Italian

BERNARD IZZO *A Major-Domo*
MARIO ZANASI *Charles Gérard*
SHAKEH VARTENISSIAN *Madeleine de Coigny*
MARGERY MacKAY *Countess de Coigny*
***VERA MAGRINI *Bersi*
MICHAEL BONDON *Fléville*
MARIANO CARUSO *The Abbé*
JON VICKERS *Andrea Chénier*
RENATO CESARI *Mathieu*
PIERO DE PALMA *Incredibile*
HENRI NOEL *Roucher*
MARY MacKENZIE *Madelon*
EDWARD WARNER *Dumas*
BERNARD IZZO *Fouquier-Tinville*
KAY CHARLES GRAVES *Schmidt*

Solo Dancers PATRICIA KLEKOVIC,
KENNETH JOHNSON

Conductor ANTONINO VOTTO
Stage Director ENRICO FRIGERIO
Chorus Master MICHAEL LEPORE
Choreographer RUTH PAGE

MEFISTOFELE BOITO
October 21, 23 and 27 / In Italian
Scenery of the House of Sormani,
Milan after the designs of Enzo Deho

BORIS CHRISTOFF *Mefistofele*
CARLO BERGONZI *Faust*
***ILVA LIGABUE *Margherita*
VERA MAGRINI *Martha*
PIERO DE PALMA *Wagner*
CHRISTA LUDWIG *Elena*
MARY MacKENZIE *Pantalis*
MARIANO CARUSO *Nereo*

Solo Dancers DOLORES LIPINSKI, ORRIN
KAYAN, PATRICIA KLEKOVIC

Conductor ANTONINO VOTTO
***Stage Director RICCARDO MORESCO
Chorus Master MICHAEL LEPORE
Choreographer RUTH PAGE
Children's Chorus CHILDREN'S CHOIR, FIRST
UNITARIAN CHURCH

LA FORZA DEL DESTINO VERDI
October 30, November 4 and 10 / In Italian

EILEEN FARRELL *Donna Leonora di Vargas*
CHRISTA LUDWIG *Preziozilla*
CARLO BERGONZI *Don Alvaro (Oct. 30 and*
Nov. 10)
DAVID POLERI *Don Alvaro (Nov. 4)*
GIAN GIACOMO GUELFI *Don Carlo di Vargas*
BORIS CHRISTOFF *Padre Guardiano*
EDWARD WARNER *Marchese di Calatrava*
RENATO CESARI *Fra Melitone*
SHARON NAWROCKI *Curra*
MICHAEL BONDON *The Mayor of*
Hornachuelos
MARIANO CARUSO *Trabucco*
BERNARD IZZO *A Surgeon*
PIERO DE PALMA *A Peddler*

Solo Dancers   PATRICIA KLEKOVIC, KENNETH
JOHNSON, ELLEN GIMPEL,
DOLORES LIPINSKI

***Conductor   CARLO FELICE CILLARIO
Stage Director   RICCARDO MORESCO
Chorus Master   MICHAEL LEPORE
Choreographer   RUTH PAGE

COSÌ FAN TUTTE   MOZART
November 1 and 3 / In Italian
Sets by courtesy of the San Francisco Opera

ELISABETH SCHWARZKOPF   Fiordiligi
CHRISTA LUDWIG   Dorabella
LEOPOLD SIMONEAU   Ferrando
WALTER BERRY   Guglielmo
RENATO CESARI   Don Alfonso
SYLVIA STAHLMAN   Despina

Conductor   PETER MAAG
Stage Director   CHRISTOPHER WEST
Chorus Master   MICHAEL LEPORE
Designed by   GEORGE JENKINS

DON GIOVANNI   MOZART
November 6, 8 and 11 / In Italian

WILLIAM WILDERMANN   The Commendatore
TERESA STICH-RANDALL   Donna Anna
LEOPOLD SIMONEAU   Don Ottavio
EBERHARD WAECHTER   Don Giovanni
WALTER BERRY   Leporello
LISA DELLA CASA   Donna Elvira (Nov. 6)
ELISABETH SCHWARZKOPF   Donna Elvira
(Nov. 8 and 11)
IRMGARD SEEFRIED   Zerlina
RENATO CESARI   Masetto

Conductor   PETER MAAG
***Stage Director   WOLFGANG WEBER
Chorus Master   MICHAEL LEPORE
Choreographer   RUTH PAGE

FIDELIO   BEETHOVEN
November 13, 17 and 22 / In German

JON VICKERS   Florestan
BIRGIT NILSSON   Leonora
WALTER BERRY   Don Fernando
HANS HOTTER   Don Pizarro
WILLIAM WILDERMANN   Rocco
IRMGARD SEEFRIED   Marcellina
RICHARD CARL KNOLL   Jacquino
JEFFREY WOLFE   Prisoner
ROBERT SMITH   Prisoner

Conductor   PETER MAAG
Stage Director   CHRISTOPHER WEST
Chorus Master   MICHAEL LEPORE

IL BARBIERE DI SIVIGLIA
ROSSINI
November 15, 18, 20 and 24 / In Italian

LUIGI ALVA   Count Almaviva
FERNANDO CORENA   Doctor Bartolo
BORIS CHRISTOFF   Basilio
***SESTO BRUSCANTINI   Figaro
BERNARD IZZO   Fiorello
GIULIETTA SIMIONATO   Rosina

VERA MAGRINI   Berta
LLOYD HARRIS   A Sergeant

Conductor   CARLO FELICE CILLARIO
Stage Director   ENRICO FRIGERIO
Chorus Master   MICHAEL LEPORE

THE HARVEST   GIANNINI
Nov. 25, 27, 29 and Dec. 1 / In English
New Production
The world premiere of THE HARVEST was the
first Lyric Opera production under the Ford
Foundation program for the promotion of
American opera.

WILLIAM WILDERMANN   Sam
MARILYN HORNE   Lora
GERAINT EVANS   Lem
RICHARD CARL KNOLL   Jesse
BARRY MORELL   Mark
ROBERT SCHMORR   Grandpa Jones
VERA MAGRINI   Sara
JEANNE DIAMOND   A Young Girl
JEFFREY WOLFE   Jason

Solo Dancers   PATRICIA KLEKOVIC, KENNETH
JOHNSON, ORRIN KAYAN,
ELLEN GIMPEL, LARRY LONG

Conductor   VITTORIO GIANNINI
Stage Director   HERBERT MACHIZ
Chorus Master   MICHAEL LEPORE
Choreographer   RUTH PAGE
Production designed by   OLIVER SMITH
Costumes designed by   OLIVER SMITH AND
HELENE PONS

1962

October 12 – November 30

PRINCE IGOR   BORODIN
October 12, 15, 20 and 24 / In Russian
New Production — gift of Mr. and Mrs. Leigh B.
Block, Mr. James C. Hemphill, Mr. Grant J. Pick,
Mrs. Clive Runnells
Broadcast by CBS-WBBM AM and FM,
as a public service
First Chicago performances

IGOR GORIN   Igor Sviatoslavitch
CONSUELO RUBIO   Jaroslavna
DAVID POLERI   Vladimir Igorevitch
BORIS CHRISTOFF   Prince Galitsky and
Konchak
CAROL SMITH   Konchakovna
RICHARD CARL KNOLL   Ovlour
RENATO CESARI   Skoula
MARIANO CARUSO   Eroshka
PRUDENCIJA BICKUS   Jaroslavna's Nurse
JEANNE DIAMOND   Polovtsian Maiden

Solo Dancers   SONIA AROVA,
**RUDOLF NUREYEV

***Conductor   OSKAR DANON
Stage Director   VLADIMIR ROSING
Chorus Master   MICHAEL LEPORE
Choreographer   RUTH PAGE
Sets and costumes designed by NICOLA BENOIS
Polovtsian dances after choreography of
MICHEL FOKINE

LA BOHEME   PICCINI
October 17, 19, 22 and 27 / In Italian

RICHARD TUCKER   Rodolfo
MARIO ZANASI   Marcello
WILLIAM WILDERMANN   Colline (Oct. 17, 19)
BORIS CHRISTOFF   Colline (Oct. 22, 27)
RENATO CESARI   Schaunard
FERNANDO CORENA   Benoit and Alcindoro
CONSUELO RUBIO   Mimi (Oct. 17, 27)
***MIETTA SIGHELE   Mimi (Oct. 19, 22)
JOAN MARIE MOYNAGH   Musetta
RICHARD CARL KNOLL   Parpignol
LESTER WAGEMAKER   Custom-House Sergeant
ROBERT SMITH   Guard

Conductor   CARLO FELICE CILLARIO
Stage Director   RICCARDO MORESCO
Chorus Master   MICHAEL LEPORE
Children's Chorus   CHILDREN'S CHOIR, FIRST
UNITARIAN CHURCH

TOSCA   PUCCINI
October 26, 29 and November 3 / In Italian

†REGINE CRESPIN   Floria Tosca
GIUSEPPE ZAMPIERI   Mario Cavaradossi
TITO GOBBI   Baron Scarpia
RENATO CESARI   Cesare Angelotti
FERNANDO CORENA   A Sacristan
MARIANO CARUSO   Spoletta
KAY CHARLES GRAVES   A Jailer
ELIZABETH FISCHER   A Shepherd Boy
BERNARD IZZO   Sciarrone

Conductor   CARLO FELICE CILLARIO
Stage Director   RICCARDO MORESCO
Chorus Master   MICHAEL LEPORE
Children's Chorus   CHILDREN'S CHOIR, FIRST
UNITARIAN CHURCH

L'ELISIR D'AMORE   DONIZETTI
October 31, November 2 and 5 / In Italian
Production through the courtesy of the
Metropolitan Opera Association, Inc.

***ALFREDO KRAUS   Nemorino
***MARIELLA ADANI   Adina
MARIO ZANASI   Belcore
FERNANDO CORENA   Dulcamara
JOAN MARIE MOYNAGH   Giannetta

Solo Dancers   PATRICIA KLEKOVIC,
KENNETH JOHNSON

Conductor   CARLO FELICE CILLARIO
Stage Director   ENRICO FRIGERIO
Chorus Master   MICHAEL LEPORE
Choreographer   RUTH PAGE
Sets and costumes designed by
ROBERT O'HEARN

LE NOZZE DI FIGARO   MOZART
November 7, 9 and 12 / In Italian

TITO GOBBI   Count Almaviva
RENATO CAPECCHI   Figaro
FERNANDO CORENA   Doctor Bartolo
MARIANO CARUSO   Don Basilio
TERESA BERGANZA   Cherubino
RENATO CESARI   Antonio
RICHARD CARL KNOLL   Don Curzio

LISA DELLA CASA *Countess Almaviva*
RITA STREICH *Susanna*
EDITH EVANS *Marcellina*
JEANNE DIAMOND *Barbarina*
PRUDENCIJA BICKUS *Peasant Girl*
ELIZABETH FISCHER *Peasant Girl*

Solo Dancers PATRICIA KLEKOVIC,
ORRIN KAYAN

Conductor PETER MAAG
Stage Director CHRISTOPHER WEST
Chorus Master MICHAEL LEPORE
Choreographer RUTH PAGE
Scenic Prod. designed by GERALD L. RITHOLZ

SAMSON ET DALILA
SAINT-SAENS
November 10, 14, 16 and 19 / In French

RITA GORR *Dalila*
***HANS KAART *Samson*
GABRIEL BACQUIER *High Priest of Dagon*
WILLIAM WILDERMANN *Abimelech*
FERNANDO CORENA *An Old Hebrew*
MARIANO CARUSO *The Philistines' Messenger*
RICHARD CARL KNOLL *1st Messenger*
BERNARD IZZO *2nd Messenger*

***Conductor* PIERRE DERVAUX
***Stage Director* ROBERT GILLES
Chorus Master MICHAEL LEPORE
Choreographer RUTH PAGE

RIGOLETTO   VERDI
November 17, 21, 23 and 26 / In Italian

RICHARD TUCKER *The Duke of Mantua*
ETTORE BASTIANINI *Rigoletto*
ROBERT SMITH *Count Ceprano*
RENATO CESARI *Count Monterone*
WILLIAM WILDERMANN *Sparafucile*
RICHARD CARL KNOLL *Matteo Borsa*
BERNARD IZZO *Cavaliere Marullo*
PRUDENCIJA BICKUS *Countess Ceprano*
GIANNA D'ANGELO *Gilda*
ELIZABETH FISCHER *Giovanna*
CAROL SMITH *Maddalena*
JEANNE DIAMOND *A Page*

Solo Dancers ELLEN EVERETT, LARRY LONG

Conductor PIERRE DERVAUX
Stage Director ENRICO FRIGERIO
Chorus Master MICHAEL LEPORE
Choreographer RUTH PAGE

ORFEO ED EURIDICE   GLUCK
November 24, 28 and 30 / In Italian
Production purchased from Royal Opera House,
Covent Garden, London — Gift of the Lyric Guild.

GABRIEL BACQUIER *Orfeo*
LISA DELLA CASA *Euridice*
RITA STREICH *Amore*

Solo Dancers MARIA TALLCHIEF, KENNETH
JOHNSON, ORRIN KAYAN,
ELLEN EVERETT

Conductor PIERRE DERVAUX
Stage Director CHRISTOPHER WEST
Chorus Master MICHAEL LEPORE
Choreographer RUTH PAGE

GALA BALLET PERFORMANCE
October 21

IDYLLE
SERRETTE, *orchestrated by Kayan*
First Chicago Performance

DOLORES LIPINSKI *White Horse*
CHARLES SCHICK *Black Horse*
LARRY LONG *Circus Horse*

Choreography GEORGE SKIBINE
Story and costumes ALWIN CAMBLE

FLOWER FESTIVAL IN GENZANO
Pas de Deux   HELSTED

Choreography AUGUST BOURNONVILLE

SONIA AROVA AND RUDOLF NUREYEV

CONCERTINO POUR TROIS
CONSTANT
First Chicago performance

Choreography RUTH PAGE

KENNETH JOHNSON, PATRICIA KLEKOVIC
ORRIN KAYAN

LE CORSAIR
Pas de Deux   DRIGO

Choreography RUDOLF NUREYEV

SONIA AROVA AND RUDOLF NUREYEV

THE MERRY WIDOW
Lehar, arranged and orchestrated
by Van Grove
Ballet adaptation by Ruth Page
and Hassard Short

SONIA AROVA *Sonia, The Merry Widow*
RUDOLF NUREYEV *Prince Danilo*
CHARLES SCHICK *Baron Popoff*
ELLEN EVERETT *Baroness Popoff*
ORRIN KAYAN *Count Jolidon*
LARRY LONG *Nish*
ANN BRADFORD *Zozo*
JEANNE ARMIN *Frou-Frou*

Choreography RUTH PAGE
Director RUTH PAGE
Conductor NEAL KAYAN
Scenery and costumes by ROLF GERARD
Costumes executed by KARINSKA

THE ANNUAL MEETING, 1963, WITH SETTINGS OF **PRINCE IGOR.**

1963

October 4 – November 29

NABUCCO   VERDI
October 4, 7, 11 and 19 / In Italian
Broadcast over CBS-WBBM AM and FM,
sponsored by Marshall Savings and Loan
Association
Production by courtesy of the Metropolitan
Opera, New York.
First Chicago Performances

***DANICA MASTILOVIC *Abigaille*
ANNA MARIA ROTA *Fenena*
***ALFONSO LA MORENA *Ismaele*
TITO GOBBI *Nabucco*
BORIS CHRISTOFF *Zaccaria*
WILLIAM WILDERMANN *High Priest*
***CARLO COSSUTTA *Abdallo*
CORINNA VOZZA *Anna*

Solo Dancer PATRICIA KLEKOVIC

Conductor BRUNO BARTOLETTI
Stage Director RICCARDO MORESCO
Chorus Master MICHAEL LEPORE
Choreographer RUTH PAGE
Production designed by TEO OTTO AND
WOLFGANG ROTH

UN BALLO IN MASCHERA   VERDI
October 5, 9, 14 and 18 / In Italian

RICHARD TUCKER *Riccardo (Oct. 5, 9 & 14)*
JON VICKERS *Riccardo (Oct. 18)*
REGINE CRESPIN *Amelia*
MARIO ZANASI *Renato*
RENATO CESARI *Samuele*
MALCOLM SMITH *Tomaso*
BERNARD IZZO *Silvano*
*LUCILLE KAILER *Oscar*
*GRACE BUMBRY *Ulrica*
*ROBERT ANGUS *Judge, Servant*

Conductor PIERRE DERVAUX
Stage Director CHRISTOPHER WEST
Chorus Master MICHAEL LEPORE
Choreographer RUTH PAGE

FAUST   GOUNOD
October 12, 16, 21 and 25 / In French
New Production — Gift of an anonymous donor

***GUY CHAUVET *Faust*
***NICOLAI GHIAUROV *Méphistophélès*
***ANDRÉA GUIOT *Marguerite*
***ROBERT MASSARD *Valentin*
ANNA MARIA ROTA *Siebel*
BERNARD IZZO *Wagner*
CORINNA VOZZA *Marthe*

Solo Dancers PATRICIA KLEKOVIC, KENNETH
JOHNSON, ORRIN KAYAN,
DOLORES LIPINSKI, CHARLES
SCHICK, ELLEN EVERETT,
LARRY LONG, JEANNE ARMIN

Conductor PIERRE DERVAUX
Stage Director ROBERT GILLES
Chorus Master MICHAEL LEPORE
Choreographer RUTH PAGE
Sets and Costumes designed by FRANCO BRAY

Ballet Costumes designed by ANDRE DELFAU
Produced in cooperation with INOPRA

FIDELIO BEETHOVEN
Oct. 23, 26, 28 and Nov. 1 / In German

JON VICKERS *Florestan (Oct. 23 & 26)*
*SEBASTIAN FEIERSINGER *Florestan (Oct. 28 &*
Nov. 1)
REGINE CRESPIN *Leonora*
RENATO CESARI *Don Fernando*
BORIS CHRISTOFF *Don Pizarro*
WILLIAM WILDERMANN *Rocco*
***HANNY STEFFEK *Marcellina*
RICHARD CARL KNOLL *Jacquino*
ROBERT ANGUS *Prisoner*
ROBERT SMITH *Prisoner*

***Conductor FRITZ RIEGER
Stage Director CHRISTOPHER WEST
Chorus Master MICHAEL LEPORE

OTELLO VERDI
Nov. 2, 4, 8 and 13 / In Italian

JON VICKERS *Otello (Nov. 2, 8 & 13)*
*DIMITER UZUNOV *Otello (Nov. 4)*
TITO GOBBI *Iago*
CARLO COSSUTTA *Cassio*
RICHARD CARL KNOLL *Roderigo*
WILLIAM WILDERMANN *Lodovico*
BERNARD IZZO *Montano*
*HOWARD NELSON *Herald*
*SENA JURINAC *Desdemona*
CORINNA VOZZA *Emilia*

Conductor BRUNO BARTOLETTI
Stage Director RICCARDO MORESCO
Chorus Master MICHAEL LEPORE
Choreographer RUTH PAGE

IL BARBIERE DI SIVIGLIA
ROSSINI *Nov. 6, 9, 11 and 15 / In Italian*

ALFREDO KRAUS *Count Almaviva*
FERNANDO CORENA *Doctor Bartolo*
BORIS CHRISTOFF *Basilio*
MARIO ZANASI *Figaro*
HOWARD NELSON *Fiorello*
TERESA BERGANZA *Rosina*
CORINNA VOZZA *Berta*
ROBERT SMITH *Sergeant*

Conductor CARLO FELICE CILLARIO
Stage Director RICCARDO MORESCO
Chorus Master MICHAEL LEPORE

TANNHÄUSER WAGNER
Nov. 16, 18, 22 and 27 / In German
*Production by courtesy of the Metropolitan
Opera, New York*

WILLIAM WILDERMANN *Hermann*
DIMITER UZUNOV *Tannhäuser*
***RAYMOND WOLANSKY *Wolfram*
CARLO COSSUTTA *Walter*
RENATO CESARI *Biterolf*
RICHARD CARL KNOLL *Heinrich*
MALCOLM SMITH *Reinmar*
REGINE CRESPIN *Elisabeth*
GRACE BUMBRY *Venus*
JEANNE DIAMOND *Shepherd*

Solo Dancers PATRICIA KLEKOVIC, KENNETH
JOHNSON, DOLORES LIPINSKI,
ELLEN EVERETT, JEANNE
ARMIN, ORRIN KAYAN,
CHARLES SCHICK, LARRY LONG.

Conductor OSKAR DANON
***Stage Director* KURT PUHLMANN
Chorus Master MICHAEL LEPORE
Choreographer RUTH PAGE
Sets and Costumes designed by ROLF GERARD

DON PASQUALE DONIZETTI
*Nov. 20, 23, 25, 27 (Student Performance)
and 29 / In Italian*
*Production by courtesy of the
Metropolitan Opera, New York*

FERNANDO CORENA *Don Pasquale*
SESTO BRUSCANTINI *Dr. Malatesta*
ALFREDO KRAUS *Ernesto*
MARIELLA ADANI *Norina*
BERNARD IZZO *A Notary*

Conductor CARLO FELICE CILLARIO
Stage Director RICCARDO MORESCO
Chorus Master MICHAEL LEPORE
Sets and costumes designed by
WOLFGANG ROTH

1964
October 9 – December 5

IL TROVATORE VERDI
October 9, 14, 17, 19 / In Italian

MARIO ZANASI *Count di Luna*
***IVO VINCO *Ferrando*
*FRANCO CORELLI *Manrico*
ROBERT SCHMORR *Ruiz*
HOWARD NELSON *An Old Gypsy*
ILVA LIGABUE *Leonora*
*ELIZABETH MANNION *Inez*
GRACE BUMBRY *Azucena*

Conductor BRUNO BARTOLETTI
Staged by CHRISTOPHER WEST
Chorus Master MICHAEL LEPORE
Production designed by MOTLEY
*This production was lent to the Lyric Opera of
Chicago by the Metropolitan Opera
Association, Inc.*

LA FAVORITA DONIZETTI
October 12, 16, 21, 24 / In Italian

SESTO BRUSCANTINI *Alfonso XI*
ALFREDO KRAUS *Ferdinand*
*JEAN DEIS *Don Gaspar*
IVO VINCO *Balthazar*
***FIORENZA COSSOTTO *Leonora di Gusman*
*LUISA DE SETT *Inez*

Solo Dancers PATRICIA KLEKOVIC, KENNETH
JOHNSON, ORRIN KAYAN,
CHARLES SCHICK, DOLORES
LIPINSKI, LARRY LONG,
JEANNE ARMIN

Conductor CARLO FELICE CILLARIO
***Staged by* RENZO FRUSCA
Chorus Master MICHAEL LEPORE

Choreographer RUTH PAGE
*Scenery of the House of Sormani, Milan after the
designs of Enzo Deho.
Costumes from Teatro alla Scala, Milan after the
designs of Alessandro Benois.*

CARMEN BIZET
*October 23, 26, 29 (Student Matinee), 31,
November 4 / In French
This production was made possible by
a generous and deeply appreciated gift of
Mrs. D. Eckhart Williams*

FRANCO CORELLI *Don Jose*
ROBERT MASSARD *Escamillo*
RENATO CESARI *El Dancairo*
*HERBERT KRAUS *El Remendado*
*MORLEY MEREDITH *Zuniga*
BERNARD IZZO *Morales*
*NICOLETTA PANNI *Micaela (Oct. 26, 29, 31
and Nov. 4)*
*IRMA GONZALES *Micaela (Oct. 23)*
*CAROL TOSCANO *Frasquita*
ELIZABETH MANNION *Mercedes*
GRACE BUMBRY *Carmen*

Solo Dancers PATRICIA KLEKOVIC, KENNETH
JOHNSON, ORRIN KAYAN,
CHARLES SCHICK, DOLORES
LIPINSKI, LARRY LONG,
JEANNE ARMIN

Conductor PIERRE DERVAUX
Staged by MARCEL LAMY
*Costumes and Scenery after the design of
PIERO ZUFFI
Chorus Master MICHAEL LEPORE
Choreographer RUTH PAGE
*Children's Choir of the First Unitarian Church
of Chicago* REV. CHRISTOPHER MOORE

DON CARLO VERDI
October 28, 30, November 2, 7 / In Italian

*LEYLA GENCER *Elisabetta di Valois*
GRACE BUMBRY *Principessa Eboli (Nov. 2 & 7)*
FIORENZA COSSOTTO *Principessa Eboli
Oct. 28 & 30)*
RICHARD TUCKER *Don Carlo*
TITO GOBBI *Rodrigo*
NICOLAI GHIAUROV *Filippo II*
***BRUNO MARANGONI *The Grand Inquisitor*
*RAYMOND MICHALSKI *A Monk*
JEANNE DIAMOND *Tebaldo*
ROBERT SCHMORR *Count Lerma*
CAROL TOSCANO *A Heavenly Voice*

Deputies K. CHARLES GRAVES, BERNARD
IZZO, ROBERT SMITH, *EDWARD
PIERSON, *RICHARD SCHREIBER,
HOWARD NELSON
Monks FRANK BAKER, LAWRENCE GRAY,
PAUL KIESGEN, WILLIAM POWERS,
MARTIN ROSEN, RICHARD
STADELMANN, KENNETH
THOMPSON, JONAS VAZNELIS

Conductor BRUNO BARTOLETTI
Staged by CHRISTOPHER WEST
Scenery designed by ROBERT FLETCHER
Chorus Master MICHAEL LEPORE

ARIADNE AUF NAXOS
November 6, 9, 14, 18 / In German

PROLOGUE
MORLEY MEREDITH   *The Major-Domo*
*THEODOR UPPMAN   *Music Master*
IRMGARD SEEFRIED   *The Composer*
*JEAN COX   *The Tenor (later Bacchus)*
ROBERT SCHMORR   *An Officer*
***GERHARD UNGER   *The Dancing Master*
ROBERT SMITH   *The Wig-maker*
BERNARD IZZO   *A Lackey*
*RERI GRIST   *Zerbinetta*
REGINE CRESPIN   *Prima Donna (later Ariadne)*
*ERICH KUNZ   *Harlequin*
HERBERT KRAUS   *Scaramuccio*
***GIORGIO TADEO   *Truffaldino*
GERHARD UNGER   *Brighella*

THE OPERA
REGINE CRESPIN   *Ariadne*
JEAN COX   *Bacchus*
CAROL TOSCANO   *Naiade*
*SHIRLEY LOVE   *Dryade* } *Nymphs*
*KAROL LORAINE   *Echo*
RERI GRIST   *Zerbinetta*
ERICH KUNZ   *Harlequin*
HERBERT KRAUS   *Scaramuccio*
GIORGIO TADEO   *Truffaldino*
GERHARD UNGER   *Brighella*

*Conductor   EUGEN JOCHUM
***Staged by   JOSEF WITT
Chorus Master   MICHAEL LEPORE
This production was lent to the Lyric Opera of Chicago by the Metropolitan Opera Association, Inc.

LA BOHEME   PUCCINI
November 8, 12, 17, 24 / In Italian

*RENATO CIONI   *Rodolfo*
SESTO BRUSCANTINI   *Marcello*
BRUNO MARANGONI   *Colline*
RENATO CESARI   *Schaunard*
*JAMES BILLINGS   *Benoit and Alcindoro*
RENATA TEBALDI   *Mimi*
LUISA DESETT   *Musetta*
HERBERT KRAUS   *Parpignol*
RICHARD SCHREIBER   *Custom-house Sergeant*
HOWARD NELSON   *Guard*

Conductor   PIERRE DERVAUX
Staged by   RENZO FRUSCA
Chorus Master   MICHAEL LEPORE
Children's Choir of the First Unitarian Church of Chicago   REV. CHRISTOPHER MOORE

TOSCA   PUCCINI
November 27, 30, December 2, 5 / In Italian

REGINE CRESPIN   *Floria Tosca*
RICHARD TUCKER   *Mario Cavaradossi*
TITO GOBBI   *Baron Scarpia*
RENATO CESARI   *Cesare Angelotti*
GIORGIO TADEO   *A Sacristan*
ROBERT SCHMORR   *Spoletta*
BERNARD IZZO   *Sciarrone*
K. CHARLES GRAVES   *A Gaoler*
ELIZABETH FISCHER   *A Shepherd Boy*

Conductor   BRUNO BARTOLETTI

Staged by   RICCARDO MORESCO
Chorus Master   MICHAEL LEPORE
Children's Choir of the First Unitarian Church of Chicago   REV. CHRISTOPHER MOORE

DON GIOVANNI   MOZART
November 16, 20, 22, 25 / In Italian

BRUNO MARANGONI   *The Commendatore*
TERESA STICH-RANDALL   *Donna Anna*
ALFREDO KRAUS   *Don Ottavio*
NICOLAI GHIAUROV   *Don Giovanni*
ERICH KUNZ   *Leporello*
*PHYLLIS CURTIN   *Donna Elvira*
NICOLETTA PANNI   *Zerlina*
THEODOR UPPMAN   *Masetto*

Conductor   JOSEPH KRIPS
Staged By   WOLFGANG WEBER
Costumes designed by   PETER HALL
Sets designed by   FRANCO ZEFFIRELLI
Chorus Master   MICHAEL LEPORE
Choreographer   RUTH PAGE
This production was lent to the Lyric Opera of Chicago by the Dallas Civic Opera.

LA CENERENTOLA   ROSSINI
November 11, 13, 19 (Student Matinee), 21, 23 / In Italian

***RENZO CASELLATO   *Don Ramiro*
SESTO BRUSCANTINI   *Dandini*
GIORGIO TADEO   *Don Magnifico*
LUISA DeSETT   *Clorinda*
ELIZABETH MANNION   *Thisbe*
TERESA BERGANZA   *Angelina*
RENATO CESARI   *Alidoro*

Conductor   CARLO FELICE CILLARIO
Staged by   RICCARDO MORESCO
Chorus Master   MICHAEL LEPORE

1965

October 8 – December 8

MEFISTOFELE   BOITO
October 8, 13, 16, 18 / In Italian

NICOLAI GHIAUROV   *Mefistofele*
ALFREDO KRAUS   *Faust*
RENATA TEBALDI   *Margherita*
MARY MacKENZIE   *Martha*
PIERO DePALMA   *Wagner*
***ELENA SULIOTIS   *Elena*
*MARGARET ROGGERO   *Pantalis*
HERBERT KRAUS   *Nereo*

Solo Dancers ACT I: DOLORES LIPINSKI, ORRIN KAYAN
ACT II: KENNETH JOHNSON, ORRIN KAYAN, CHARLES SCHICK, LARRY LONG, JUDITH THELEN
ACT IV: PATRICIA KLEKOVIC

Conductor   **NINO SANZOGNO
Staged by   **FILIPPO CRIVELLI
Chorus Master   MICHAEL LEPORE
Choreographer   RUTH PAGE
Chicago Children's Choir First Unitarian Church

of Chicago and the Institute for Cultural Development   REV. CHRISTOPHER MOORE
Scenery of the House of Sormani, Milan after the designs of Enzo Deho

SIMON BOCCANEGRA   VERDI
October 11, 15, 20, 23 / In Italian

TITO GOBBI   *Simon Boccanegra*
ILVA LIGABUE   *Amelia Grimaldi*
*RAFFAELE ARIE   *Jacopo Fiesco*
RENATO CIONI   *Gabriele Adorno*
RENATO CESARI   *Paolo Albiani*
RAYMOND MICHALSKI   *Pietro*
PIERO DePALMA   *A Captain*
ELIZABETH FISCHER   *A Servant of Amelia*

Conductor   BRUNO BARTOLETTI
Staged by   **TITO GOBBI
Chorus Master   MICHAEL LEPORE
Scenery of the House of Sormani, Milan after the designs of Giancarlo Bartolini-Salimbeni

LA BOHEME   PUCCINI
October 22, 25, 27, 30 / In Italian

FRANCO CORELLI   *Rodolfo*
SESTO BRUSCANTINI   *Marcello*
RAFFAELE ARIE   *Colline*
RENATO CESARI   *Schaunard*
GIORGIO TADEO   *Benoit*
GIORGIO TADEO   *Alcindoro*
*MIRELLA FRENI   *Mimi*
***EDITH MARTELLI   *Musetta*
HERBERT KRAUS   *Parpignol*
BERNARD IZZO   *Custom-house Sergeant*
HOWARD NELSON   *Guard*

Conductor   CARLO FELICE CILLARIO
Staged by   RENZO FRUSCA
Chorus Master   MICHAEL LEPORE
Chicago Children's Choir First Unitarian Church of Chicago and the Institute for Cultural Development   REV. CHRISTOPHER MOORE

MADAMA BUTTERFLY   PUCCINI
October 29, November 1, 4, 6, 10 / In Italian

RENATA SCOTTO   *Madama Butterfly*
*NEDDA CASEI   *Suzuki*
ELIZABETH FISCHER   *Kate Pinkerton*
RENATO CIONI   *B. F. Pinkerton*
SESTO BRUSCANTINI   *Sharpless*
PIERO DePALMA   *Goro*
RENATO CESARI   *Prince Yamadori*
RAYMOND MICHALSKI   *The Bonze*
BERNARD IZZO   *The Imperial Commissioner*
HOWARD NELSON   *The Official Registrar*

Conductor   CARLO FELICE CILLARIO
Staged by   FILIPPO CRIVELLI
Chorus Master   MICHAEL LEPORE

SAMSON ET DALILA
SAINT-SAENS
November 3, 5, 8, 13 / In French

GRACE BUMBRY   *Dalila*
JON VICKERS   *Samson*

SESTO BRUSCANTINI *High Priest of Dagon*
MORLEY MEREDITH *Abimelech*
RAYMOND MICHALSKI *An Old Hebrew*
HERBERT KRAUS *The Philistines' Messenger*
*STEFAN WICIK *1st Philistine*
BERNARD IZZO *2nd Philistine*

Solo Dancers PATRICIA KLEKOVIC, KENNETH
JOHNSON, ORRIN KAYAN,
DOLORES LIPINSKI, CHARLES
SCHICK, LARRY LONG, JUDITH
THELEN

Conductor JEAN FOURNET
Staged by JOSEF WITT
Chorus Master MICHAEL LEPORE
Choreographer RUTH PAGE

DOUBLE BILL / *November 12, 15, 17, 20*

L'HEURE ESPAGNOLE RAVEL
First Chicago performances / In French

TERESA BERGANZA *Concepcion*
ALFREDO KRAUS *Gonzalve*
HERBERT KRAUS *Torquemada*
SESTO BRUSCANTINI *Ramiro*
GIORGIO TADEO *Don Inigo*

Conductor JEAN FOURNET
Staged by JOSEF WITT
*Scenery of the House of Sormani, Milan and
Costumes of the Casa d'Arte Cerratelli, Florence
after the designs of Emanuele Luzzati*

CARMINA BURNANA ORFF
*First Chicago performances / In Latin and
Medieval German*

Singers
EDITH MARTELLI *Soprano*
ALFREDO KRAUS *Tenor*
SESTO BRUSCANTINI *Baritone*

Dancers
FORTUNA IMPERATRIX MUNDI
*HARALD KREUTZBERG *Death*
MARGOT GRIMMER *Fortuna*
CHARLES SCHICK *King*
DOLORES LIPINSKI *Prostitute*
LARRY LONG *Peasant Man*
NANCY ANNA MILLER *Bourgeois Woman*
JERRY KENT *Bishop*

UF DEM ANGER
HARALD KREUTZBERG *Winter*
HARALD KREUTZBERG *Chramer*

Solo Couple PATRICIA KLEKOVIC, CHARLES
SCHICK
Solo Dancer DOLORES LIPINSKI
Spring Maidens JUDITH THELEN, NANCY
ANNA MILLER,
VIOLETTA KAROSAS

COURS D'AMOURS
Lovers PATRICIA KLEKOVIC,
KENNETH JOHNSON
Court of Love VICKI FISERA, RAYA LEE,

MADELEINE ROZAK, SARAH
JANE SMITH, JOHN
LANDOWSKI, PAUL KRUMM,
GIORGIO FILIATO, RICHARD
LICHTER

BLANZIFLOR ET HELENA
HARALD KREUTZBERG *Major Domo*

FORTUNA IMPERATRIX MUNDI
FULL COMPANY

Conductor JEAN FOURNET
Staged by JOSEF WITT
Chorus Master MICHAEL LEPORE
Supplementary Chorus MEMBERS OF
ROCKEFELLER
CHAPEL CHOIR
Lyric Opera Children's Chorus MARY MAJ,
LAURENCE DAVIS
Choreographer RUTH PAGE
*Scenery of the House of Sormani, Milan and
Costumes of the Casa d'Arte Cerratelli, Florence
after the designs of Emanuele Luzzati*

WOZZECK BERG
*First Chicago performances
November 19, 22, December 1 / In English
This production was designed by Luciano
Damiani for the Teatro Comunale di Firenze*

GERAINT EVANS *Wozzeck*
***NICOLA TAGGER *The Drum-major*
RICHARD CARL KNOLL *Andrew*
*HERBERT HANDT *The Captain*
MORLEY MEREDITH *The Doctor*
PETER HARROWER *First Workman*
BERNARD IZZO *Second Workman*
HERBERT KRAUS *A Fool*
*HELGA PILARCZYK *Marie (Nov. 22)*
BRENDA LEWIS *Marie (Nov. 19 & Dec. 1)*
MARGARET ROGGERO *Margret*
STEFAN WICIK *A Soldier*

Conductor BRUNO BARTOLETTI
Staged by VIRGINIO PUECHER
Chorus Master MICHAEL LEPORE
Lyric Opera Children's Chorus MARY MAJ,
LAURENCE DAVIS
Choreographer RUTH PAGE

AIDA VERDI
November 24, 27, 30, December 3, 6 / In Italian

LEONTYNE PRICE *Aida (Nov. 24, 27, 30
& Dec. 3)*
*ELLA LEE *Aida (Dec. 6)*
FIORENZA COSSOTTO *Amneris*
ETTORE BASTIANINI *Amonasro (Nov. 24, 27,
30 & Dec. 6)*
*ANSELMO COLZANI *Amonasro (Dec. 3)*
***GIORGIO CASELLATO *Radames*
IVO VINCO *Ramphis*
RAYMOND MICHALSKI *King of Egypt*
HERBERT KRAUS *Messenger*
*DOLORES WHITE *Priestess*

Solo Dancers (Triumphal Scene)
PATRICIA KLEKOVIC,
KENNETH JOHNSON
Solo Dancer, ACT II, Scene I ORRIN KAYAN

Conductor CARLO FELICE CILLARIO
Staged by RENZO FRUSCA
Chorus Master MICHAEL LEPORE
Choreographer RUTH PAGE
*Scenery of the House of Sormani, Milan after the
designs of Enzo Deho*

RIGOLETTO VERDI
*November 26, 29, December 4, 8; Student
Matinees Dec. 2 & 6 / In Italian*

ALFREDO KRAUS *The Duke of Mantua*
CORNELL MacNEIL *Rigoletto (Nov. 26, 29
& Dec. 2)*
SESTO BRUSCANTINI *Rigoletto (Dec. 4, 6, & 8)*
*RICHARD WRIGHT *Count Ceprano*
RAYMOND MICHALSKI *Count Monterone*
IVO VINCO *Sparafucile*
HERBERT KRAUS *Matteo Borsa*
BERNARD IZZO *Cavaliere Marullo*
DOLORES WHITE *Countess Ceprano*
RENATA SCOTTO *Gilda*
ELIZABETH FISCHER *Giovanna*
NEDDA CASEI *Maddalena*
JEANNE DIAMOND *A Page*

Solo Dancers JUDITH THELEN, LARRY LONG

Conductor BRUNO BARTOLETTI
Staged by RENZO FRUSCA
Chorus Master MICHAEL LEPORE
Choreographer RUTH PAGE
*Scenery of the House of Sormani, Milan after the
designs of Ercole Sormani*

1966

October 7 – December 15

BORIS GODUNOV
MUSSORGSKY
*October 7, 12, 15, 17 / In Russian
The 1966 presentation of "Boris Godunov" is
made possible by the most generous and deeply
appreciated gift of Mrs. John L. Kellogg in
memory of her son, Thomas Updegraff
Flanner IV.*

NICOLAI GHIAUROV *Boris Godounov*
SYLVIA STAHLMAN *Feodor* ⎫
*LORNA HAYWOOD *Xenia* ⎬ *His Children*
MARGARET ROGGERO *The old Nurse* ⎭
***MILEN PAUNOV *Prince Shuisky*
†LOTHAR OSTENBURG *Andrey Tchelkalov*
WILLIAM WILDERMANN *Pimen*
CARLO COSSUTTA *The Pretender Dimitri*
*RUZA POSPINOV *Marina Mnishek*
***LADKO KOROSEC *Varlaam* ⎫
HERBERT KRAUS *Missail* ⎬ *Vagabonds*
*FLAVIA ACOSTA *The Hostess of the Inn*
PETER HARROWER *Nikitich*
***ERMANNO LORENZI *The Idiot*
HOWARD NELSON ⎫
BERNARD IZZO ⎬ *Two Jesuits*
STEFAN WICIK *Khrushchov*
PETER HARROWER *A Guard*
ROBERT SMITH *Mitiukh*
STEFAN WICIK *A Boyar*
JEAN EVANS *A Peasant*

Conductor BRUNO BARTOLETTI
Staged by **PETER SHTARBANOV
*Costumes and scenery after the design
of Nicola Benois*
Chorus Master MICHAEL LEPORE
Lyric Opera Children's Chorus
LAURENCE DAVIS
Choreographer RUTH PAGE

OTELLO VERDI
October 14, 16, 19, 22 / In Italian

JON VICKERS *Otello (Oct. 14 & 22)*
***CHARLES CRAIG *Otello (Oct. 16 & 19)*
TITO GOBBI *Iago*
ERMANNO LORENZI *Cassio*
*FREDERIC MAYER *Roderigo*
WILLIAM WILDERMANN *Lodovico*
BERNARD IZZO *Montano*
HOWARD NELSON *A Herald*
*RAINA KABAIVANSKA *Desdemona*
MARGARET ROGGERO *Emilia (Oct. 14, 19,
& 22)*
*BISERKA CVEJIC *Emilia (Oct. 16)*

Conductor NINO SANZOGNO
Staged by TITO GOBBI
*Costumes and scenery after the designs of
Giancarlo Bartolini-Salimbeni*
Chorus Master MICHAEL LEPORE

LA GIOCONDA PONCHIELLI
October 21, 24, 26, 29 / In Italian

ELENA SULIOTIS *La Gioconda*
***ELENA ZILIO *La Cieca*
IVO VINCO *Alvise Badoero*
FIORENZA COSSOTTO *Laura*
RENATO CIONI *Enzo Grimaldo*
GIAN GIACOMO GUELFI *Barnaba*
BERNARD IZZO *Zuane*
ROBERT SMITH *A Pilot*
HERBERT KRAUS *Isepo*
HOWARD NELSON *A Monk*
BERNARD IZZO *A Singer*
HERBERT KRAUS, HOWARD NELSON
Off Stage Voices

Solo Dancers CARLA FRACCI (Oct. 21 only)
PATRICIA KLEKOVIC (Oct. 24,
26 & 29), KENNETH JOHNSON

Conductor NINO SANZOGNO
Staged by RENZO FRUSCA
Chorus Master MICHAEL LEPORE
Lyric Opera Children's Chorus
LAURENCE DAVIS
Choreographer RUTH PAGE

DOUBLE BILL / *October 28, 31,
November 2, 5*

LA GIARA CASELLA
Ballet in One Act
First Chicago performances

PATRICIA KLEKOVIC *Nela*
†ERIK BRUHN *A Youth*
CHARLES SCHICK *Don Lollo*
LARRY LONG *Zi'Dima*
LYRIC OPERA CORPS DE BALLET *Townspeople*

ERMANNO LORENZI *Tenor*

Conductor NINO SANZOGNO
Staged by **BEPPE MENEGATTI
Choreographer RUTH PAGE
*This production of "La Giara" was lent to the
Lyric Opera of Chicago by the Maggio Musicale
Fiorentino, Teatro Comunale di Firenze. Scenery
and costumes designed by Renato Guttuso*

CAVALLERIA RUSTICANA
MASCAGNI / *In Italian*

GRACE BUMBRY *Santuzza*
FLAVIA ACOSTA *Lucia*
GIAN GIACOMO GUELFI *Alfio*
***GIAN FRANCO CECCHELE *Turiddu*
MARGARET ROGGERO *Lola*

Conductor NINO SANZOGNO
Staged by RENZO FRUSCA
Chorus Master MICHAEL LEPORE

L'INCORONAZIONE DI POPPEA
MONTEVERDI
*First Chicago performances
November 4, 7, 9, 12 / In Italian*

*EVELYN LEAR *Poppea*
*ANDRE MONTAL *Nerone*
LOTHAR OSTENBURG *Ottone*
TERESA BERGANZA *Ottavia*
SYLVIA STAHLMAN *Drusilla*
WILLIAM WILDERMANN *Seneca*
*ORALIA DOMINGUEZ *Arnalta*
FLAVIA ACOSTA *Ottavia's Nurse*
MARGARET ROGGERO *Valletto*
FREDERIC MAYER *Lucano*
HOWARD NELSON *Liberto*
JEFF MORRIS } *Two Soldiers*
ERMANNO LORENZI }

Solo Dancers DOLORES LIPINSKI,
ORRIN KAYAN

Conductor BRUNO BARTOLETTI
Staged by *LUCIANA NOVARO
Chorus Master MICHAEL LEPORE
Choreographer RUTH PAGE
*The complete production of the Dallas Civic
Opera Company, Inc. of "The Coronation of
Poppea." Costumes designed by Peter Hall.
Settings and properties designed by Attilio
Colonnello*

LES PÊCHEURS DE PERLES
BIZET
November 11, 14, 16, 19 / In French

***CHRISTIANE EDA-PIERRE *Leïla*
ALFREDO KRAUS *Nadir*
SESTO BRUSCANTINI *Zurga*
*NICOLA GHIUSELEV *Nourabad*

Solo Dancers PATRICIA KLEKOVIC,
KENNETH JOHNSON

Conductor JEAN FOURNET
Staged by FILIPPO CRIVELLI
*Scenery and Costumes after the designs
of Peter Hall*
Chorus Master MICHAEL LEPORE
Choreographer RUTH PAGE

DIE ZAUBERFLÖTE MOZART
November 18, 21, 23, 26 / In German

†ERNST HAEFLIGER *Tamino*
*RITA SHANE
LORNA HAYWOOD } *Three ladies in attendance
on the Queen of the Night*
***SABINE ZIMMER
ERICH KUNZ *Papageno*
MADY MESPLE *Queen of the Night*
JEFF MORRIS *Monostatos*
*CLAIRE WATSON *Pamina*
CAROL TOSCANO
JEANNE DIAMOND } *Three Genii*
*JEAN KRAFT
HANS HOTTER *The Orator*
***KARL RIDDERBUSCH *Sarastro*
*ARNOLD VOKETAITIS } *Two Priests*
FREDERIC MAYER
***OLIVERA MILJAKOVIC *Papagena*
FREDERIC MAYER } *Two Men in Armor*
HOWARD NELSON

Conductor EUGEN JOCHUM
Staged by *HERBERT GRAF
Chorus Master MICHAEL LEPORE
Choreographer RUTH PAGE
*This production of "Die Zauberflöte" was lent
to the Lyric Opera of Chicago by the Grand
Théâtre de Geneve. Production designed
by Oscar Kokoschka*

ITALIAN FLOOD RELIEF
BENEFIT CONCERT
November 20
Singers:
SESTO BRUSCANTINI
ORALIA DOMÍNGUEZ
NICOLA GHIUSELEV
ERNST HAEFLIGER
ALFREDO KRAUS
ADRIANA MALIPONTE
KARL RIDDERBUSCH
MARGHERITA RINALDI
CLAIRE WATSON
WILLIAM WILDERMAN

Conductors and Accompanists:
BRUNO BARTOLETTI
LAURENCE DAVIS
GIULIO FAVARIO
WILLIAM HUGHES
EUGEN JOCHUM
MICHAEL LEPORE, *Chorus Master*
EDOARDO MUELLER
MARIO ROSSI
THE LYRIC OPERA CHORUS
THE LYRIC OPERA ORCHESTRA

Dancers:
PATRICIA KLEKOVIC
KENNETH JOHNSON

LA TRAVIATA VERDI
*November 25, 28 & 30 December 2, 5, 7, 10
(Student Matinees Dec. 13 & 15) / In Italian*

MARGHERITA RINALDI *Violetta Valéry
(Nov. 25, 28, 30)*
*ADRIANA MALIPONTE *Violetta Valéry (Dec. 2,
5, 7, 10, 13 & 15)*

ELENA ZILIO   *Flora Bervoix*
JEAN KRAFT   *Annina*
ALFREDO KRAUS   *Alfredo Germont*
SESTO BRUSCANTINI   *Giorgio Germont*
FREDERIC MAYER   *Gastone de Letorières*
ROBERT SMITH   *Baron Douphol*
BERNARD IZZO   *Marquis d'Obigny*
ARNOLD VOKETAITIS   *Doctor Grenvil*

Solo Dancers   DOLORES LIPINSKI, LARRY
LONG

**Conductor   MARIO ROSSI
Staged by   BEPPE MENEGATTI
*Costumes and scenery after the designs
of Peter Hall*
Chorus Master   MICHAEL LEPORE
Choreographer   RUTH PAGE

ANGEL OF FIRE   PROKOFIEV
First Chicago performances
*December 3, 6 (Student Performance), 9, 12
& 14 / In English*

FLAVIA ACOSTA   *The Hostess*
*NORMAN MITTELMANN   *Ruprecht*
*FELICIA WEATHERS   *Renata*
BERNARD IZZO   *A Laborer*
MARGARET ROGGERO   *A Fortuneteller*
FREDERIC MAYER   *Jacob Glock*
HERBERT KRAUS   *Agrippa*
BERNARD IZZO   *Matthew*
FREDERIC MAYER   *A Physician*
ROBERT SMITH   *An Innkeeper*
ANDRE MONTAL   *Mephistopheles*
LOTHAR OSTENBURG   *Dr. Faustus*
*SHEILA NADLER   *The Abbess*
JEANNE DIAMOND ⎫
DOLORES WHITE   ⎬ *Two Young Nuns*
WILLIAM WILDERMANN   *The Inquisitor*

Conductor   BRUNO BARTOLETTI
Staged by   VIRGINIO PUECHER
Chorus Master   MICHAEL LEPORE
*This production of "Angel Of Fire" was lent to
the Lyric Opera of Chicago by the Teatro
dell'Opera, Rome. Costumes and scenery
designed by Luciano Damiani.*

1968

September 27 – December 14

SALOME   R. STRAUSS
September 27, 30; October 4, 9, 12 / In German

*HANS HOPF   *Herod Antipas*
ASTRID VARNAY   *Herodias*
FELICIA WEATHERS   *Salome*
+GERD NIENSTEDT   *Jokanaan*
*HARRY THEYARD   *Narraboth*
*DEBORAH KIEFFER   *The Page of Herodias*
*DALE MALONE ⎫
ERMANNO LORENZI ⎪
*BERNARD FITCH   ⎬ *Five Jews*
*JOHN WALKER ⎪
*JOSEF GUSTERN ⎭
*HERSCHELE GARBER ⎫ *Two Nazarenes*
ARNOLD VOKETAITIS ⎭

*EUGENE GREEN ⎫ *Two Soldiers*
ROBERT SMITH ⎭
*PETER VAN GINKEL   *A Cappadocian*
*ELSA CHARLSTON   *A Slave*

Conductor   BRUNO BARTOLETTI
Staged by   VIRGINIO PUECHER
Lighting designed by   JOHN HARVEY
*This production of "Salome" was lent to the
Lyric Opera of Chicago by the Metropolitan
Opera of New York. Scenery and costumes
designed by Rudolf Heinrich. This production of
"Salome" was made possible by a generous gift
to the Metropolitan Opera from the Gramma
Fisher Foundation, Marshalltown, Iowa.*

NORMA   BELLINI
October 2, 5, 7, 14, 18, 23 / In Italian

GIANFRANCO CECCHELE   *Pollione*
IVO VINCO   *Oroveso*
ELENA SULIOTIS   *Norma*
FIORENZA COSSOTTO   *Adalgisa*
*DEBORAH KIEFFER   *Clotilde*
DALE MALONE   *Flavio*

Conductor   NINO SANZOGNO
Staged by   LUCIANA NOVARO
Chorus Master   MICHAEL LEPORE
Supplementary Chorus   GIULIO FAVARIO
Lighting designed by   JOHN HARVEY
*The Teatro alla Scala of Milan Production of
"Norma." Scenery and costumes designed by
Salvatore Fiume.*

TOSCA   PUCCINI
October 11, 16, 19, 25, 28 / In Italian

*ANTONIETTA STELLA   *Floria Tosca*
RENATO CIONI   *Mario Cavaradossi*
GIAN GIACOMO GUELFI   *Baron Scarpia*
PETER VAN GINKEL   *Angelotti*
ARNOLD VOKETAITIS   *A Sacristan*
ERMANNO LORENZI   *Spoletta*
BERNARD IZZO   *Sciarrone*
ROBERT SMITH   *A Jailer*
DEBORAH KIEFFER   *A Shepherd Boy*

Conductor   BRUNO BARTOLETTI
Production staged by   **MAURO BOLOGNINI
Realized by   FRANCO GUANDALINI
Chorus Master   MICHAEL LEPORE
Children's Chorus   LAURENCE DAVIS
Lighting designed by   JOHN HARVEY
*The Teatro dell'Opera di Roma production of
"Tosca" Scenery designed by Adolf Hohenstein.
Costumes designed by Anna Anni.*

FALSTAFF   VERDI
October 21, 26, 30; November 1, 4, 8 / In Italian

TITO GOBBI   *Sir John Falstaff*
*OTTAVIO GARAVENTA   *Fenton*
NORMAN MITTELMANN   *Ford*
ERMANNO LORENZI   *Dr. Cajus*
*FLORINDO ANDREOLLI   *Bardolph*
***PAOLO WASHINGTON   *Pistol*
RAINA KABAIVANSKA   *Alice Ford*
*LYDIA MARIMPIETRI   *Nanetta*
***STEFANIA MALAGÙ   *Mistress Meg Page*
ORALIA DOMÍNGUEZ   *Dame Quickly*

Conductor   NINO SANZOGNO
Original Production Staged by   FRANCO
ZEFFIRELLI
Staged for Chicago by   TITO GOBBI
Choreographer   RUTH PAGE
Chorus Master   MICHAEL LEPORE
Lighting Designed by   JOHN HARVEY
*The Teatro dell'Opera di Roma production of
"Falstaff." Scenery and costumes designed by
Franco Zeffirelli.*

UN BALLO IN MASCHERA   VERDI
*November 2, 6, 9, 11, 15, 18 (Student
Performance) / In Italian*

RENATO CIONI   *Riccardo*
*LUISA MARAGLIANO   *Amelia*
*PETER GLOSSOP   *Renato*
PAOLO WASHINGTON   *Samuele*
PETER VAN GINKEL   *Tomaso*
*RONALD COMBS   *Silvano*
SYLVIA STAHLMAN   *Oscar*
***FRANCA MATTIUCCI   *Ulrica*
BERNARD FITCH   *Judge*
BERNARD FITCH   *A Servant to Amelia*

Solo Dancers   PATRICIA KLEKOVIC, ORRIN
KAYAN

Conductor   NINO SANZOGNO
Staged by   RENZO FRUSCA
Choreographer   RUTH PAGE
Chorus Master   MICHAEL LEPORE
Lighting designed by   JOHN HARVEY

DOUBLE BILL / *November 13, 16, 20,
22, 25, 30; December 3 (Student
Performance)*

LE ROSSIGNOL   STRAVINSKY / *In
French*

DANCERS
CARLA FRACCI   *The Nightingale*
KENNETH JOHNSON   *The Fisherman*
LARRY LONG   *The Mechanical Nightingale*
ORRIN KAYAN   *Death*
JOHN LANDOVSKI   *Bearer*
RAYA LEE   *Chinese March Soloist*
DOLORES LIPINSKI   *Chinese March Soloist*
ORRIN KAYAN   *Chinese March Soloist*

SINGERS
CHRISTIANE EDA-PIERRE   *The Nightingale*
STEFANIA MALAGÙ   *The Cook*
OTTAVIO GARAVENTA   *The Fisherman*
PETER VAN GINKEL   *The Emperor of China*
PAOLO WASHINGTON   *The Chamberlain*
ARNOLD VOKETAITIS   *The Bonze*
ORALIA DOMÍNGUEZ   *Death*
*JOHN WALKER   *Japanese Envoy*
BERNARD IZZO   *Japanese Envoy*
BERNARD FITCH   *Japanese Envoy*
DOLORES WHITE   *Soprano*
*ANNE PORAYKO   *Alto*
*ROBERT JOHNSON   *Tenor*

Conductor   JEAN FOURNET
Staged and choreographed by
LUCIANA NOVARO

1969

September 26 – December 13

Scenery and costumes designed by
EMANUELE LUZZATI
Chorus Master   MICHAEL LEPORE
Lighting designed by   JOHN HARVEY

OEDIPUS REX   STRAVINSKY / In
Latin and English

*WILLIAM MARSHALL   Speaker
MIRTO PICCHI   Oedipus
ORALIA DOMÍNGUEZ   Jocasta
DONALD GRAMM   Creon
PAOLO WASHINGTON   Tiresias
JOHN WALKER   The Shepherd
DONALD GRAMM   The Messenger
PETER VAN GINKEL   A Guard

Conductor   JEAN FOURNET
Staged by   LUIGI SQUARZINA AND GIAN
PIETRO CALASSO
Chorus Master   MICHAEL LEPORE
Lighting designed by   JOHN HARVEY
The Teatro dell'Opera di Roma production of
"Oedipus Rex." Scenery and Costumes designed
by Giacomo Manzù.

DON PASQUALE   DONIZETTI
November 23, 27; December 2, 4, 7, 13 (Student
Matinee and evening performances on
December 2) / In Italian

GERAINT EVANS   Don Pasquale (Nov. 23, 27;
Dec. 2, 4)
PAOLO WASHINGTON   Don Pasquale
(Dec. 7, 13)
SESTO BRUSCANTINI   Doctor Malatesta
ALFREDO KRAUS   Ernesto
RERI GRIST   Norina
BERNARD IZZO   Notary

Conductor   BRUNO BARTOLETTI
Staged by   BEPPE MENEGATTI
Scenery and Costumes after the design of
ANNA ANNI
Chorus Master   MICHAEL LEPORE
Lighting designed by   JOHN HARVEY

MANON LESCAUT   PUCCINI
December 6, 8, 9, 11, 14 / In Italian

LUISA MARAGLIANO   Manon Lescaut
***ALBERTO RINALDI   Lescaut
*PLACIDO DOMINGO   Chevalier des Grieux (Dec.
6, 8, 11, 14)
MICHELE MOLESE   Chevalier des Grieux
(Dec. 9)
CARLO BADIOLI   Geronte di Ravior
ERMANNO LORENZI   Edmondo
BERNARD IZZO   The Innkeeper
FLORINDO ANDREOLLI   A Music Master
*HUGUETTE TOURANGEAU   A Musician
FLORINDO ANDREOLLI   A Lamplighter
RONALD COMBS   A Naval Captain
BERNARD IZZO   A Sergeant of Archers

Conductor   BRUNO BARTOLETTI
Staged by   SANDRO SEQUI
Chorus Master   MICHAEL LEPORE
Lighting designed by   ARTHUR CALLAGHAN
The Teatro Massimo di Palermo production of
"Manon Lescaut." Scenery designed by Fiorella
Mariani. Costumes designed by David Walker.

KHOVANSHCHINA   MUSSORGSKY
September 26, 29, October 3, 8, 11, 17 (Student
Performance) / In Russian

NICOLAI GHIAUROV   Prince Ivan Khovansky
HARRY THEYARD   Prince Andrew Khovansky
***LUBOMIR BODUROV   Prince Vassily Galitsin
NORMAN MITTELMANN   The Boyar Shaklovity
***BORIS SHTOKOLOV   Dositheus
RUZA POSPINOV-BALDANI   Martha
FLORINDO ANDREOLLI   The Scrivener
*CLARICE CARSON   Emma
BERNARD IZZO   Varsonofiev
EUGENE GREEN   Kouzka
RICHARD BEST
*CHARLES KOEHN   } Two Streltsy
*CLIFTON WARE   Streshniev
*ANAMARIE SARAZIN   Solo Dancer

Conductor   BRUNO BARTOLETTI
**Staged by   NICOLA BENOIS AND
SONJA FRISELL
**Scenery and costumes designed by
NICOLA BENOIS
Choreographer   RUTH PAGE
Chorus Master   MICHAEL LEPORE
Supplementary Chorus   GIULIO FAVARIO
Lighting Designed by   JOHN HARVEY

MACBETH   VERDI
October 1, 4, 6, 10, 15, 18 / In Italian

GIAN GIACOMO GUELFI   Macbeth
*SIMON ESTES   Banquo
GRACE BUMBRY   Lady Macbeth
*SYLVIA COOPER   Lady-in-waiting to
Lady Macbeth
*BERNABE MARTI   Macduff
*ROBERT THOMAS   Malcolm (Oct. 1, 4, 6, 10)
LUBOMIR BODUROV   Malcolm (Oct. 15, 18)
PETER VAN GINKEL   A Physician
BERNARD IZZO   Servant to Macbeth
CHARLES KOEHN   Assassin
BERNARD IZZO   First Apparition
***ROBERT WILLIAMS   Second Apparition
***DAVID DELL   Third Apparaition

Conductor   BURNO BARTOLETTI
Staged by   DOUGLAS CAMPBELL
Chorus Master   MICHAEL LEPORE
Lighting Designed by   JOHN HARVEY
The complete production of the Dallas Civic
Opera, Inc. of "Macbeth." Scenery and costumes
designed by PETER HALL.

MADAMA BUTTERFLY   PUCCINI
October 13, 22, 25, 27, 31, December 4,
7 (Student Performance) / In Italian

FELICIA WEATHERS   Madama Butterfly
*DOROTHY KREBILL   Suzuki
SYLVIA COOPER   Kate Pinkerton
RENATO CIONI   B. F. Pinkerton
ALBERTO RINALDI   Sharpless
FLORINDO ANDREOLLI   Goro
BERNARD IZZO   Prince Yamadori
PETER VAN GINKEL   The Bonze

CHARLES KOEHN   The Imperial Commissioner
RICHARD BEST   The Official Registrar

***Conductor   ARGEO QUADRI
*Staged by   YOSHIO AOYAMA
Chorus Master   MICHAEL LEPORE
Lighting Designed by   JOHN HARVEY
The Metropolitan Opera National Company
production of "Madama Butterfly," lent to
the Lyric Opera of Chicago by the Metropolitan
Opera of New York. Scenery and costumes
designed by Ming Cho Lee.

DER FLIEGENDE HOLLÄNDER
WAGNER
October 21, 24, 29, November 3, 7, 15 / In German

*MARTTI TALVELA   Daland
THOMAS STEWART   The Dutchman
ROBERT THOMAS   The Steersman
JEAN COX   Erik
*CORINNE CURRY   Mary
*ANJA SILJA   Senta

**Conductor   CHRISTOPH VON DOHNANYI
*Staged by   RENATE EBERMANN
Scenery and costumes designed by
WOLF SIEGFRIED WAGNER
Chorus Master   MICHAEL LEPORE
Supplementary Chorus   GIULIO FAVARIO
Lighting designed by   JOHN HARVEY

I PURITANI   BELLINI
November 1, 5, 8, 14, 17 / In Italian

PETER VAN GINKEL   Lord Walter Walton
PAOLO WASHINGTON   Sir George Walton
ALFREDO KRAUS   Lord Arthur Talbot
*PIERO CAPPUCCILLI   Sir Richard Forth
ROBERT THOMAS   Sir Bruno Robertson
CORINNE CURRY   Henrietta of France
MARGHERÍTA RINALDI   Elvira

***Conductor   ALDO CECCATO
Staged by   BEPPE MENEGATTI
Scenery and costumes designed by
SILVANO FALLENI AND
BEPPE MENEGATTI
Chorus Master   MICHAEL LEPORE
Lighting designed by   JOHN HARVEY

DON GIOVANNI   MOZART
November 12, 18 (Student Performance), 21, 24,
29, December 3, 6 / In Italian
The production of Mozart's "Don Giovanni" is
made possible by a generous and deeply
appreciated gift of The Lyric Guild.

PAOLO WASHINGTON   The Commendatore
CLAIRE WATSON   Donna Anna
ALFREDO KRAUS   Don Ottavio (Nov. 12, 21, 24,
29, Dec. 3 and 6)
OTTAVIO GARAVENTA   Don Ottavio (Nov. 18)
TITO GOBBI   Don Giovanni
GERAINT EVANS   Leporello
ILVA LIGABUE   Donna Elvira
*JUDITH RASKIN   Zerlina
PETER VAN GINKEL   Masetto

*Conductor   FERDINAND LEITNER
Staged by   TITO GOBBI
Scenery and Costumes designed by PETER HALL

Choreographer SAMUEL KURKJIAN
Chorus Master MICHAEL LEPORE
Lighting designed by JOHN HARVEY

DOUBLE BILL / *November 19, 22, 26, Dec 1, 9 (Student Performance), 12*

EL AMOR BRUJO FALLA / *In Spanish*

Dancers:
***ELETTRA MORINI *Candelas*
***LUCIANA SAVIGNANO *Lucia*
*ANTONIO GADES *The Spectre*
***BRUNO TELLOLI *Carmelo*
VICTOR DE LAMADRID ⎫
ESTEBAN DE LEON ⎪
VINCENTE GOYA ⎬ *Gypsies*
ANTONIO MORENO ⎪
OSCAR NEITO ⎪
LUIS PETRA ⎭
AND THE LYRIC OPERA CORPS DE BALLET
*LINDA MATOUSEK *Mezzo soprano*

Conductor BRUNO BARTOLETTI
Staged and choreographed by
LUCIANA NOVARO
Scenery and costumes designed by
EMANUELE LUZZATI
Lighting designed by JOHN HARVEY

CAVALLERIA RUSTICANA
MASCAGNI / *In Italian*

FIORENZA COSSOTTO *Santuzza*
*EDNA GARABEDIAN-GEORGE *Lucia*
GIAN GIACOMO GUELFI *Alfio*
*FRANCO TAGLIAVINI *Turiddu*
DOROTHY KREBILL *Lola*

Conductor BRUNO BARTOLETTI
Staged by LUCIANA NOVARO
Scenery designed by LORENZO GHIGLIA
Costumes designed by ANNA SALVATORI
Chorus Master MICHAEL LEPORE
Supplementary Chorus GIULIO FAVARIO
Lighting designed by JOHN HARVEY

IL BARBIERE DI SIVIGLIA
ROSSINI
November 28, December 5, 8, 10, 13 / In Italian
The production of "Il Barbiere di Siviglia" is made possible by a generous and deeply appreciated gift of the Gramma Fisher Foundation, Marshalltown, Iowa

OTTAVIO GARAVENTA *Count Almaviva*
GERAINT EVANS *Doctor Bartolo*
IVO VINCO *Basilio*
SESTO BRUSCANTINI *Figaro*
BERNARD IZZO *Fiorello*
MARILYN HORNE *Rosina*
CORINNE CURRY *Berta*
RICHARD BEST *A Sergeant*

*Conductor JOHN PRITCHARD
Staged by TITO GOBBI
Scenery and costumes designed by PETER HALL
Chorus Master MICHAEL LEPORE
Lighting designed by JOHN HARVEY

1970

September 25 – December 12

DER ROSENKAVALIER
STRAUSS
September 25, 28, October 2, 7, 10, 15 / In German

CHRISTA LUDWIG *Princess von Werdenberg (The Feldmarschallin)*
**YVONNE MINTON *Octavian, Count Rofrano*
GERALD CALHOUN *Mohammed, the Feldmarschallin's page*
ROBERT JOHNSON ⎫
*DENNIS SINCLAIR ⎬ *Footmen of the Princess*
BERNARD IZZO ⎪
ROBERT SMITH ⎭
WALTER BERRY *Baron Ochs auf Lerchenau*
CASIMIR ZIELINSKI *Leopold*
ROBERT THOMAS *The Major-domo of the Marschallin*
ARNOLD VOKETAITIS *A Notary*
*EILEEN DENEEN *A Milliner*
*FRANK LITTLE *An Animal Vendor*
FLORINDO ANDREOLLI *Valzacchi, an Italian intriguer*
ELENA ZILIO *Annina, his partner*
JEANNE DIAMOND ⎫
ELIZABETH FISCHER ⎬ *Three Noble Orphans*
EDNA GARABEDIAN-GEORGE ⎭
OTTAVIO GARAVENTA *An Italian Singer*
***ERNST GUTSTEIN *Herr von Faninal*
*PATRICIA BROOKS *Sophie, his daughter*
SYLVIA COOPER *Marianne Leitmetzerin, her duenna*
*DAVID ASTOR *The Major-domo of Faninal*
HERBERT KRAUS *An Innkeeper*
ROBERT JOHNSON ⎫
DENNIS SINCLAIR ⎬ *Waiters*
BERNARD IZZO ⎪
ROBERT SMITH ⎭
ARNOLD VOKETAITIS *A Police Commissioner*

Conductor CHRISTOPH VON DOHNANYI
Associate Conductor ALEXANDER SANDER
***Staged by HANS NEUGEBAUER
*Scenery designed by GÜNTHER SCHNEIDER-SIEMSSEN
Assistants to Mr. Schneider-Siemssen
BERND MUELLER,
JORG NEUMANN
Chorus Master MICHAEL LEPORE
Lyric Opera Children's Chorus
LAURENCE DAVIS

MRS. EDWARD B. BENSINGER

Lighting designed by JOHN HARVEY
Costumes of the Cologne Opera production of "Der Rosenkavalier," designed by Sophia Schroeck

TURANDOT PUCCINI
October 5, 8, 11, 14, 17 / In Italian

BERNARD IZZO *A Mandarin*
FELICIA WEATHERS *Liu, a young slave girl*
FRANCO TAGLIAVINI *Calaf, the Unknown Prince*
PAOLO WASHINGTON *Timur, exiled king of Tartary*
GIORGIO GIORGETTI *Ping, the Grand Chancellor*
HERBERT KRAUS *Pang, the General Purveyor*
FLORINDO ANDREOLLI *Pong, the Chief Cook*
ROBERT JOHNSON *Emperor Altoum of China*
BIRGIT NILSSON *Turandot, his daughter*

Conductor ANTONINO VOTTO
*Staged by NATHANIEL MERRILL
*Choreographer MATTLYN GAVERS
Chorus Master MICHAEL LEPORE
Supplementary Chorus GIULIO FAVARIO
Lyric Opera Children's Chorus
LAURENCE DAVIS
Lighting designed by JOHN HARVEY
This production of "Turandot" has been lent to the Lyric Opera of Chicago by the Metropolitan Opera of New York.
Costumes and scenery designed by Cecil Beaton.

LUCIA DI LAMMERMOOR
DONIZETTI
October 16, 19, 24, 28, 31, November 4 / In Italian

FRANK LITTLE *Normanno, (Oct. 16, 19, 24, Nov. 4)*
HERBERT KRAUS *Normanno (Oct. 28, 31)*
NORMAN MITTELMANN *Lord Enrico Ashton*
PAOLO WASHINGTON *Raimondo Bidebent*
*CRISTINA DEUTEKOM *Lucia*
EDNA GARABEDIAN-GEORGE *Alisa*
RICHARD TUCKER *Sir Edgardo di Ravenswood*
ROBERT THOMAS *Lord Arturo Bucklaw*

Conductor ANTONINO VOTTO
Staged by SONJA FRISELL
Chorus Master MICHAEL LEPORE
Lighting designed by JOHN HARVEY
The Teatro alla Scala of Milan production of "Lucia di Lammermoor," designed by Alessandro Benois.

LA TRAVIATA VERDI
October 22, 26, 30, November 2, 7, 11, 14 / In Italian
This production of "La Traviata" is made possible by a generous and deeply appreciated gift of the Gramma Fisher Foundation of Marshalltown, Iowa.

*MONTSERRAT CABALLE *Violetta Valéry*
DOROTHY KREBILL *Flora Bervois*
*DAVID CORNELL *Doctor Grenvil*
BERNARD IZZO *Marquis d'Obigny*
GIORGIO GIORGETTI *Baron Douphol*
NORMAN PAIGE *Gastone*
*NICOLAI GEDDA *Alfredo Germont*

GIORGIO DE LULLO, CAROL FOX, AND BRUNO BARTOLETTI.

EDNA GARABEDIAN-GEORGE *Annina*
*ARVID KNUTSEN *The Messenger*
PIERO CAPPUCCILLI *Giorgio Germont*
ROBERT JOHNSON *Giuseppe*
JOHN CLEVELAND *A Servant*

Conductor BRUNO BARTOLETTI
Staged by GIORGIO DE LULLO
Costumes and scenery designed by
PIER-LUIGI PIZZI
Choreographer SAMUEL KURKJIAN
Chorus Master MICHAEL LEPORE
Lighting designed by JOHN HARVEY

AMERICAN STAGE PREMIERE

BILLY BUDD BRITTEN
1961 Revision
*November 6, 9, 12 (Student Performance), 18,
21, 23 / In English*

RICHARD LEWIS *Edward Fairfax Vere*
DAVID CORNELL *First Mate*
BERNARD IZZO *Second Mate*
RAYMOND MICHALSKI *Mr. Flint*
WILLIE BROWN, JR. *A Sailor*
JAMES FARRAR *Bosun*
DAVID HOLLOWAY *Donald*
HFRBERT KRAUS *Maintop*
JOHN WALKER *Novice*
ANDREA VELIS *Squeak*
BRUCE YARNELL *Mr. Redburn*
ARNOLD VOKETAITIS *Mr. Ratcliffe*
GERAINT EVANS *John Claggart*
ROBERT THOMAS *Red Whiskers*
ROBERT SMITH *Arthur Jones*
THEODOR UPPMAN *Billy Budd*
PAUL GEIGER *The Novice's Friend*
DENNIS WICKS *Dansker*
BERNARD PRAPUOLENIS *Gunner's Mate*
KEN DUDDLEY *Cabin Boy*
GREG ARNOLD, ANDY BRESNAHAN,
ALFRED MUELLER, ROB WILLIAMS,   } *Midship-*
BRADLEY WOLF   } *men*
MICHAEL ALTENHOFF
PETER BALDWIN
VICTORIA FLANAGAN,   } *Drummers*
STEVEN KACHLIK,
ELISE PASCHEN
DAVID SELLERS

Conductor BRUNO BARTOLETTI
Staged by GERAINT EVANS AND ANDE
ANDERSON

Chorus Master MICHAEL LEPORE
Supplementary Chorus GIULIO FAVARIO
Lyric Opera Children's Chorus
LAURENCE DAVIS
Lighting Designed by JOHN HARVEY
*The Royal Opera, Covent Garden, London
production of "Billy Budd," scenery and costumes
designed by John Piper.*

CHICAGO STAGE PREMIERE

L'ITALIANA IN ALGERI
ROSSINI
*November 13, 16, 25, 29, December 1 (Student
Performance) 5 / In Italian*

LYDIA MARIMPIETRI *Elvira*
DOROTHY KREBILL *Zulma*
GIUSEPPE TADDEI *Mustafa*
GIORGIO GIORGETTI *Haly*
OTTAVIO GARAVENTA *Lindoro*
MARILYN HORNE *Isabella*
DOMENICO TRIMARCHI *Taddeo*

Conductor ARGEO QUADRI
Staged by LOTFI MANSOURI
Scenery and costumes designed by
EMANUELE LUZZATI
Choreographer SAMUEL KURKJIAN
Chorus Master MICHAEL LEPORE
Lighting designed by JOHN HARVEY

MADAMA BUTTERFLY PUCCINI
*The production of "Madama Butterfly" is made
possible by a generous and deeply appreciated
gift of Mr. James C. Hemphill.
November 20, 28, 30, December 3, 6, 9, 11 / In
Italian*

FRANCO TAGLIAVINI *B. F. Pinkerton*
FLORINDO ANDREOLLI *Goro*
DOROTHY KREBILL *Suzuki*
DOMENICO TRIMARCHI *Sharpless*
EDY AMEDEO *Madama Butterfly (Cio-Cio San)*
GIORGIO GIORGETTI *The Imperial
Commissioner*
TOM MASUKO *The Official Registrar*
ARNOLD VOKETAITIS *The Bonze*
BERNARD IZZO *Prince Yamadori*
DEBBIE GOLD *Trouble*
JEANNE DIAMOND *Kate Pinkerton*
Cio-Cio-San's relations and friends, servants

Conductor ARGEO QUADRI
Staged by YOSHIO AOYAMA
Scenery and costumes designed by
MING CHO LEE
Chorus Master MICHAEL LEPORE
Lighting designed by JOHN HARVEY

DOUBLE BILL / *November 27,
December 2, 4, 7, 10, 12*

BLUEBEARD'S CASTLE BARTOK
/ In English

DOUGLAS CAMPBELL *The Bard*
*DAVID WARD *Bluebeard*
*JANIS MARTIN *Judith*

Conductor BRUNO BARTOLETTI
Staged by VIRGINIO PUECHER

Scenery designed by VIRGINIO PUECHER
Costumes designed by VITTORIO ROSSI
Lighting designed by JOHN HARVEY

GIANNI SCHICCHI PUCCINI
In Italian

MURIEL GREENSPON *Zita*
PAOLO WASHINGTON *Simone*
OTTAVIO GARAVENTA *Rinuccio*
GIORGIO GIORGETTI *Marco*
EDNA GARABEDIAN-GEORGE *La Ciesca*
FLORINDO ANDREOLLI *Gherardo*
ANNDRE HOUSE *Nella*
BERNARD IZZO *Betto di Signa*
LISA KVETON *Gherardino*
TITO GOBBI *Gianni Schicchi*
LYDIA MARIMPIETRI *Lauretta*
JAMES BILLINGS *Maestro Spinelloccio*
DAVID HOLLOWAY *Ser Amantio di Nicolao*
ARVID KNUTSEN *Pinellino*
ROBERT SMITH *Guccio*

Conductor BRUNO BARTOLETTI
Staged by TITO GOBBI
Costumes and scenery designed by
LORENZO GHIGLIA
Lighting designed by JOHN HARVEY

1971

September 24 – December 18

SEMIRAMIDE ROSSINI
*First Lyric Opera performances
September 24, 27, 29, October 2, 8, 11 / In Italian
The opening night performance of "Semiramide"
was broadcast over Chicago's Fine Arts Station
WFMT presented by Commonwealth Edison
Company, The First National Bank of Chicago
and Texaco, Inc.*

*PIETRO BOTTAZZO *Idreno*
*SPIRO MALAS *Assur*
*AGOSTINO FERRIN *Oroe*
JOAN SUTHERLAND *Semiramide*
MARILYN HORNE *Arsace*
SYLVIA COOPER *Azema*
SIMON ESTES *Ghost of Nino*

*Conductor RICHARD BONYNGE
Staged by SANDRO SEQUI
Chorus Master MICHAEL LEPORE
Supplementary Chorus GIULIO FAVARIO
Lighting designed by JOHN HARVEY
*The Teatro Comunale di Firenze production of
"Semiramide." Scenery designed by Pier Luigi
Samaritani. Costumes designed by Peter Hall.*

NEW PRODUCTION

RIGOLETTO VERDI
*October 4, 6, 9, 12 (Student Performance),
15, 20 / In Italian
A generous and deeply appreciated gift by
Mrs. Nathaniel Leverone has helped to make
this production of "Rigoletto" possible.*

ALFREDO KRAUS *The Duke of Mantua*
*LEONARD JOHNSON *Matteo Borsa*

ANNDRE HOUSE   *Countess Ceprano*
PIERO CAPPUCCILLI   *Rigoletto*
BERNARD IZZO   *Cavaliere Marullo*
ROBERT SMITH   *Count Ceprano*
GIORGIO GIORGETTI   *Count Monterone*
IVO VINCO   *Sparafucile*
*GAIL ROBINSON   *Gilda*
*ROSE TAYLOR   *Giovanna*
SYLVIA COOPER   *A page*
WILLIE BROWN, JR.   *An usher*
**BIANCA ROSA ZANIBELLI   *Maddalena*

Conductor   BRUNO BARTOLETTI
Staged by   SANDRO SEQUI
Designed by   PIER LUIGI PIZZI
Choreographer   SAMUEL KURKJIAN
Chorus Master   MICHAEL LEPORE
Lighting designed by   JOHN HARVEY

NEW PRODUCTION

TOSCA   PUCCINI

October 13, 16, 18, 22, 26 (Student Performance), 30 / In Italian
The new production of "Tosca" is made possible by a generous and deeply appreciated gift of Mr. James C. Hemphill.

GIORGIO GIORGETTI   *Cesare Angelotti*
*ITALO TAJO   *A Sacristan*
CARLO BERGONZI   *Mario Cavaradossi*
JANIS MARTIN   *Floria Tosca (Oct. 13, 16, 22, 26, 30)*
*TERESA KUBIAK   *Floria Tosca (Oct. 18)*
TITO GOBBI   *Baron Scarpia*
FLORINDO ANDREOLLI   *Spoletta*
BERNARD IZZO   *Sciarrone*
SYLVIA COOPER   *A young shepherd*
ROBERT SMITH   *A jailer*

Conductor   NINO SANZOGNO
Staged by   TITO GOBBI
Assistant to Mr. Gobbi   DAVID SELL
Designed by   PIER LUIGI PIZZI
Chorus Master   MICHAEL LEPORE
Lyric Opera Children's Chorus
                LAURENCE DAVIS
Lighting Designed by   JOHN HARVEY

FIRST LYRIC OPERA PERFORMANCES

WERTHER   MASSENET

October 23, 27, 29, November 2 (Student Performance), 5, 8 / In French

ARNOLD VOKETAITIS   *The Bailiff*
GIORGIO GIORGETTI   *Johann*
FLORINDO ANDREOLLI   *Schmidt*
***ANA MARIA MIRANDA   *Sophie*
ALFREDO KRAUS   *Werther*
*TATIANA TROYANOS   *Charlotte*
PAUL GUDAS   *Brühlmann*
ALICE SWANSON   *Kätchen*
***JEAN ANGOT   *Albert*

Conductor   JEAN FOURNET
Staged by   LOTFI MANSOURI
Chorus Master   MICHAEL LEPORE
Lyric Opera Children's Chorus
                LAURENCE DAVIS
Lighting designed by   JOHN HARVEY

DON CARLO   VERDI

November 3, 6, 10, 12, 15, 20 / In Italian

SIMON ESTES   *A friar*
CARLO COSSUTTA   *Don Carlo*
*SHERRILL MILNES   *Rodrigo*
SYLVIA COOPER   *Tebaldo*
FIORENZA COSSOTTO   *Princess Eboli*
*PILAR LORENGAR   *Elisabeth de Valois*
NICOLAI GHIAUROV   *Philip II*
PAULA PAYNE   *Countess d'Aremberg*
DAVID ASTOR   *A royal herald*
BERNARD IZZO   *A Flemish envoy*
TOM MASUKO   *A Flemish envoy*
ROBERT SMITH   *A Flemish envoy*
RICHARD SCHREIBER   *A Flemish envoy*
*RICHARD ALDERSON   *A Flemish envoy*
GIORGIO GIORGETTI   *A Flemish envoy*
*GLORIA CUTSFORTH   *A celestial voice*
LEONARD JOHNSON   *Count Lerma*
*HANS SOTIN   *The Grand Inquisitor*

Conductor   BRUNO BARTOLETTI
Staged by   LOTFI MANSOURI
Stage settings by   ROBERT DARLING
Chorus Master   MICHAEL LEPORE
Supplementary Chorus   GIULIO FAVARIO
Lighting designed by   JOHN HARVEY

NEW PRODUCTION
FIRST LYRIC
OPERA PERFORMANCES

DAS RHEINGOLD   WAGNER

November 13, 17, 19, 22, 27, 29 / In German
The new "Der Ring der Nibelungen" is a generous and deeply appreciated gift from The Gramma Fisher Foundation of Marshalltown, Iowa. This season's production of "Das Rheingold" is the prologue to the Ring Cycle.

*LISELOTTE REBMANN   *Woglinde*
ELENA ZILIO   *Wellgunde*
*URSULA BOESE   *Flosshilde*
*GUSTAV NEIDLINGER   *Alberich*
GRACE HOFFMAN   *Fricka*
*HUBERT HOFMANN   *Wotan*
*JEANNINE ALTMEYER   *Freia*
***BENGT RUNDGREN   *Fasolt*
HANS SOTIN   *Fafner*
FRANK LITTLE   *Froh*
GERD NIENSTEDT   *Donner*
*RICHARD HOLM   *Loge*
***GEORG PASKUDA   *Mime*
*URSULA BOESE   *Erda*

Conductor   FERDINAND LEITNER
Staged by   HANS-PETER LEHMANN
Designed by   EKKEHARD GRÜBLER
Lighting designed by   JOHN HARVEY

IL BARBIERE DI SIVIGLIA
ROSSINI

November 26, December 2 (Student Performance), 4, 8, 11, 13, 17 / In Italian
The production of "Il Barbiere di Siviglia" is a generous and deeply appreciated gift of the Gramma Fisher Foundation of Marshalltown, Iowa.

FERDINAND LEITNER

GIORGIO GIORGETTI   *Fiorello*
OTTAVIO GARAVENTA   *Count Almaviva*
*HERMANN PREY   *Figaro*
*SPIRO MALAS   *Doctor Bartolo*
MARILYN HORNE   *Rosina*
*AGOSTINO FERRIN   *Basilio*
ELENA ZILIO   *Berta*
FLORINDO ANDREOLLI   *A sergeant*

Conductor   BRUNO BARTOLETTI
Staged by   TITO GOBBI
Scenery and costumes designed by
                PETER HALL
Chorus Master   MICHAEL LEPORE
Lighting designed by   JOHN HARVEY
Assistant to Mr. Gobbi   DAVID SELL

SALOME   STRAUSS

December 3, 6, 10, 15, 18 / In German

FRANK LITTLE   *Narraboth (Dec. 6, 10, 15, 18)*
*ROD MAC WHERTER   *Narraboth (Dec. 3)*
ELENA ZILIO   *The page of Herodias*
*RICHARD MUNDT   *First soldier*
***ATTILIO BURCHIELLARO   *Second soldier*
*ROY SAMUELSEN   *A Cappadocian*
GERD NIENSTEDT   *Jokanaan*
ANJA SILJA   *Salome*
*ROSE TAYLOR   *A slave*
*RAGNAR ULFUNG   *Herod Antipas*
*SONA CERVENA   *Herodias*
DALE MALONE   *A Jew*
LEONARD JOHNSON   *A Jew*
FLORINDO ANDREOLLI   *A Jew*
NORMAN PAIGE   *A Jew*
*ARCHIE DRAKE   *A Jew*
MORLEY MEREDITH   *First Nazarene*
ROBERT JOHNSON   *Second Nazarene*

Conductor   CHRISTOPH VON DOHNANYI
Staged by   HANS-PETER LEHMANN
Lighting designed by   JOHN HARVEY
Designs by   WIELAND WAGNER
realized by   ROBERT DARLING
Scenery and costumes owned by the San Francisco Opera

1972

September 22 – December 16

CHICAGO PREMIERE

I DUE FOSCARI   VERDI

September 22, 25, 29; October 2, 4, 7 / In Italian
The opening night performance of "I due Foscari" was broadcast over Station WFMT presented by Texaco, Inc.

FRANK LITTLE   Barbarigo
ARNOLD VOKETAITIS   Jacopo Loredano
* ERNESTO GASCO   Officer of the Council of Ten
FRANCO TAGLIAVINI   Jacopo Foscari
***KATIA RICCIARELLI   Lucrezia Contarini
*CHRISTINA ASHER   Pisana
PIERO CAPPUCCILLI   Francesco Foscari
BERNARD IZZO   Servant of the Doge

Conductor   BRUNO BARTOLETTI
Staged by   GIORGIO DE LULLO
Realized by   PIER-LUIGI PIZZI
Chorus Master   MICHAEL LEPORE
Supplementary Chorus   GIULIO FAVARIO
Lighting designed by   GIL WECHSLER
The Teatro dell'Opera di Roma production of "I due Foscari."
Scenery and costumes designed by
PIER-LUIGI PIZZI

NEW PRODUCTION

DIE WALKÜRE   WAGNER

September 27, 30; October 3, 6, 9, 13 / In German
The new "Der Ring des Nibelungen" is a generous and deeply appreciated gift of The Gramma Fisher Foundation of Marshalltown, Iowa. This season's production of "Die Walküre" is the first opera of the Ring Cycle. "Das Rheingold," the prologue of the cycle, was presented in 1971.

***HERMIN ESSER   Siegmund
JANIS MARTIN   Sieglinde
BENGT RUNDGREN   Hunding
HUBERT HOFMANN   Wotan
BIRGIT NILSSON   Brünnhilde
GRACE HOFFMAN   Fricka
*ANA RIERA   Gerhilde
GRACE HOFFMAN   Waltraute
*LOUISE PARKER   Schwerleite
CHRISTINA ASHER   Ortlinde
*JEANNETTE HALL-WOOD   Helmwige
ELENA ZILIO   Siegrune
ROSE TAYLOR   Rossweisse
*MAJDA RADIC-DESPALJ   Grimgerde

Conductor   FERDINAND LEITNER
Associate Conductor   ANTONIO TAURIELLO
Staged by   HANS-PETER LEHMANN
Designed by   EKKEHARD GRÜBLER
Lighting designed by   GIL WECHSLER

LA TRAVIATA   VERDI

October 11, 14, 18 (Student Performance), 20, 23, 27, 30 (Student Performance); November 4 / In Italian
The production of "La Traviata" is a generous and deeply appreciated gift of the Gramma Fisher Foundation of Marshalltown, Iowa.

***CELESTINA CASAPIETRA   Violetta Valéry
ELENA ZILIO   Flora Bervoix
ARNOLD VOKETAITIS   Doctor Grenvil
BERNARD IZZO   Marquis d'Obigny
*RONALD HUDLUND   Baron Douphol
NORMAN PAIGE   Gastone
*GIORGIO MERIGHI   Alfredo (Oct. 11)
FRANCO TAGLIAVINI   Alfredo (Oct. 14, 20, 27)
***WIESLAW OCHMAN   Alfredo (Oct. 23; Nov. 4)
ROSE TAYLOR   Annina
ROBERT SMITH   The messenger
*FRANCO BORDONI   Giorgio Germont
ERNESTO GASCO   Giuseppe
JOHN H. CLEVELAND, JR.   A servant

***Conductor   MAURIZIO ARENA
Staged by   GIORGIO DE LULLO
Costumes and scenery designed by
PIER-LUIGI PIZZI
Chorus Master   MICHAEL LEPORE
Lighting designed by   GIL WECHSLER
Choreographer   SAMUEL KURKJIAN

NEW PRODUCTION

LA BOHEME   PUCCINI

October 21, 25, 28; November 1, 3, 6, 11;
Student Performances: December 11, 14 / In Italian
The new production of "La Boheme" is a generous and deeply appreciated gift of Mr. James C. Hemphill

*JULIAN PATRICK   Marcello
GIORGIO MERIGHI   Rodolfo
AGOSTINO FERRIN   Colline
DAVID HOLLOWAY   Schaunard
ITALO TAJO   Benoit
*MARINA KRILOVICI   Mimi (Oct. 21, 25; Nov. 3, 6, 11)
*JOANNA BRUNO   Mimi (Oct. 28; Nov. 1)
ERNESTO GASCO   Parpignol
ITALO TAJO   Alcindoro
ELENA ZILIO   Musetta
BERNARD IZZO   Custom House Sergeant
ROBERT SMITH   Custom House Guard

Conductor   BRUNO BARTOLETTI
Staged by   GIORGIO DE LULLO
Designed by   PIER-LUIGI PIZZI
Chorus Master   MICHAEL LEPORE
Lighting Designed by   GIL WECHSLER
Children's Chorus   LAURENCE DAVIS

NEW PRODUCTION

UN BALLO IN MASCHERA   VERDI

November 8, 10, 13, 18; December 1, 4 / In Italian
The new production of "Un Ballo in Maschera" is a generous and deeply appreciated gift of Mr. and Mrs. Lee A. Freeman and Mr. James C. Hemphill.

AGOSTINO FERRIN   Sam
ARNOLD VOKETAITIS   Tom
*URSZULA KOSZUT   Oscar
FRANCO TAGLIAVINI   Riccardo
SHERRILL MILNES   Renato
ERNESTO GASCO   Judge
RUZA BALDANI   Ulrica
RONALD HUDLUND   Silvano

ERNESTO GASCO   A servant of Amelia
*MARTINA ARROYO   Amelia

Conductor   CHRISTOPH VON DOHNANYI
Associated Conductor   GERHARD GEIST
Staged by   TITO GOBBI
Designed by   ROBERT DARLING
Chorus Master   MICHAEL LEPORE
Lighting designed by   GIL WECHSLER
Supplementary Chorus   GIULIO FAVARIO
Choreographer   SAMUEL KURKJIAN

COSI FAN TUTTE   MOZART

November 15, 17, 20, 22, 25, 29 / In Italian

*RYLAND DAVIES   Ferrando
*TOM KRAUSE   Guglielmo
GERAINT EVANS   Don Alfonso
*MARGARET PRICE   Fiordiligi
***ANNE HOWELLS   Dorabella
URSZULA KOSZUT   Despina

Conductor   CHRISTOPH VON DOHNANYI
Associate Conductor   GERHARD GEIST
*Staged by   JEAN-PIERRE PONNELLE
Chorus Master   MICHAEL LEPORE
Lighting Designed by   GIL WECHSLER
Scenery and costumes owned by the San Francisco Opera.

PELLEAS ET MELISANDE   DEBUSSY

November 27; December 2, 6, 9, 12, 15 / In French
The 1972 presentation of "Pelléas et Mélisande" was made possible by a most generous and deeply appreciated gift from Mrs. John L. Kellogg.

*FRANTZ PETRI   Golaud
*JEANNETTE PILOU   Mélisande
***JOCELYNE TAILLON   Geneviève
RAFFAELE ARIE   Arkel
*RICHARD STILWELL   Pelléas
ELENA ZILIO   Yniold
WILLIE BROWN, JR.   Shepherd
ARNOLD VOKETATIS   Physician

Conductor   JEAN FOURNET
*Staged by   PAUL-EMILE DEIBER
Chorus Master   MICHAEL LEPORE
Lighting designed by   GIL WECHSLER
The Metropolitan Opera of New York production of "Pélleas et Mélisande"
Scenery and costumes designed by
DESMOND HEELEY

WOZZECK   BERG

December 5, 8, 11, 13, 16 / In English

*VINCENZO MANNO   Captain
GERAINT EVANS   Franz Wozzeck
*EDWARD HERRNKIND   Andres
ANJA SILJA   Marie
SHEILA NADLER   Margaret
MORLEY MEREDITH   Doctor
FRANK LITTLE   Drum Major
PETER HARROWER   First Apprentice
BERNARD IZZO   Second Apprentice
ERNESTO GASCO   A Fool
PAUL GUDAS   A Soldier
ROBERT JOHNSON   A Townsman
H. L. SILETS, JR.   Marie's Child

Conductor BRUNO BARTOLETTI
Associate Conductor ANTONIO TAURIELLO
Staged by VIRGINIO PUECHER
Designed by LUCIANO DAMIANI
Chorus Master MICHAEL LEPORE
Lighting designed by GIL WECHSLER
Children's Chorus LAURENCE DAVIS

1973

September 21 – December 15

The first performance of each opera of the 1973 repertoire was broadcast over Station WFMT presented by Texaco, Inc. and Continental Bank and by Commonwealth Edison, Illinois Bell Telephone Company, Kraftco and MusiCraft.

CHICAGO PREMIERE

MARIA STUARDA DONIZETTI
September 21, 24, 28, October 3, 6, 8 / In Italian

*VIORICA CORTEZ Elisabetta
DONALD GRAMM Giorgio Talbot
BRENT ELLIS Guglielmo Cecil
FRANCO TAGLIAVINI Leicester
*SANDRA WALKER Anna Kennedy
*DONNA MOREIN Anna Kennedy (Sept. 28)
MONTSERRAT CABALLE Maria Stuarda
(Sept. 21, 24, 28)
***YASUKO HAYASHI Maria Stuarda
(Oct. 3, 6 and 8)
BERNARD IZZO A Servant

Conductor BRUNO BARTOLETTI
Designed by PIER-LUIGI PIZZI
Lighting designed by GIL WECHSLER
Staged by GIORGIO DE LULLO
Chorus Master MICHAEL LEPORE
Scenery owned by the San Francisco Opera

LYRIC OPERA PREMIERE, NEW PRODUCTION

MANON MASSENET
*September 29, October 1, 4, 8, 15, 17 / In French
The new production of "Manon" is a generous and deeply appreciated gift of Mr. James C. Hemphill.*

NORMAN PAIGE Guillot de Morfontaine
GIORGIO GIORGETTI de Bretigny
***MIWAKO KUO MATSUMOTO Poussette
‡PATRICIA GUTHRIE Javotte
**NICOLETTA CILIENTO Rosette
‡RICHARD SUTLIFF Innkeeper
JULIAN PATRICK Lescaut
*WESLEY GARRISON, ‡GLEN CUNNINGHAM
Two Soldiers
*TERESA ZYLIS-GARA Manon Lescaut
ALFREDO KRAUS Chevalier des Grieux
‡PAUL GUDAS A Vendor
DONALD GRAMM Count des Grieux

Conductor JEAN FOURNET
Designed by JACQUES DUPONT
Lighting designed by GIL WECHSLER
Assistant to Mr. Dupont MARC PAYEN
Staged by PAUL-EMILE DEIBER
Chorus Master MICHAEL LEPORE

Choreographer SAMUEL KURKJIAN
*Scenery constructed in the studios of Robert Petit and painted in the studios of Pierre Laverdet.
Costumes executed by* IRENE KARINSKA

TOSCA PUCCINI
*October 10, 13, 15, 19, 22, 27 / In Italian
The production of "Tosca" is a generous and deeply appreciated gift of Mr. James C. Hemphill.*

GIORGIO GIORGETTI Cesare Angelotti
ITALO TAJO A Sacristan
FRANCO TAGLIAVINI Mario Cavaradossi
TERESA KUBIAK Floria Tosca
TITO GOBBI Baron Scarpia
FLORINDO ANDREOLLI Spoletta
BERNARD IZZO Sciarrone
ENRICHETTA MANCA A young shepherd
‡PAUL GEIGER A jailer

Conductor BRUNO BARTOLETTI
Designed by PIER-LUIGI PIZZI
Chorus Master MICHAEL LEPORE
Lyric Opera Children's Chorus
LAURENCE DAVIS
Staged by TITO GOBBI
Assistant to Mr. Gobbi DAVID SELL
Lighting designed by GIL WECHSLER

LYRIC OPERA PREMIERE
DONIZETTI
*October 20, 24, 26, November 2, 5 and 7 / In French
The 1973 presentation of "La Fille du Régiment" is made possible by a most generous and deeply appreciated gift from Mr. and Mrs. H. G. Cartwright.*

NORMAN PAIGE Hortensius
*REGINA RESNIK Marquise de Berkenfeld
FLORINDO ANDREOLLI Peasant
SPIRO MALAS Sergeant Sulpice
JOAN SUTHERLAND Marie
ALFREDO KRAUS Tonio
GIORGIO GIORGETTI Corporal
CHARLES PIZARRO Dancing Master
*JENNIE TOUREL Duchess of Crakenthorp
LILI CHOOKASIAN Duchess of Crakenthrop
(Nov. 2, 5 and 7)
FLORINDO ANDREOLLI A Soldier

Conductor RICHARD BONYNGE
Chorus Master MICHAEL LEPORE
Staged by SANDRO SEQUI
Lighting designed by GIL WECHSLER
*The Metropolitan Opera of New York production of "La Fille du Régiment".
Scenery designed by* ANNA D'ANNI
Costumes designed by MARCEL ESCOFFIER

LYRIC OPERA PREMIERE, NEW PRODUCTION

SIEGFRIED WAGNER
*October 31, November 3, 6, 9, 12 and 15 / In German
The "Ring of the Nibelungen", including the 1973 production of "Siegfried", is the generous gift of the Gramma Fisher Foundation of Marshalltown, Iowa.*

GERHARD UNGER Mime
JEAN COX Siegfried
THEO ADAM The Wanderer (Wotan)
KLAUS HIRTE Alberich
OTTOKAR SCHOEFER Fafner
JAN REDICK The Forest Bird
LILI CHOOKASIAN Erda
BIRGIT NILSSON Brünnhilde

Conductor FERDINAND LEITNER
Assoc. Conductor ANTONIO TAURIELLO
Staged by HANS-PETER LEHMANN
Designed by EKKEHARD GRUEBLER
Lighting designed by GIL WECHSLER

CARMEN BIZET
*The production of "Carmen" was a generous and deeply appreciated gift of the late Mrs. D. Eckhart Williams.
November 14, 17, 19, 24, 29 (Student Matinee), December 3, 6, 12 and 14.*

‡GLENN CUNNINGHAM Morales (Nov. 14, 17, 19, 24, 29)
‡RICHARD SUTLIFF Morales (Dec. 3, 6, 12, 14)
MARINA KRILOVICI Micaela
PATRICIA WELLS Micaela (Dec. 6)
JAMES KING Don José
ARNOLD VOKETAITIS Zuniga
VIORICA CORTEZ Carmen
MIWAKO KUO MATSUMOTO Frasquita
NICOLETTA CILIENTO Mercedes
LORENZO SACCOMANI Escamillo
FLORINDO ANDREOLLI El Remendado
GIORGIO GIORGETTI El Dancairo

Dancers ANTONIO GADES, LYDIA GOMEZ,
CHRISTINA HOYOS, FELIX
ORDONEZ, ENRIQUE RODENAS

Conductor JESUS LOPEZ-COBOS
Choreographed by ANTONIO GADES
Chorus Master MICHAEL LEPORE
Lyric Opera Children's Chorus
LAURENCE DAVIS
Staged by LUCIANA NOVARO
Designed by PIERO ZUFFI
Lighting Designed by GIL WECHSLER

DER ROSENKAVALIER STRAUSS
*The scenery in the 1973 production of "Der Rosenkavalier" is a generous and deeply appreciated gift of Mr. and Mrs. B. Edward Bensinger.
November 23, 26, 30, December 5, 7, 10 / In German*

CHRISTA LUDWIG The Feldmarschallin
(Nov. 23, Dec. 5)
HELGA DERNESCH The Feldmarschallin
(Nov. 26, 30, Dec. 8, 10)
CHARLOTTE BERTHOLD Octavian,
Count Rofrano
CHARLES LAWRENCE Mohammed, the
Feldmarschallin's page
‡JOSEPH PINEDO
*FREDERICK SCHREINER ⎫ Footmen of the
‡RICHARD SUTLIFF ⎬ Marschallin
‡PAUL GEIGER ⎭

HANS SOTIN   *Baron Ochs auf Lerchenau*
CASIMIR ZIELINSKI   *Leopold*
FRANK LITTLE   *Major-domo of the Marschallin*
ARNOLD VOKETAITIS   *A Notary*
‡PATRICIA GUTHRIE   *A Milliner*
WESLEY GARRISON   *An Animal Vendor*
FLORINDO ANDREOLLI   *Valzacchi*
ELENA ZILIO   *Annina*
*HELEN-KAY EBERLEY
DONNA MOREIN   } *Three Noble Orphans*
SANDRA WALKER
GIORGIO MERIGHI   *An Italian Singer*
ERNST GUTSTEIN   *von Faninal*
JUDITH BLEGEN   *Sophie*
BETTY JONES   *Marianne Leitmetzerin*
‡DAVID GORDON   *Major-domo of Faninal*
‡PAUL GUDAS   *An Innkeeper*
‡JOSEPH PINEDO
FREDERICK SCHREINER   } *Waiters*
‡RICHARD SUTLIFF
‡PAUL GEIGER
ARNOLD VOKETAITIS   *A Police Commissioner*

Conductor   FERDINAND LEITNER
Staged by   HANS NEUGEBAUER
Scenery designed by   GÜNTHER
SCHNEIDER-SIEMSSEN
Lyric Opera Children's Chorus   LAURENCE
DAVIS
Associate Conductor   ANTONIO TAURIELLO
Chorus Master   MICHAEL LEPORE
Lighting designed by   GIL WECHSLER
*Costumes of the Cologne Opera production of
"Der Rosenkavalier", designed by Sophia Schroeck*

LA BOHEME   PUCCINI

*November 28, December 1, 3, 7, 11, 13 (Student
Matinee & Evening) 15 / In Italian
The production of "La Boheme" is a generous and
deeply appreciated gift of Mr. James C. Hemphill.*

JULIAN PATRICK   *Marcello*
*LUCIANO PAVAROTTI   *Rodolfo*
GIORGIO MERIGHI   *Rodolfo (Student
Performance Dec. 13)*
PAOLO WASHINGTON   *Colline*
GIORGIO GIORGETTI   *Schaunard*
ITALO TAJO   *Benoit and Alcindoro*
***ILEANA COTRUBAS   *Mimi*
PATRICIA WELLS   *Mimi (Student Performance
Dec. 13)*
‡PAUL GUDAS   *Parpignol*
ELENA ZILIO   *Musetta*
‡PAUL GEIGER   *Custom House Sergeant*
‡GLENN CUNNINGHAM   *Custom House Guard*

Conductor   BRUNO BARTOLETTI
Realized by   BRUNO NOFRI
Designed by   PIER-LUIGI PIZZI
Chorus Master   MICHAEL LEPORE
Lyric Opera Children's Chorus   LAURENCE
DAVIS
Staged by   GIORGIO DE LULLO
Special Assistant for the Production   MARCUS L.
OVERTON
Scenery constructed by   SCENOGRAFIA BROGGI
Costumes by   SARTORIA ARTIGIANA
TEATRALE TIRELLI

1974

September 20 – December 14, 1974

---

*The first performance of each opera in the 1974
repertoire was broadcast over Station WFMT
presented by Texaco, Inc. and the Continental
Bank, and by Commonwealth Edison, Illinois
Bell Telephone Company, Kraftco Corporation
and MusiCraft.*

NEW PRODUCTION

SIMON BOCCANEGRA
VERDI, revised edition of 1881
*September 20, 23, 27, October 2, 5, 8 / In Italian
The production of "Simon Boccanegra" is a
generous and deeply appreciated gift of the
Gramma Fisher Foundation of Marshalltown,
Iowa.*

CONFERENCE OF THE VERDI CONGRESS, 1974.
RIGHT: BRUNO BARTOLETTI.

---

*DAVID CLATWORTHY   *Paolo Albiani*
*HAROLD ENNS   *Pietro*
PIERO CAPPUCCILLI   *Simon Boccanegra*
*RUGGERO RAIMONDI   *Jacopo Fiesco*
MARTINA ARROYO   *Amelia Grimaldi*
CARLO COSSUTTA   *Gabriele Adorno*
‡KAREN YARMAT   *Servant to Amelia*
‡DEAN RHODUS   *Captain*

Conductor   BRUNO BARTOLETTI
Staged by   GIORGIO DE LULLO
Designed by   PIER-LUIGI PIZZI
Chorus Master   MICHAEL LEPORE
Suppl. Chorus   GIULIO FAVARIO
Lighting designed by   GIL WECHSLER

LEFT TO RIGHT: BRUNO BARTOLETTI, SAUL BELLOW, CAROL
FOX AND THOMAS WILLIS DURING THE VERDI CONGRESS, 1974.

LYRIC OPERA PREMIERE, NEW PRODUCTION

PETER GRIMES   BRITTEN
*September 30, October 4, 7, 10, 12, 15 / In English
This new production of "Peter Grimes" was made
possible by the Gramma Fisher Foundation of
Marshalltown, Iowa through a deeply
appreciated joint gift to the San Francisco Opera
and Lyric Opera of Chicago.*

---

‡PAUL GEIGER   *Hobson*
MORLEY MEREDITH   *Swallow*
JON VICKERS   *Peter Grimes*
*DONNA PETERSEN   *Mrs. Sedley*
TERESA KUBIAK   *Ellen Orford*
LILI CHOOKASIAN   *Auntie*
FRANK LITTLE   *Bob Boles*
GERAINT EVANS   *Captain Balstrode*
NORMAN PAIGE   *Rev. Horace Adams*
‡PATRICIA GUTHRIE   *First Niece*
HELEN-KAY EBERLEY   *Second Niece*
*TIMOTHY NOLEN   *Ned Keene*
H. L. SILETS   *John*
‡PAUL GUDAS   *Lawyer*
DAVID NOVY   *Dr. Thorpe*
GLEN CUNNINGHAM
‡RICHARD SUTLIFF   } *Fishermen*
‡CARL GLAUM
‡KAREN YARMAT   *Fisherwoman*

Conductor   BRUNO BARTOLETTI
Staged by   GERAINT EVANS AND
ANDE ANDERSON
Designed by   CARL TOMS
Chorus Master   MICHAEL LEPORE
Suppl. Chorus   GIULIO FAVARIO
Lighting designed by   GIL WECHSLER
Costumes by   METROPOLITAN OPERA
OF NEW YORK

LA FAVORITA   DONIZETTI
October 11, 14, 17, 19, 21, 25 / In Italian

IVO VINCO   *Baldassare*
ALFREDO KRAUS   *Fernando*
ELENA ZILIO   *Inez*
FIORENZA COSSOTTO   *Leonora di Gusman*
PIERO CAPPUCCILLI   *Alfonso XI*
NORMAN PAIGE   *Don Gasparo*

**Solo Dancers*   JOHNNA KIRKLAND, JOHN
CLIFFORD

Conductor   NICOLA RESCIGNO
Staged by   ANDE ANDERSON
Choreographer   JOHN CLIFFORD
Chorus Master   MICHAEL LEPORE
Lighting designed by   GIL WECHSLER
*The San Francisco Opera production of "La
Favorita."
Scenery and costumes by*   MING CHO LEE

FALSTAFF   VERDI
*October 18, 23, 26, 28, November 1 and 6 / In
Italian*

NORMAN PAIGE   *Dr. Cajus*
GERAINT EVANS   *Sir John Falstaff*
FLORINDO ANDREOLLI   *Bardolph*
*LUIGI RONI   *Pistol*

ELENA ZILIO   *Meg Page*
ILVA LIGABUE   *Alice Ford*
LILI CHOOKASIAN   *Dame Quickly*
***MADDALENA BONIFACCIO   *Nannetta*
THOMAS STEWART   *Ford*
LUIGI ALVA   *Fenton*

Conductor   PETER MAAG
Original production staged by
FRANCO ZEFFIRELLI
Staged for Chicago by   GERAINT EVANS AND
ANDE ANDERSON
Choreographer   JOHN CLIFFORD
Chorus Master   MICHAEL LEPORE
Lighting designed by   GIL WECHSLER
Ass't Stage Director   WILLIAM MASON
*The Teatro dell'Opera di Roma production
of "Falstaff."*
Scenery and costumes by   FRANCO ZEFFIRELLI

NEW PRODUCTION

DON PASQUALE   DONIZETTI
November 2, 4, 8, 11, 16 and 19 / In Italian
*The production of "Don Pasquale" is a generous
and deeply appreciated gift from Mr. James C.
Hemphill.*

***WLADIMIRO GANZAROLLI   *Don Pasquale*
*VINCENZO SARDINERO   *Doctor Malatesta*
ALFREDO KRAUS   *Ernesto*
ILEANA COTRUBAS   *Norina*
‡RICHARD SUTLIFF   *Notary*

Conductor   BRUNO BARTOLETTI
**Staged by*   EDUARDO DE FILIPPO
Designed by   EZIO FRIGERIO
Chorus Master   MICHAEL LEPORE
Lighting designed by   GIL WECHSLER

MADAMA BUTTERFLY   PUCCINI
*November 9, 13, 15, 23, 26, December 2 (Student
Performance), 4, and (Student Performances)
December 10 and 12. / In Italian*
*The production of "Madama Butterfly" is a
generous and deeply appreciated gift of Mr. James
C. Hemphill.*

GIORGIO MERIGHI   *B. F. Pinkerton, Lt.*
FLORINDO ANDREOLLI   *Goro*
NORMAN PAIGE   *Goro (Dec. 4, 10, 12)*
ELENA ZILIO   *Suzuki*
JULIAN PATRICK   *Sharpless*
‡GLENN CUNNINGHAM   *Sharpless (Dec. 10)*
MARINA KRILOVICI   *Madama Butterfly*
EDY AMEDEO   *Madama Butterfly (Nov. 26,
Dec. 4)*
‡PAUL GEIGER   *The Imperial Commissioner*
‡CARL GLAUM   *The Official Registrar*
PETER VAN GINKEL   *The Bonze*
‡RICHARD SUTLIFF   *Prince Yamadori*
ANDRE ZIELINSKI   *Trouble*
‡KAREN YARMAT   *Kate Pinkerton*

**Conductor*   RICCARDO CHAILLY
Staged by   YOSHIO AOYAMA
Scenery & costumes by   MING CHO LEE
Chorus Master   MICHAEL LEPORE
Lighting designed by   GIL WECHSLER

EDUARDO DE FILIPPO

LYRIC OPERA PREMIERE, NEW PRODUCTION

DON QUICHOTTE   MASSENET
*November 22, 29, December 2, 5 (Student
Performance), 7, 11 and 14 / In French*

‡DEAN RHODUS   *Rodriguez*
NORMAN PAIGE   *Juan*
‡PATRICIA GUTHRIE   *Pedro*
‡KAREN YARMAT   *Garcias*
VIORICA CORTEZ   *Dulcinée*
NICOLAI GHIAUROV   *Don Quichotte*
ANDREW FOLDI   *Sancho*
‡PAUL GEIGER   *Bandit Chief*
‡PAUL GUDAS   ⎫
‡CARL GLAUM   ⎪
‡WALTER RYALS   ⎬ *Bandits*
‡JONATHAN WELCH   ⎭
BERNARD IZZO   *First Valet*
HAROLD POTTER   *First Valet (Dec. 14)*
‡RICHARD SUTLIFF   *Second Valet*

Conductor   JEAN FOURNET
Staged by   ITALO TAJO
Designed by   PIER LUIGI SAMARITANI
Chorus Master   MICHAEL LEPORE
Lighting designed by   GIL WECHSLER

LYRIC OPERA PREMIERE, NEW PRODUCTION

GÖTTERDÄMMERUNG   WAGNER
*November 27, 30, December 3, 6, 9, 13 / In
German*

MR. AND MRS. LEE A. FREEMAN, SR.

*The "Ring of the Nibelungen," including the
1974 production of "Götterdämmerung" is the
generous gift of the Gramma Fisher Foundation
of Marshalltown, Iowa.*

*CLAUDIA CAPORALE   *First Norn*
*ANNA REYNOLDS   *Second Norn*
JEANNINE ALTMEYER   *Third Norn*
BIRGIT NILSSON   *Brünnhilde (Nov. 27, Dec. 3, 6)*
BERIT LINDHOLM   *Brünnhilde (Nov. 30,
Dec. 9, 13)*
JEAN COX   *Siegfried*
*DONALD MCINTYRE   *Gunther*
BENGT RUNDGREN   *Hagen*
JEANNINE ALTMEYER   *Gutrune*
*ANNA REYNOLDS   *Waltraute*
PETER VAN GINKEL   *Alberich*
‡PATRICIA GUTHRIE   *Woglinde*
ELENA ZILIO   *Welgunde*
*CLAUDIA CAPORALE   *Flosshilde*
‡CARL GLAUM   *First Vassal*
‡JONATHAN WELCH   *Second Vassal*

Conductor   FERDINAND LEITNER
Associate Cond.   ANTONIO TAURIELLO
Staged by   HANS-PETER LEHMANN
Designed by   EKKEHARD GRÜBLER
Chorus Master   MICHAEL LEPORE
Suppl. Chorus   GIULIO FAVARIO
Lighting designed by   GIL WECHSLER

1975

September 19–December 13, 1975

*The first performance of each opera in the 1975
repertoire was broadcast over Station WFMT
presented by Texaco, Inc. and the Continental
Bank, and by Commonwealth Edison, Illinois
Bell Telephone Company, Kraftco Corporation
and MusiCraft.*

NEW PRODUCTION

OTELLO   VERDI
*September 19, 22, 27; October 1, 3, 6, 11, 15 / In
Italian*
*The production of "Otello" is a generous and
deeply appreciated gift of Mr. and Mrs. Lee A.
Freeman and James C. Hemphill.*

‡THOMAS BOOTH   *Montano*
*VITTORIO TERRANOVA   *Cassio*
PIERO CAPPUCCILLI   *Iago*
‡ENOCH SHERMAN   *Roderigo*
CARLO COSSUTTA   *Otello*
*GILDA CRUZ-ROMO   *Desdemona*
‡ADRIENNE PASSEN   *Emilia*
‡DANA TALLEY   *A Herald*
*MAURIZIO MAZZIERI   *Lodovico*

Conductor   BRUNO BARTOLETTI
Staged by   GIORGIO DE LULLO
Designed by   PIER-LUIGI PIZZI
Chorus Master   HERBERT HANDT
Associate Chorus Master   GIULIO FAVARIO
Lyric Opera Children's Chorus
LAURENCE DAVIS
Lighting designed by   GIL WECHSLER

LA TRAVIATA   VERDI

*September 26, 30; October 4, 8, 13, 17 and 21
(student performance) / In Italian
The production of "La Traviata" is a generous
and deeply appreciated gift of the Gramma
Fisher Foundation of Marshalltown, Iowa.*

ILEANA COTRUBAS   *Violetta Valéry*
ELENA ZILIO   *Flora Bervoix*
ARNOLD VOKETAITIS   *Doctor Grenvil*
BERNARD IZZO   *Marquis d'Obigny*
‡THOMAS BOOTH   *Baron Douphol*
NORMAN PAIGE   *Gastone*
ALFREDO KRAUS   *Alfredo*
‡TRUDY HINES   *Annina*
‡JAMES STITH   *The messenger*
PIERO CAPPUCCILLI   *Giorgio Germont*
‡ENOCH SHERMAN   *Giuseppe*
‡DANA TALLEY   *A servant*

Conductor   BRUNO BARTOLETTI
Staged by   GIORGIO DE LULLO
Costumes and scenery designed by
          PIER-LUIGI PIZZI
Chorus Master   HERBERT HANDT
Associate Chorus Master   GIULIO FAVARIO
Lighting designed by   GIL WECHSLER
Assistant Director   MARCUS L. OVERTON

LYRIC OPERA PREMIERE

ELEKTRA   STRAUSS

*October 10, 14, 18; December 3, 6, 9, 12 / In
German*

*ISOLA JONES
‡ADRIENNE PASSEN
‡TRUDY HINES   } *Five Maidservants*
‡JO ANN PICKENS
‡LINDA BRINKERHOFF
*AVIVA ORVATH   *Overseer*
*BRENDA ROBERTS   *Elektra (Oct. 10, 14, 18)*
*URSULA SCHROEDER-FEINEN   *Elektra (Dec. 3,
          6, 9, 12)*
*CAROL NEBLETT   *Chrysothemis*
URSULA BOESE   *Klytämnestra (Oct. 10, 14, 18)*
MIGNON DUNN   *Klytämnestra (Dec. 3, 6, 9, 12)*
*BEVERLY HOFFMANN   *Confidante*
‡WINIFRED BROWN   *Trainbearer*
‡ENOCH SHERMAN   *Young Servant*
‡JAMES STITH   *Old Servant*
THOMAS STEWART   *Orest (Oct. 10, 14, 18)*
*NOEL TYL   *Orest (Dec. 3, 6, 9, 12)*
‡CARL GLAUM   *Orest's Tutor*
FRANK LITTLE   *Aegisth*

*Conductor   BERISLAV KLOBUČAR
          (Oct 10, 14, 18)
          BRUNO BARTOLETTI
          Dec. 3, 6, 9, 12)
Associate Conductor   ANTONIO TAURIELLO
*Staged by   NIKOLAUS LEHNHOFF
Chorus Master   HERBERT HANDT
Associate Chorus Master   GIULIO FAVARIO
Lighting designed by   GIL WECHSLER
Assistant Director   MARCUS L. OVERTON
The Teatro alla Scala of Milan production
of "Elektra."
Scenery and costumes designed by
          RUDOLF HEINRICH
Additional costume designs by   UTA WILHELM*

NEW PRODUCTION

LE NOZZE DI FIGARO
MOZART

*October 22, 25, 28, 31; Nov. 5, 8, 13 (student
performance) and 17 / In Italian
The production of "Le Nozze di Figaro" is a
generous and deeply appreciated gift of
Mr. and Mrs. H. G. Cartwright and The
Seabury Foundation.*

*STAFFORD DEAN   *Figaro*
*CATHERINE MALFITANO   *Susanna*
ARNOLD VOKETAITIS   *Bartolo*
*HEATHER BEGG   *Marcellina*
*MARIA EWING   *Cherubino*
THOMAS STEWART   *Count Almaviva*
FLORINDO ANDREOLLI   *Don Basilio*
MARGARET PRICE   *Countess Almaviva*
‡CARL GLAUM   *Antonio*
‡DEAN RHODUS   *Don Curzio*
‡WINIFRED BROWN   *Barbarina*
‡WINIFRED BROWN   } *Two Peasant Girls*
‡LINDA BRINKERHOFF
*Conductor   JOHN PRITCHARD
Staged and designed by
          JEAN-PIERRE PONNELLE
Chorus Master   HERBERT HANDT
Associate Chorus Master   GIULIO FAVARIO
Lighting designed by   GIL WECHSLER*

FIDELIO   BEETHOVEN

October 29; November 1, 4, 7, 10, 14 / In German

‡ENOCH SHERMAN   *Jacquino*
*PATRICIA WISE   *Marzelline*
*FRANZ CRASS   *Rocco*
*GWYNETH JONES   *Leonora (Oct. 29, Nov. 1, 4)*
*ROSE WAGEMANN   *Leonora (Nov. 7, 10, 14)*
WALTER BERRY   *Don Pizarro*
PETER PRIOR   } *Two Prisoners*
‡CARL GLAUM
JON VICKERS   *Florestan*
ARNOLD VOKETAITIS   *Don Fernando*

*Conductor   YURI AHRONOVITCH
Staged by   ANDE ANDERSON
Chorus Master   HERBERT HANDT
Associate Chorus Master   GIULIO FAVARIO
Lighting designed by   GIL WECHSLER
Assistant Director   MARCUS L. OVERTON*

LUCIA DI LAMMERMOOR
DONIZETTI

Nov. 12, 15, 18, 21, 24, 28; Dec. 1, 4 / In Italian

‡ENOCH SHERMAN   *Normanno*
LORENZO SACCOMANI   *Lord Enrico Ashton*
AGOSTINO FERRIN   *Raimondo Bidebent*
JOAN SUTHERLAND   *Lucia*
‡TRUDY HINES   *Alisa*
LUCIANO PAVAROTTI
          Sir Edgardo di Ravenswood
HARRY THEYARD   *Sir Edgardo di Ravenswood
          (Dec. 4)*
FRANK LITTLE   *Lord Arturo Bucklaw*

*Conductor   RICHARD BONYNGE
**Staged by   JOHN COPLEY
Chorus Master   HERBERT HANDT*

*Associate Chorus Master   GIULIO FAVARIO
Lighting designed by   GIL WECHSLER
Assistant Director   MARCUS L. OVERTON
The Dallas Civic Opera production of "Lucia di
Lammermoor."
Scenery designed by   HENRY BARDON
Costumes by   PETER HALL*

NEW PRODUCTION

ORFEO ED EURIDICE   GLUCK

*Nov. 22, 25 (student performance), December 2,
5, 8, 10 and 13 / In Italian*

RICHARD STILWELL   *Orfeo*
ELENA ZILIO   *Amore*
ILEANA COTRUBAS   *Euridice*

*Conductor   JEAN FOURNET
Staged by   SANDRO SEQUI
Designed by   PIER LUIGI SAMARITANI
Choreographer   GEORGE BALANCHINE
Director of Ballet   MARIA TALLCHIEF
Chorus Master   HERBERT HANDT
Associate Chorus Master   GIULIO FAVARIO
Lighting designed by   GIL WECHSLER*

GEORGE BALANCHINE

1976

September 25–December 18, 1976

*The first performance of each opera in the 1976
repertoire was broadcast over Station WFMT
presented by Texaco, Inc. and the Continental
Bank, and by Commonwealth Edison, Illinois
Bell Telephone Company, Kraftco Corporation
and MusiCraft.
The same performances were rebroadcast
nationwide on more than 250 stations in the
spring of 1977, sponsored by Allstate.*

LYRIC OPERA PREMIERE, NEW PRODUCTION

LES CONTES D'HOFFMANN
OFFENBACH

*September 25, 29, October 1, 4, 9, 12, 15 / In
French
The production of "Les Contes d'Hoffmann" is a
generous and deeply appreciated gift of
Mrs. Thomas B. Burke.*

NORMAN MITTELMANN   *Councillor Lindorf*
FLORINDO ANDREOLLI   *Andres*
‡CARL GLAUM   *Luther*
‡DEAN SHOFF   *Nathanaël*
‡THOMAS BOOTH   *Hermann*
ELENA ZILIO   *Nicklausse*
PLACIDO DOMINGO   *Hoffmann (September 25, 29, October 9, 12, 15)*
**WILLIAM JOHNS   *Hoffmann (October 1 and 4)*
GIORGIO GIORGETTI   *Spalanzani*
FLORINDO ANDREOLLI   *Cochenille*
NORMAN MITTELMANN   *Coppelius*
*RUTH WELTING   *Olympia*
VIORICA CORTEZ   *Giulietta*
‡ROBERT TOTA   *Schlemil*
FLORINDO ANDREOLLI   *Pittichinaccio*
NORMAN MITTELMANN   *Dappertutto*
CHRISTIANE EDA-PIERRE   *Antonia*
ARNOLD VOKETAITIS   *Crespel*
*WILLIAM POWERS   *Crespel (September 25)*
FLORINDO ANDREOLLI   *Frantz*
NORMAN MITTELMANN   *Dr. Miracle*
‡KATHLEEN KUHLMANN   *Voice of Antonia's mother*
‡TRUDY HINES   *The Muse of Poetry*
‡WINIFRED BROWN   *Stella*

Conductor   BRUNO BARTOLETTI
Staged by   VIRGINIO PUECHER
Designed by   EZIO FRIGERIO
Chorus Master   DOUGLAS ROBINSON
Associate Chorus Master   GIULIO FAVARIO
Lighting Designed by   GIL WECHSLER
Assistant to Mr. Puecher   PATRICIA GRACIS
Assistant to Mr. Frigerio   MAURO PAGANO
2nd Assistant to Mr. Puecher
LUCA BARBARESCHI

LA CENERENTOLA   ROSSINI
October 2, 6, 8, 14 (student performance), 18, 21 (student performance), 23 and 26 / In Italian

*LUCIA VALENTINI-TERRANI   *Cenerentola*
*NASSRIN AZARMI   *Clorinda*
‡TRUDY HINES   *Tisbe*
*ANGELO ROMERO   *Alidoro*
PAOLO MONTARSOLO   *Don Magnifico*
LUIGI ALVA   *Don Ramiro*
TIMOTHY NOLEN   *Dandini*

Conductor   NICOLA RESCIGNO
Staged by   JEAN-PIERRE PONNELLE
Assistant Stage Director to
Mr. Ponnelle   GRISHA ASAGAROFF
Chorus Master   DOUGLAS ROBINSON
Lighting designed by   GIL WECHSLER
Assistant Stage Director   MARCUS L. OVERTON
Set and Costume designs by
JEAN-PIERRE PONNELLE
Production owned by   THE SAN FRANCISCO
OPERA

UN BALLO IN MASCHERA   VERDI
October 13, 16, 19, 22, 19; November 1 and 4 (student performance) / In Italian
The production of "Un Ballo in Maschera" is a generous and deeply appreciated gift of Mr. and Mrs. Lee A. Freeman and the late Mr. James C. Hemphill.

EZIO FRIGERIO   VIRGINIO PUECHER

*GIANFRANCO CASARINI   *Sam*
ARNOLD VOKETAITIS   *Tom*
PATRICIA WISE   *Oscar*
*JOSE CARRERAS   *Riccardo*
*RENATO BRUSON   *Renato*
‡DEAN SHOFF   *Judge*
*BEVERLY WOLFF   *Ulrica*
‡ROBERT TOTA   *Silvano*
‡THOMAS BOOTH   *Servant to Amelia*
KATIA RICCIARELLI   *Amelia*

Conductor   JESUS LOPEZ-COBOS
Staged by   TITO GOBBI
Designed by   ROBERT DARLING
Choreographer   EUGENE TANNER
Chorus Master   DOUGLAS ROBINSON
Associate Chorus Master   GIULIO FAVARIO
Lighting designed by   GIL WECHSLER

RIGOLETTO   VERDI
October 27, 30; November 2, 5, 8, 10, 13, 16 (student performance), 19 and 23 / In Italian
The production of "Rigoletto" is a generous and deeply appreciated gift of Martha Ericsson Leverone.

ALFREDO KRAUS   *The Duke of Mantua*
‡DEAN SHOFF   *Matteo Borsa*
‡WINIFRED BROWN   *Countess Ceprano*
NORMAN MITTELMANN   *Rigoletto (Oct. 27, 30; Nov. 2, 5 and 10)*
***MATTEO MANUGUERRA   *Rigoletto (Nov. 8, 13, 16, 19 and 23)*
‡THOMAS BOOTH   *Cavaliere Marullo*
‡ROBERT TOTA   *Count Ceprano*
‡GIORGIO GIORGETTI   *Count Monterone*
‡GIANFRANCO CASARINI   *Sparafucile*
*ELENA MAUTI-NUNZIATA   *Gilda*
‡KATHLEEN KUHLMANN   *Giovanna*
H. L. SILETS   *A page (Oct. 27, 30, Nov. 2, 8, 10 and 13)*
DAVID SHUBINSKI   *A page (Nov. 5, 16)*
RONALD SOFFER   *A page (Nov. 19, 23)*
‡CARL GLAUM   *An usher*
***SILVANA MAZZIERI   *Maddalena*
Courtiers, ladies and gentlemen of the court, servants

Conductor   RICCARDO CHAILLY
Staged by   SANDRO SEQUI
Designed by   PIER-LUIGI PIZZI
Chorus Master   DOUGLAS ROBINSON

Associate Chorus Master   GIULIO FAVARIO
Lighting designed by   GIL WECHSLER
Assistant Stage Director   MARCUS L. OVERTON

KHOVANSHCHINA   MUSSORGSKY
RIMSKY-KORSAKOFF VERSION
November 6, 9, 12, 17, 20, 22, 27 / In Russian

‡CARL GLAUM   *Kouzka, A Streletz*
‡ROBERT TOTA AND ‡THOMAS BOOTH   *Two Streltsy*
FLORINDO ANDREOLLI   *The Scrivener*
NORMAN MITTELMANN   *The Boyar Shaklovity*
NICOLAI GHIAUROV   *Prince Ivan Khovansky*
*ELLEN SHADE   *Emma*
FRANK LITTLE   *Prince Andrew Khovansky*
VIORICA CORTEZ   *Martha*
*PETER LAGGER   *Dositheus*
*JACK TRUSSEL   *Prince Vassily Galitsin*
BERNARD IZZO   *Varsonofiev*
‡MARIO ROCHER   *Streshniev*
Streltsy (Guardsmen), Their Wives, Old Believers, Waiting Maids, Persian Dancers of Prince Ivan Khovansky, Poteshny (Body Guards of Peter the Great), the Populace.

Solo Dancer   HELENE ALEXOPOULOS

Conductor   BRUNO BARTOLETTI
Scenery and Costumes designed by
NICOLA BENOIS
Choreographer   GEORGE SKIBINE
Chorus Master   DOUGLAS ROBINSON
Associate Chorus Master   GIULIO FAVARIO
Lighting Designed by   GIL WECHSLER

TOSCA   PUCCINI
November 26, 29, December 6, 8, 11, 14, 17 / In Italian
The production of "Tosca" is a generous and deeply appreciated gift of the late Mr. James C. Hemphill.

GIORGIO GIORGETTI   *Cesare Angelotti*
ITALO TAJO   *A sacristan*
LUCIANO PAVAROTTI   *Mario Cavaradossi*
CAROL NEBLETT   *Floria Tosca*
CORNELL MacNEIL   *Baron Scarpia*
FLORINDO ANDREOLLI   *Spoletta*
‡THOMAS BOOTH   *Sciarrone (Nov. 26, 29, Dec. 6, 8, 11)*
BERNARD IZZO   *Sciarrone (Dec. 14 and 17)*
‡TRUDY HINES   *A young shepherd (Nov. 26; Dec. 6, 11, 17)*
‡KATHLEEN KUHLMANN   *A young shepherd (Nov. 29, Dec. 8, 14)*
‡CARL GLAUM   *A jailer (Nov. 26, 29, Dec. 8, 17)*
‡NOEL RAMIREZ   *A jailer (Dec. 6, 11, 14)*
Soldiers, Police, noblemen, ladies, townspeople

Conductor   JESUS LOPEZ-COBOS
Staged by   TITO GOBBI
Designed by   PIER-LUIGI PIZZI
Chorus Master   DOUGLAS ROBINSON
Associate Chorus Master   GIULIO FAVARIO
Lighting Designed by   GIL WECHSLER
Lyric Opera Children's Chorus
LAURENCE DAVIS
Assistant Stage Director   MARCUS L. OVERTON

NEW PRODUCTION, LYRIC OPERA PREMIERE

THE LOVE FOR THREE ORANGES
PROKOFIEV
December 4, 7, 10, 13, 15, 18 / In English
The production of "The Love for Three Oranges" is a generous and deeply appreciated gift of the late James C. Hemphill.

‡CARL GLAUM   *Herald*
*RICHARD GILL   *King of Hearts*
*ALAN TITUS   *Pantaloon*
*JACK TRUSSEL   *Truffaldino*
*WILLIAM DOOLEY   *Leandro*
*WILLIAM POWERS   *Celio*
*KLARA BARLOW   *Fata Morgana*
*JOY DAVIDSON   *Clarissa*
‡KATHLEEN KUHLMANN   *Smeraldina*
FRANK LITTLE   *The Prince*
*TOM FOX   *Farfarello*
ITALO TAJO   *The Cook*
‡TRUDY HINES   *Princess Linetta*
‡LINDA BRINKERHOFF   *Princess Nicoletta*
*MARIANNA CHRISTOS   *Princess Ninetta*
LISA COLLINS   *Mouse*
‡DEAN SHOFF   *Master of Ceremonies*

Conductor   BRUNO BARTOLETTI
***Staged by   GIULIO CHAZALETTES
***Designed by   ULISSE SANTICCHI
Choreographer   EUGENE TANNER
Chorus Master   DOUGLAS ROBINSON
Associate Chorus Master   GIULIO FAVARIO
Lighting designed by   GIL WECHSLER
Prompter   PHILIP EISENBERG

1977

September 23 – December 17, 1977

The first performance of each opera in the 1977 repertoire was broadcast over Station WFMT presented by Texaco, Inc. and the Continental Bank, and by Commonwealth Edison, Illinois Bell Telephone Company, Kraftco Corporation, MusiCraft and Playback.
The same performances were rebroadcast nationwide on over 250 stations in the spring of 1978, sponsored by Allstate.

NEW PRODUCTION

L'ELISIR D'AMORE   DONIZETTI
Sept. 23, 26, 28; Oct. 1, 4, 7, 10, 12 / In Italian
The production of "L'Elisir d'Amore" is a generous and deeply appreciated gift of Mrs. Thomas B. Burke.

LUCIANO PAVAROTTI   *Nemorino*
MARGHERITA RINALDI   *Adina*
‡WINIFRED BROWN   *Giannetta*
ANGELO ROMERO   *Sergeant Belcore*
GERAINT EVANS   *Dr. Dulcamara*

Conductor   BRUNO BARTOLETTI
Staged by   GIULIO CHAZALETTES
Designed by   ULISSE SANTICCHI
Chorus Master   GIULIO FAVARIO
Lighting designed by   DUANE SCHULER

LYRIC OPERA PREMIERE

IDOMENEO   MOZART
Oct. 5, 8, 11, 14, 17, 21, 24 / In Italian

CHRISTIANE EDA-PIERRE   *Ilia (Oct. 5, 8, 11, 14, 24)*
ELLEN SHADE   *Ilia (Oct. 17 and 21)*
MARIA EWING   *Idamante*
‡SARAH REESE, ‡KATHLEEN KUHLMANN   *Cretan Ladies*
CAROL NEBLETT   *Electra*
FRANK LITTLE   *Arbace*
*ERIC TAPPY   *Idomeneo*
*GEORGE SHIRLEY   *High Priest of Neptune*
‡JULIEN ROBBINS   *Voice of Neptune*

Conductor   JOHN PRITCHARD
Staged by   JEAN-PIERRE PONNELLE
Assistant Stage Director to
Mr. Ponnelle   GRISHA ASAGAROFF
Chorus Master   GIULIO FAVARIO
Lighting designed by   GILBERT V. HEMSLEY, JR.
Set and costume designs by
JEAN-PIERRE PONNELLE
Production of the Cologne Opera.

PETER GRIMES   BRITTEN
Oct. 15, 19, 22, 25, 28, 31, Nov. 3 (student performance) and 5 / In English
The production of "Peter Grimes" is a generous and deeply appreciated gift of the Gramma Fisher Foundation of Marshalltown, Iowa presented jointly to the San Francisco Opera and Lyric Opera of Chicago.

‡JULIEN ROBBINS   *Hobson*
ARNOLD VOKETAITIS   *Swallow*
JON VICKERS   *Peter Grimes*
DONNA PETERSEN   *Mrs. Sedley*
TERESA KUBIAK   *Ellen Orford*
***ELIZABETH BAINBRIDGE   *Auntie*
FRANK LITTLE   *Bob Boles*
MORLEY MEREDITH   *Captain Balstrode (Oct. 11, 19, 22, 25)*
GERAINT EVANS   *Captain Balstrode (Oct. 28, 31, Nov. 3, 5)*
NORMAN PAIGE   *Rev. Horace Adams*
‡WINIFRED BROWN   *First Niece*
*JUNE ANDERSON   *Second Niece*
TIMOTHY NOLEN   *Ned Keene*
H. L. SILETS   *John*
EDWARD QUILLIN   *Lawyer*
MARSHALL WEINBERG   *Dr. Thorpe*
Burgesses, townspeople, fishermen

MRS. THOMAS B. BURKE

Conductor   BRUNO BARTOLETTI
Staged by   GERAINT EVANS
Assistant to Sir Geraint   PAMELA McRAE
Designed by   CARL TOMS
Chorus Master   GIULIO FAVARIO
Lighting designed by   STEPHEN ROSS

ORFEO ED EURIDICE   GLUCK
October 26, 29, Nov. 2, 4, 8, 11, 14 / In Italian

RICHARD STILWELL   *Orfeo*
ELENA ZILIO   *Amore*
ELLEN SHADE   *Euridice*
‡SARAH REESE
‡KATHLEEN KUHLMANN
‡GREGORY MERCER   *Quartet of Shepherds, and*
‡DAVID DREHER   *Blessed Spirits*
‡EDWARD HULS

Conductor   JEAN FOURNET
Staged by   SANDRO SEQUI
Designed by   PIER LUIGI SAMARITANI
Choreographer   GEORGE BALANCHINE
Director of Ballet   MARIA TALLCHIEF
Chorus Master   GIULIO FAVARIO
Lighting designed by   GILBERT V. HEMSLEY, JR.

MARIA CALLAS TRIBUTE
November 1

Speakers:
NORMAN ROSS
CAROL FOX
TITO GOBBI
JOHN COVENEY
MASSIMO BOGIANKINO

Singers:
RICHARD STILWELL
SARAH REESE, KATHLEEN KUHLMANN
DAVID DREHER
FRANK LITTLE
CAROL NEBLETT
JOHN VICKERS

Conductors:
JEAN FOURNET
GIULIO FAVARIO
BRUNO BARTOLETTI
THE LYRIC OPERA CHORUS
THE LYRIC OPERA ORCHESTRA

NEW PRODUCTION

MANON LESCAUT   PUCCINI
Nov. 9, 12, 15, 19, 23, 29 (student performance), Dec. 2 and 5 / In Italian
The production of "Manon Lescaut" is a generous and deeply appreciated gift of the late James C. Hemphill.

*JAMES HOBACK   *Edmondo*
GIORGIO MERIGHI   *Chevalier des Grieux*
TIMOTHY NOLEN   *Lescaut*
BERNARD IZZO   *The Innkeeper*
PAOLO MONTARSOLO   *Geronte di Ravoir*
***MARIA CHIARA   *Manon Lescaut*
‡KATHLEEN KUHLMANN   *A Musician*
FLORINDO ANDREOLLI   *A Music Master*
‡EDWARD HULS   *Sergeant*
FLORINDO ANDREOLLI   *A Lamplighter*
‡JULIEN ROBBINS   *A Naval Captain*

Conductor   NINO SANZOGNO (Nov. 9, 12, 15,
              19, 23);
              BRUNO BARTOLETTI (Nov. 29,
              Dec. 2, 5)
Staged by   GIORGIO DE LULLO
Designed by   PIER-LUIGI PIZZI
Chorus Master   GIULIO FAVARIO
Lighting designed by   DUANE SCHULER

IL BARBIERE DI SIVIGLIA   ROSSINI

Nov. 18, 21, 26, Dec. 1 (student performance), 6,
9, 12 (student performance), 14 and 17 / In Italian
The production of "Il Barbiere di Siviglia" is a
generous and deeply appreciated gift of the
Gramma Fisher Foundation of Marshalltown,
Iowa.

TOM FOX   Fiorello
LUIGI ALVA   Count Almaviva
RICHARD STILWELL   Figaro
*CLAUDIO DESDERI   Doctor Bartolo
MARIA EWING   Rosina
PAOLO MONTARSOLO   Basilio
‡TRUDY HINES   Berta
FLORINDO ANDREOLLI   A sergeant

*Conductor   PIERO BELLUGI
Staged by   TITO GOBBI
Scenery and costumes designed by   PETER HALL
Chorus Master   GIULIO FAVARIO
Lighting designed by   STEPHEN ROSS

LYRIC OPERA PREMIERE

DIE MEISTERSINGER VON NÜRNBERG   WAGNER

Nov. 25, 28, Dec. 3, 7, 10, 13, 16 / In German

WILLIAM JOHNS   Walther von Stolzing
PILAR LORENGAR   Eva
*SARAH WALKER   Magdalene
*KENNETH RIEGEL   David
MASTERSINGERS:
*GWYNNE HOWELL   Veit Pogner
GERAINT EVANS   Sixtus Beckmesser
KARL RIDDERBUSCH   Hans Sachs
FRANK LITTLE   Kunz Vogelgesang
WILLIAM POWERS   Konrad Nachtigall
WILLIAM DOOLEY   Fritz Kothner
*EUGENE JOHNSON   Hermann Ortel
JAMES HOBACK   Balthasar Zorn
*RICHARD VERSALLE   Augustin Moser
‡DEAN SHOFF   Ulrich Eisslinger
‡JULIEN ROBBINS   Hans Foltz
‡CARL GLAUM   Hans Schwarz
TOM FOX   Nightwatchman

Conductor   FERDINAND LEITNER
Staged by   NATHANIEL MERRILL
Designed by   ROBERT O'HEARN
Choreographer   JOHN TARAS
Director of Ballet   MARIA TALLCHIEF
Chorus Master   GIULIO FAVARIO
Lighting designed by   GILBERT V. HEMSLEY, JR.
This production of "Die Meistersinger von
Nürnberg" on loan from the Metropolitan
Opera was made possible by a generous gift
to the Metropolitan Opera from Mrs. John D.
Rockefeller, Jr. The costs of transporting and
refurbishing this production have been defrayed
by an anonymous donor.

LEFT TO RIGHT: HAL PRINCE, EUGENE LEE,
AND BRUNO BARTOLETTI.

1978

The first performance of each opera in the 1978
repertoire was broadcast over Station WFMT
presented by Continental Bank and by
Commonwealth Edison Company, Illinois
Bell Telephone Company, Kraft Inc. and
Texaco Inc.
The same performances were rebroadcast
nationwide on more than 250 stations in the
spring of 1979, sponsored by Allstate.

NEW PRODUCTION

LA FANCIULLA DEL WEST
PUCCINI

September 22, 26, 29, October 4, 7, 12, 16, 20 / In
Italian
This new production of "La Fanciulla del West"
is a generous and deeply appreciated gift of
the Gramma Fisher Foundation of
Marshalltown, Iowa.

*MICHAEL BALLAM   Harry
‡DAVID HOWELL   Joe
TOM FOX   Handsome
‡EDWARD HULS   Sid
‡DANIEL McCONNELL   Happy
BERNARD IZZO   Billy Jackrabbit
FLORINDO ANDREOLLI   Nick
*JOSEPH SHORE   Sonora
RICHARD VERSALLE   Trin
*JOHN BRANDSTETTER   Larkens
*GIAN-PIERO MASTROMEI   Sheriff Jack Rance
‡JULIEN ROBBINS   Jake Wallace

J.W. FISHER OF THE GRAMMA FISHER FOUNDATION.

ARNOLD VOKETAITIS   Ashby
CAROL NEBLETT   Minnie
*MARILYN ZSCHAU   Minnie (Sept. 26, 29)
‡WILLIAM MITCHELL   U.S. Postman
CARLO COSSUTTA   Dick Johnson
CARL GLAUM   José Castro
‡KATHLEEN KUHLMANN   Wowkle

Conductor   BRUNO BARTOLETTI
*Staged by   HAROLD PRINCE
*Designed by   EUGENE AND FRANNE LEE
Lighting Designed by   KEN BILLINGTON
Chorus Master   GIULIO FAVARIO
Scenery and properties
constructed by   THEATRE TECHNIQUES, INC.
Costumes executed by   BROOKS-VAN HORN
              COSTUME CO., NEW YORK

SALOME   STRAUSS

September 27, 30; October 3, 6, 9, 13, 17 / In
German

FRANK LITTLE   Narraboth
‡KATHLEEN KUHLMANN   The page of Herodias
*JOHN WEST   First soldier
‡DANIEL McCONNELL   Second soldier
‡JULIEN ROBBINS   A Cappadocian
*NORMAN BAILEY   Jokanaan
GRACE MELZIA BUMBRY   Salome
‡SUSAN BRUMMELL   A slave
RAGNAR ULFUNG   Herod Antipas
MIGNON DUNN   Herodias
RICHARD VERSALLE ⎫
*MELVIN LOWERY ⎪
‡WILLIAM MITCHELL ⎬ Five Jews
‡DAVID HOWELL ⎪
WILLIAM POWERS ⎭
*THOMAS O'LEARY   First Nazarene
‡GREGORY KUNDE   Second Nazarene

Conductor   BERISLAV KLOBUČAR
***Staged by   ERNST POETTGEN
Lighting designed by   DUANE SCHULER
Designs by   WIELAND WAGNER
Realized by   ROBERT DARLING
Scenery and costumes owned by
THE SAN FRANCISCO OPERA ASSOCIATION

MADAMA BUTTERFLY   PUCCINI

October 11, 14, 18, 21, 24 (Student Performance),
27, 31, Nov. 6 / In Italian
The production of "Madama Butterfly" is a
generous and deeply appreciated gift of the late
Mr. James C. Hemphill.

GIORGIO MERIGHI   B. F. Pinkerton
              (Oct. 11, 14, 18, 21, 24, 27)
*VASILE MOLDOVEANU   B. F. Pinkerton
              (Oct. 31, Nov. 6)
FLORINDO ANDREOLLI   Goro
ELENA ZILIO   Suzuki
ANGELO ROMERO   Sharpless
YASUKO HAYASHI   Madama Butterfly
*NICOLE LORANGE   Madama Butterfly (Oct. 27)
‡EDWARD HULS   The Imperial Commissioner
‡DANIEL McCONNELL   The Official Registrar
WILLIAM POWERS   The Bonze
RICHARD SUTLIFF   Prince Yamadori
BENJAMIN C. HEALD   Trouble
‡KATHLEEN KUHLMANN   Kate Pinkerton

LYRIC OPERA

Conductor RICCARDO CHAILLY
Original Production Staged by
YOSHIO AOYAMA
Realized by MARCUS L. OVERTON
Scenery and costumes designed by
MING CHO LEE
Chorus Master GIULIO FAVARIO
Lighting designed by DUANE SCHULER

WERTHER   MASSENET

October 25, 28, 30, November 3, 7, 10, 13 / In French

ARNOLD VOKETAITIS   *The Bailiff*
JOHN BRANDSTETTER   *Johann*
MICHAEL BALLAM   *Schmidt*
*LOUISE RUSSELL   *Sophie*
ALFREDO KRAUS   *Werther*
YVONNE MINTON   *Charlotte*
‡GREGORY KUNDE   *Brühlmann*
‡SUSAN BRUMMELL   *Kätchen*
TIMOTHY NOLEN   *Albert*

PIER LUIGI SAMARITANI

*Conductor   REYNALD GIOVANINETTI
Staged by   PIER LUIGI SAMARITANI
Chorus Master   GIULIO FAVARIO
Lyric Opera Children's Chorus
LAURENCE DAVIS
Lighting designed by   DUANE SCHULER
Set and Costume designs by
PIER LUIGI SAMARITANI
Production of the Teatro Comunale, Florence

DOUBLE BILL / *November 4, 8, 11, 14 (Student Performance), 17, 20, 24, 28*

CAVALLERIA RUSTICANA
MASCAGNI / *In Italian*

*OLIVIA STAPP   *Santuzza*
*GERALDINE DECKER   *Mamma Lucia*
MATTEO MANUGUERRA   *Alfio*
GIORGIO MERIGHI   *Turiddu*
*BRENDA BOOZER   *Lola*

Conductor   RICCARDO CHAILLY
Staged by   LUCIANA NOVARO
Scenery designed by   LORENZO GHIGLIA

Costumes designed by   FRANCO ZEFFIRELLI
Chorus Master   GIULIO FAVARIO
Lighting designed by   DUANE SCHULER
The costumes of this production of "Cavalleria Rusticana" were on loan from the Metropolitan Opera.

I PAGLIACCI   LEONCAVALLO
In Italian

MATTEO MANUGUERRA   *Tonio*
CARLO COSSUTTA   *Canio*
FLORINDO ANDREOLLI   *Beppe*
TERESA KUBIAK   *Nedda*
DAVID HOLLOWAY   *Silvio*
‡EDWARD QUILLIN ⎫
‡DENNIS MARSHALL ⎭ *Villagers*

Conductor   RICCARDO CHAILLY
Original Production staged by
FRANCO ZEFFIRELLI
Designed by   FRANCO ZEFFIRELLI
Staged for Chicago by   FABRIZIO MELANO
Chorus Master   GIULIO FAVARIO
Lighting designed by   DUANE SCHULER
This production of "I Pagliacci" was on loan from the Metropolitan Opera.

DON PASQUALE   DONIZETTI
November 18, 22, December 1, 4, 7 (Student Performance), 9, 12, 15 / In Italian
The production of "Don Pasquale" is a generous and deeply appreciated gift from the late Mr. James C. Hemphill.

GERAINT EVANS   *Don Pasquale*
RICHARD STILWELL   *Doctor Malatesta*
ALFREDO KRAUS   *Ernesto*
JUDITH BLEGEN   *Norina*
CARL GLAUM   *Notary*
Servants, Tradesmen, Townspeople

Conductor   JOHN PRITCHARD
Staged by   EDUARDO DE FILIPPO
Designed by   EZIO FRIGERIO
Chorus Master   GIULIO FAVARIO
Lighting designed by   DUANE SCHULER

WORLD PREMIERE

PARADISE LOST   PENDERECKI
November 29, December 2, 5, 8, 11, 13, 16 / In English and Hebrew

*ARNOLD MOSS   *John Milton*
*WILLIAM STONE   *Adam*
ELLEN SHADE   *Eve*
PETER VAN GINKEL   *Satan*
MICHAEL BALLAM   *Beelzebub*
WILLIAM POWERS   *Moloch*
MELVIN LOWERY   *Belial*
‡EDWARD HULS   *Mammon*
*ARNOLD MOSS ⎫
‡DAVID HOWELL ⎪
‡WILLIAM MITCHELL ⎪
‡EDWARD HULS ⎬ *Voices of God*
JOHN BRANDSTETTER ⎪
‡JULIEN ROBBINS ⎪
‡DANIEL McCONNELL ⎭

*PAUL ESSWOOD   *Death*
JOY DAVIDSON   *Sin*
‡SUSAN BRUMMELL   *Zephon*
**JOHN PATRICK THOMAS   *Ithuriel*
*JAMES SCHWISOW   *Gabriel*
*DALE TERBEEK   *Raphael*
*ALAN OPIE   *Messias*
FRANK LITTLE   *Michael*

Dancers
*DENNIS WAYNE   *Adam*
EDWARD TUELL   *Adam (Dec. 2)*
*NANCY THUESEN   *Eve*
DENNIS WAYNE   *Cain*
KEVIN BROWN   *Cain (Dec. 2)*
EDWARD TUELL   *Abel*
KEVIN BROWN   *Panther*
DUNCAN EMANUEL   *Panther (Dec. 2)*
LISA COLLINS   *Gazelle*

Conductor   BRUNO BARTOLETTI
Choreographer   JOHN BUTLER
Staging   IGAL PERRY
Director of Ballet   MARIA TALLCHIEF
Chorus Master for "Paradise Lost"
ROBERT PAGE
Artistic Consultant   EZIO FRIGERIO
Lighting Design Consultant   GIL WECHSLER
Lighting designed by   DUANE SCHULER
Chorus Master   GIULIO FAVARIO
Children's Chorus Master   LAURENCE DAVIS
Assistant Stage Director   VINCENT LIOTTA
Assistant to Mr. Frigerio   MAURO PAGANO
Supplementary Movement   GUS GIORDANO
DANCE CENTER
Musical Preparation   WALTER BARACCHI,
LOUIS SALEMNO
Make-up   STAN DUFFORD
World Premiere Performance presented by Lyric Opera of Chicago on November 29, 1978. The commission and the production of "Paradise Lost" is a deeply appreciated gift from the late Mr. James C. Hemphill.
The production, conceived in conjunction with Teatro alla Scala, Milan Italy, had its European premiere at Teatro alla Scala on January 21, 1979. A gift by Mr. Thomas B. Burke made Lyric Opera's participation possible.

JAMES C. HEMPHILL

The Lyric Opera Chorus performed in the European premiere through generous grants received from The City of Chicago, The First National Bank of Chicago, Stepan Chemical Co. and Kraft Inc.

Lyric Opera's principal artists and its chorus appeared in a concert version of this opera before Pope John Paul II at the Vatican on February 8, 1979. Via an international radio syndication, the world premiere performance was heard throughout Europe and as far away as Australia.

TEATRO ALLA SCALA

EUROPEAN PREMIERE

PARADISE LOST   PENDERECKI

January 21, 26, 28, 30; February 4, 6, 9, 11

ARNOLD MOSS   *John Milton*
WILLIAM STONE   *Adam*
ELLEN SHADE   *Eve*
CARLO ZARDO   *Satan*
ALDO BOTTION   *Beezlebub*
BORIS CARMELI   *Moloch*
NICOLA TAGGER   *Belial*
GIOVANNI SAVOIARDO   *Mammon*
ARNOLD MOSS   *The Voice of God*
SAVERIO FORZANO ⎫
REGOLO ROMANI ⎪
WALTER GULLION ⎪
RE DENTO COMACCHIO ⎬ *Singing Voices*
CARLO MELICIANI ⎪ *of God*
VINCENZO SAGONA ⎪
GUISEPPE MORRESI ⎭
JOY DAVIDSON   *Sin*
PAUL ESSWOOD   *Death*
FRANK LITTLE   *Michael*
CHORUS OF LYRIC OPERA OF CHICAGO

Conductor   KRZYSZTOF PENDERECKI
Staging   IGAL PERRY
Chorus Master   ROBERT PAGE
Alternate Chorus Master   GIULIO FAVARIO
On February 8, Act II of "Paradise Lost" was performed before Pope John Paul II and a special audience in the Vatican. Penelope Daner sang the part of Eve with the rest of the cast from the Scala performances.

THE LYRIC OPERA CHORUS AT THE VATICAN PERFORMING
PARADISE LOST

GERAINT EVANS AND SESTO BRUSCANTINI, **DON PASQUALE,**
1979 FESTIVAL CERVANTINO.

FESTIVAL CERVANTINO, MEXICO

DON PASQUALE   DONIZETTI

27 y 29 de Abril, 1979 en italiano
Nueva Produccion del Sr. Lee A. Freeman y Sra.

GERAINT EVANS   *Don Pasquale*
SESTO BRUSCANTINI   *Doctor Malatesta*
EDUARDO GIMENEZ   *Ernesto*
WINIFRED BROWN   *Norina*
CARL GLAUM   *Notario*

Director   PIERO BELLUGI
Escenografia   SANDRO SEQUI
Diseño   PIER LUIGI SAMARITANI
Maestro de Coros   GIULIO FAVARIO
Illumiñacion   DUANE SCHULER

1979

NEW PRODUCTION

FAUST   GOUNOD

September 22, 25, 28; October 1, 3, 6, 9, 15, 19

ALFREDO KRAUS   *Faust*
NICOLAI GHIAUROV   *Mephistopheles*
MIRELLA FRENI   *Marguerite*
RICHARD STILWELL   *Valentin*
GERALDINE DECKER   *Marthe Schwerlein*
KATHERINE CIESINSKI   *Siebel*
ROBERT WILBER   *Wagner*

Conductor   GEORGES PRETRE
Designer   PIER LUIGI SAMARITANI
Director   ALBERTO FASSINI
Choreographer   GEORGE BALANCHINE

This new production is a deeply appreciated gift of Mrs. Thomas B. Burke.

LOVE FOR THREE ORANGES
PROKOFIEV

September 29; October 2, 5, 8, 10, 13, 16

RICHARD GILL   *King of Clubs (Don Garrad)*
FRANK LITTLE   *The Prince*
KATHLEEN KUHLMANN   *Princess Clarissa*
BILL DOOLEY   *Leandro*
JACQUES TRUSSEL   *Truffaldino*

TIMOTHY NOLEN   *Pantaloon*
ERIC HALFVARSON   *Magician Tchelio*
ELENA SOULIOTIS   *Fata Morgana*
SHARON GRAHAM   *Linetta*
PAT SCHRADEN   *Nicoletta*
PENELOPE DANER   *Nicoletta*
ERIE MILLS   *Ninetta*
ITALO TAJO   *Cook*
TOM FOX   *Farfarello*
WENDY WHITE   *Smeraldina*
WILLIAM MITCHELL   *Master of Ceremonies*
DAN McCONNELL   *Herald*

Conductor   GEORGES PRETRE
Designer   ULISSE SANTICCHI
Director   GIORGIO CHAZALETTES

RIGOLETTO   VERDI

October 12, 17, 20, 23, 26, 29; November 2

LUCIANO PAVAROTTI   *The Duke of Mantua*
MATTEO MANUGUERRA   *Rigoletto*
DAN McCONNELL   *Count Ceprano*
DONNIE RAY ALBERT   *Count Monterone*
RICHARD T. GILL   *Sparafucile*
WILLIAM MITCHELL   *Matteo Borsa*
TOM FOX   *Cavaliere Marullo*
MARTHA MONASTERO   *Countess Ceprano*
JUDITH BLEGEN   *Gilda*
WENDY WHITE   *Giovanna*
SHARON GRAHAM   *Giovanna*
KATHLEEN KUHLMANN   *Maddalena*
JAMIE GANGI   *A Page*
PHILIP VAN LIDTH DE JEUDE   *Usher*

Conductor   RICCARDO CHAILLY
Designer   PIER-LUIGI PIZZI
Director   SANDRO SEQUI

LA BOHEME   PUCCINI

October 24, 27, 30; November 5, 9, 14, 17;
December 7, 13

JOSE CARRERAS   *Rodolfo, a poet*
VASILE MOLDOVEANU   *Rodolfo, a poet*
ANGELO ROMERO   *Marcello, a painter*
SAMUEL RAMEY   *Colline, a philosopher*
TIMOTHY NOLEN   *Schaunard, a musician*
WILLIAM STONE   *Schaunard, a musician*
ITALO TAJO   *Benoit, a landlord*
ITALO TAJO   *Alcindoro, a state councillor and*
                follower of Musetta
JAMES SCHWISOW   *Parpignol, an itinerant*
                toy vendor
DUANE CLENTON CARTER   *Custom-House*
                Sargeant
PHILIP VAN LIDTH DE JEUDE   *Guard*
ELENA ZILIO   *Musetta, a grisette*
KATIA RICCIARELLI   *Mimi, a maker of*
                embroidery
MARIANA NICULESCU   *Mimi, a maker of*
                embroidery
Students, work girls, citizens, shopkeepers, street vendors, soldiers, waiters, boys, girls, etc.

Conductor   RICCARDO CHAILLY,
                LEE SCHAENEN
Designer   PIER-LUIGI PIZZI
Director   SONJA FRISELL

ARDIS KRAINIK, ASSISTANT MANAGER, ARTISTIC
ADMINISTRATOR

GALA CONCERT

October 14.

BRUNO BARTOLETTI
JUDITH BLEGEN
JOSE CARRERAS
RICCARDO CHAILLY
CARLO COSSUTTA
GERAINT EVANS
MIRELLA FRENI
NICOLAI GHIAUROV
TITO GOBBI
ALFREDO KRAUS
FRANK LITTLE
MATTEO MANUGUERRA
SHERRILL MILNES
LUCIANO PAVAROTTI
KRZYSZTOF PENDERECKI
GEORGES PRÊTRE
LEONTYNE PRICE
MARGARET PRICE
JOHN PRITCHARD
NICOLA RESCIGNO
KATIA RICCIARELLI
RICHARD STILWELL
JON VICKERS
SAM WANAMAKER

SIMON BOCCANEGRA   VERDI

November 3, 7, 10, 13, 16, 19, 24

MARGARET PRICE   *Amelia Boccanegra (Maria)*
CARLO COSSUTTA   *Gabriele Adorno,*
       a patrician
SHERRILL MILNES   *Simon Boccanegra,*
       a Plebian, later Doge
JAMES MORRIS   *Jacopo Fiesco, a patrician*
WILLIAM STONE   *Paolo Albiani, a plebian*
Z. EDMUND TOLIVER   *Pietro, a plebian*
WILLIAM MITCHELL   *A Captain*
JAMES SCHWISOW   *A Captain*
PENELOPE DANER   *Maid to Amelia*

Conductor   BRUNO BARTOLETTI
Designer   PIER-LUIGI PIZZI
Director   SONJA FRISELL

NEW PRODUCTION

TRISTAN UND ISOLDE   WAGNER

November 15, 20, 26; December 1, 5, 10, 14

JON VICKERS   *Tristan*
ROBERTA KNIE   *Isolde*
HANS SOTIN   *King Marke*
SIEGMUND NIMSGERN   *Kurwenal*
RICHARD VERSALLE   *Melot*
MIGNON DUNN   *Brangane*
GREGORY KUNDE   *A Shepherd*
WILLIAM MITCHELL   *A Sailor*
DAN McCONNELL   *A Helmsman*

Conductor   FRANZ-PAUL DECKER
Designer   ROBERTO OSWALD
Director   ERNST POETTGEN

*This new production is a deeply
appreciated gift of the Gramma
Fisher Foundation.*

DANNY NEWMAN, DIRECTOR
OF PUBLIC RELATIONS

ANDREA CHENIER   GIORDANO

November 23, 27, 30; December 3, 8, 12, 15

PLACIDO DOMINGO   *Andrea Chemier*
RENATO BRUSON   *Carlo Gerard*
EVA MARTON   *Maddalena di Coigny*
KATHLEEN KUHLMANN   *Bersi*
WENDY WHITE   *La Contessa di Coigny*
DIANE CURRY   *Madelon*
SHARON GRAHAM   *Madelon*
ALAN OPIE   *Roucher*
TOM FOX   *Fleville*
DANIEL McCONNELL   *Fouquier Tinville*
ARNOLD VOKETAITIS   *Mathieu*
DAVID GORDON   *Un "Incredibile"*
JAMES SCHWISOW   *L'Abate*
ROBERT WILBUR   *Schmidt*
DUANE CARTER   *Innkeeper*
PHILIP VAN LIDTH de JEUDE   *Dumas*

Conductor   BRUNO BARTOLETTI
Designer   PIER LUIGI SAMARITANI
Director   TITO GOBBI
*Ladies, gentlemen, lackey, musicians, poets,
servants, plebians, revolutionarys, soldiers,
gendarmes, merchant, judges, officials, guards,
prisoners, rabble*

DON GIOVANNI LA BOHEME I PURITANI
CARMEN AÏDA CAVALLERIA RUSTICANA
DON CARLO NORMA FAUST TURANDOT
RIGOLETTO IL TROVATORE SIEGFRIED
LA TRAVIATA KHOVANSHCHINA TOSCA
IL TABARRO DIE GÖTTERDÄMMERUNG
SALOME DIE ZAUBERFLÖTE WERTHER
TRISTAN UND ISOLDE COSI FAN TUTTE
ANGEL OF FIRE DIE WALKÜRE OTELLO
MADAMA BUTTERFLY DON QUICHOTTE
PARADISE LOST FIDELIO LA FAVORITA
DON PASQUALE SEMIRAMIDE ELEKTRA
MACBETH I DUE FOSCARI BILLY BUDD
EL AMOR BRUJO DER ROSENKAVALIER
I PAGLIACCI MARIA STUARDA WOZZECK
FALSTAFF LE NOZZE DI FIGARO THAÏS
THE HARVEST NABUCCO LA GIOCONDA
PETER GRIMES LUCIA DI LAMMERMOOR
FEDORA SIMON BOCCANEGRA JENUFA
LA FANCIULLA DEL WEST TANNHÄUSER
OEDIPUS REX PRINCE IGOR IDOMENEO
SAMSON ET DALILA BORIS GODUNOV